CHRIST JESUS
Our
HOPE

Living in Light of Christ's Return

Ravi Hans & Julia Hans

WESTBOW
PRESS®
A DIVISION OF THOMAS NELSON
& ZONDERVAN

WestBow Press books may be ordered through booksellers or by contacting:

WestBow Press
A Division of Thomas Nelson & Zondervan
1663 Liberty Drive
Bloomington, IN 47403
www.westbowpress.com
844-714-3454

ISBN: 978-1-6642-9459-2 (sc)
ISBN: 978-1-6642-9460-8 (hc)
ISBN: 978-1-6642-9458-5 (e)

Library of Congress Control Number: 2023904295

Print information available on the last page.

WestBow Press rev. date: 10/26/2023

Dedication

To Cliff and Eileen LoVerme

Contents

Preface

How the Book Came to be Written

More than twenty years ago, I (Ravi) began a detailed study of the Hope in the Scriptures. I read from Matthew to Revelation, listing everything that spoke about the future. This process was repeated many times and the scope expanded to include the entire Bible. The wealth of information surprised me. God's Word not only has a lot to say about "things to come," but it contains countless exhortations to live in light of the Hope. In other words, the Hope is very practical. I learned that having a firm grasp of the Hope greatly helps Christians to remain faithful despite the trials and tribulations of life.

As I began to understand that the Christian's hope is a living hope, something that impacts his daily life, I found myself more excited about the things of God than ever before. Studying the topic had a transformative effect on me, and my priorities soon shifted from earthly things to seeking things above. As the song "Turn Your Eyes Upon Jesus" vividly captures, "the things of earth grow strangely dim in the light of his glory and grace."

In 2006, I taught the first seminar on the Hope material. In the years that followed, I taught numerous seminars in Canada and the U.S. and continued to develop the topic. During one of these seminars, someone suggested that I put the material down in book form.

My initial attempt failed miserably. At the risk of frightening the reader, I must admit that my writing skills are mediocre at best. I made numerous attempts to write down what I was learning but would inevitably give up, feeling that I was not equipped for the task. So, the project languished. Two things kept me going: the exhortation in God's Word to freely give what I had freely received and knowing how much a deeper understanding of their hope would bless God's people.

Some years later, God put it on Julie's heart to help me with the book, which completely changed the project's direction. Julie is a professional writer who excels at making complex subjects easy to understand. She took the disjointed materials and helped me organize and clarify the many topics that make up the Christian's Hope. But it would be erroneous to assume that she merely edited the book. She contributed significantly to the material with her understanding of and reverence for God and His Word. What you hold in your hands is the result of our combined effort. It is safe to say that without Julie's help, this book may not have seen the light of day, so I am immensely grateful for her assistance.

I have been a student of God's Word for more than 40 years. Being an engineer by profession where details are so crucial, one of the things that first thrilled me about God's Word is its remarkable precision. Engineers rely on principles and laws every day to do their work. God's Word far surpasses the details and precision of any engineering endeavor. It is 100% reliable and worthy of our complete trust. And so when the Scriptures promise that Christ is coming back and that great blessings await those who love his appearing, we can wholly rely on that information.

How the Book Came to be Edited

I (Julie) jumped into this project about seven years ago when I realized that Ravi had enough material on the Hope to fill a warehouse and that he would need help organizing and writing up all those notes. While I have written several books, I have not co-authored anything.

Yet, in many ways, my experience as a writing professor uniquely qualified me for this task. After all, what does a writing professor do but help students revise, reorganize, and improve their work? And for much of this book, that's what I did—revise material Ravi had already written. Sometimes that meant rewriting a few paragraphs; sometimes, overhauling a whole chapter. In not a few cases, that meant studying and researching the topics myself so that I could understand them better and work them into readable prose. Along the way, Ravi and I carved out a process that seemed to work. He would compile his research notes, review the material with me, and I'd reorganize it and put it into formal writing. Countless revisions later, we had a book in draft form. The draft then went to a group of readers, who gave us feedback. Their input was incorporated into a second draft, resulting in the manuscript you now have in your hands.

Working with Ravi on this book has been enjoyable because he is easy to work with, and the subject matter is thrilling! I think it's important to note that while I did the original research for the material in chapter 6 and a few appendices, Ravi has done the lion's share of the research for this book. This is his labor of love, the fruit of his hard work, believing, and prayer.

When Ravi and I were married more than 35 years ago, we did a lot of home improvement projects together: stripping wallpaper, ripping up old carpet, and installing vinyl siding on the house. Because he knew much more about home repairs than I did, I deferred to him. But he deferred to me when picking a paint color and fabric patterns. It all went swimmingly. This ability to work well together is one of the strengths of our marriage. And throughout the writing of this book, we have again seen how well we work together. Hopefully, the fruit of our efforts will be a blessing to you as you ponder the greatness of Christ Jesus, our hope.

Ravi and Julie Hans
February 9, 2023
Carthage, NC

Acknowledgments

We thank the group of individuals who read the manuscript in its draft stage and offered feedback: Rev. Walter Cummins, Rev. Susan Miller, Raj Hans, Abby and Jon Nickols, Denise Tiemissen, Daniel Hyder, and others. While their feedback was invaluable, we recognize that we alone are responsible for the final contents of this book. Though they chose to remain anonymous, we wholeheartedly thank those who proofread the manuscript, an essential service. We also wish to thank the friends and family members who have prayed for this project from inception to draft to finished product. Such assistance cannot be measured. Finally, we thank Cliff and Eileen LoVerme, to whom this book is dedicated, for their feedback on the draft and their love and kindness extended to us these many decades. We count ourselves truly blessed to have friends like you.

Above all, we thank God, our heavenly Father, for His lovingkindness, mercy, and grace, for sending His Son Jesus Christ to redeem us, and for promising to send Christ again to receive us to glory.

Introduction

Why Read this Book

In the opening chapter of the book of Acts we read:

> **Acts 1:9-11**
> [9]And when he had said these things, as they were looking on, he was lifted up, and a cloud took him out of their sight.
> [10]And while they were gazing into heaven as he went, behold, two men stood by them in white robes,
> [11]and said, "Men of Galilee, why do you stand looking into heaven? This Jesus, who was taken up from you into heaven, will come in the same way as you saw him go into heaven."

Immediately after Jesus Christ ascended into the cloud, two men in white robes promised he would return.[1] There is no time lapse between Christ's ascension to heaven and the promise of his return. How important is this information if God saw fit to deliver this message immediately after Christ ascended?

Many Christians believe that Christ is coming back, but do they clearly understand what the Scriptures say about it? Do they know about the reward, the prize and crown, the inheritance, and other topics related to the Hope? Or is their understanding somewhat hazy? Have they learned how the Hope can motivate them in their day-to-day living? This book is written to help Christians gain a deeper knowledge of this blessed Hope.

If you are looking for a book that discusses what the Scriptures say

---

[1]   These two men were angels, or spirit messengers from God. Angels are often described in the Scriptures as men wearing bright clothing. See for example Gen. 19:1-16; Matt. 28:2-3; Mark 16:5; John 20:12; Acts 10:30.

about the hope of Christ's return and what that entails, then you have come to the right place. However, this book will be a disappointment if you're looking for speculations or frothy prognostications about the future based on man's opinion.

What's in this Book

Chapter 1 discusses how Jesus Christ is the central figure of God's revelation. Jesus Christ has always been the hope for humanity, even as far back as when man sinned in the Garden. Old Testament believers like Abraham, Moses, and David looked forward to the first coming of Christ, and this knowledge greatly impacted their lives. Chapter 2 reviews some events that occur when Christ returns for the Church. Because there is much confusion about Christ's return for the Church and Christ's return during the Day of the Lord, the chapter also covers some basics about the Day of the Lord. Chapter 3 examines what the Bible says about the Christian's inheritance. Chapter 4 discusses the subject of the reward including what will be rewarded. To some the truths about rewards and grace are at odds, so chapter 5 addresses this topic. Chapter 6 considers what the Scriptures say about the prize and crown. Because many people wonder what the heavenly reward will be, chapter 7 delves into the nature of the future reward. Chapter 8 considers Jesus Christ's highly exalted position and its ramifications for the Church. Finally, chapter 9 considers what it means to run the race to the finish and what is at stake for every saint.[2]

These chapters are followed by nine appendices, which are offered as supplemental material for interested students:

A: The Day of the Lord
B: Four Apparent Contradictions about the Inheritance
C: The Judgment Seat of Christ

---

[2] We use the word "saint" here and throughout this book to refer to those who are born again of God's spirit, a Christian believer. See the numerous uses of this word in the Pauline epistles.

D: The New Body

E: Jesus Christ's Teachings on Reward

F: "Lest I Be Disqualified"-A Study of 1 Corinthians 10:1-14

G: A Study of *Kathizō* (Seated)

H: Some Words and Expressions that Signify Reward

I: Frequently Asked Questions

Both the apostle Paul and the apostle John were given vivid glimpses of the future. Yet Paul wrote, "now we see in a mirror dimly" (1 Cor. 13:12), and John said, "we are God's children now, what we will be has not yet appeared" (1 John 3:2). Even those who were given direct revelation about the future, like Paul and John, said that we could only know in part. Far be it for anyone, therefore, to presume they know everything the future holds. But thankfully, there is enough information in the Scriptures to convince the students of God's Word that the Hope is real and that it will exceed their grandest expectations. The material in this book is only a glimpse of what is to come, a compilation of our best understanding at this time.

Methodology

First and foremost, all Scripture is given by *inspiration of God* and is profitable for "teaching, reproof, correction, and training in righteousness, that the man of God may be complete, equipped for every good work" (2 Tim. 3:16-17). This, then, is our starting point for all research and teaching. While outside sources may be helpful, our final authority is the Bible. Even when we take narrative liberties and write things like, "Paul wrote to the Thessalonians," it's understood that he wrote this *by revelation*. The warnings in God's Word about adding to, subtracting from, and changing His Word are sobering, to say the least. In writing about future things, we have tried to say what the Scriptures say, avoiding speculation or guesswork. God purposely hides some things about the future, and more understanding may be gained by further study.

Second, we expect readers to have some prior biblical knowledge. That's why we may refer to a record rather than quoting it fully. We assume that readers are familiar with the record or will familiarize themselves with it when necessary.

Third, we recognize that context is king regarding biblical exposition. While we have studied each verse and passage in its full context, we don't always reprint the full context for the reader in this book. To do so would double the length of the material. However, we hope readers will take the time to consider each passage in its broader context.

Next, we consider figurative language and eastern customs in the Bible. Words can be figurative or literal, and language does not exist in a vacuum; as such, culture influences and shapes the meaning of words. So, we pay attention to figures of speech and cultural idioms or customs and include their significance when necessary. For instance, appreciating figures of speech and the Greek Games is crucial to ferreting out the truth regarding the prize and crown. It would have been nearly impossible to fully articulate what these terms signify without understanding metaphor and the Greek Games that were so popular during New Testament times.

To Greek or not to Greek—that is the question for anyone writing a book on the New Testament. While we both have a working knowledge of Greek, neither of us is fluent. So, we rely on Greek scholars such as Joseph Henry Thayer, E. W. Bullinger, and James Strong to derive definitions or to better appropriate the meaning of a word in the original languages. Along those lines, we keep the Greek to a minimum because this book is written for the general reader, not for Greek scholars.

Finally, we have selected the English Standard Version rather than the King James Version as the text for this book. Early in this project, we discovered that because of the archaisms of the King James Version, we were spending more time explaining diction and grammar rather than expounding the subject of our book. Using the English Standard Version (ESV) nicely mitigated these problems. Incidentally, we use the Chicago Manual of Style short footnotes in this book; the full bibliographic information for each source may be found in the bibliography.

The title for this book is *Christ Jesus our Hope: Living in Light of*

Christ's Return. The subtitle reflects one of the main reasons for writing this work: to encourage people to set their affections on things above, not on the things of this earth, for Christ is our life.

May God enlighten your understanding as you read these chapters and meditate on the Scriptures regarding our great and living hope.

Ephesians 1:18-19a

[18]having the eyes of your hearts enlightened, that you may know what is the hope to which he has called you, what are the riches of his glorious inheritance in the saints,

[19]and what is the immeasurable greatness of his power toward us who believe....

Chapter 1

Christ Jesus Our Hope

What advantage would you have if you knew the future?

Let's say you knew the coming 90 days in advance. And let's say you knew a particular stock, XYZ Inc., worth $10 today, would be worth $10,000 in 90 days. The information is guaranteed: there is no doubt, speculation, or uncertainty about it. In 90 days, XYZ stock is absolutely going to increase 1,000 times. Anyone can buy this stock.

What would you do in those 90 days?

If you were utterly convinced about this information, you might sell everything you owned to invest that cash in XYZ stock. You might sell your jewelry, car, and anything of value to get as much cash as possible. You might even sell your house. After all, nothing you own will likely appreciate 1000 times in 90 days. But XYZ stock will. With singular focus, you might expend all your energies selling everything you have to buy XYZ stock.

Would you ignore the ridicule from those who thought XYZ stock was worthless?

Would you be willing to tell others about this great investment despite the negative press?

Would you refuse to be discouraged if the stock price fell before it rose at the 90-day mark?

Your actions would depend on how convinced you were about the information. The more confident you were, the more you would invest,

1

even sacrificing some comforts while waiting for the payoff. But if you weren't convinced of this information, you would not take such drastic measures. Instead, you might sell a few things and invest a little in XYZ stock, "just in case." But you wouldn't be as hog wild about it as the person who was utterly convinced.

At the end of 90 days, XYZ stock hits $10,000, and you cash in—every dollar you invested multiplied a thousand times. All the sacrifices, ridicule, and lousy press, forgotten.

Of course, this illustration is hypothetical. We don't know how the stock market will perform 90 days in advance. But the Scriptures assure us that God knows the future, way beyond the next three months. And His Word reveals many things that will take place in the coming ages. While the Scriptures don't pull back the curtain on all future details, they do reveal enough information so that we can wisely invest our time, resources, and energy. God is the only One with a perfect track record of accurately knowing and revealing what is coming. When He gives information about future events, it is reliable and sure.

> **1 Kings 8:56**
> "Blessed be the LORD who has given rest to his people
> Israel, according to all that he promised. Not one word
> has failed of all his good promise, which he spoke by
> Moses his servant.

What God promised by Moses came to pass. Not one word failed.

> **Numbers 23:19**
> God is not man, that he should lie, or a son of man,
> that he should change his mind. Has he said, and will
> he not do it? Or has he spoken, and will he not fulfill it?

Note the reliability of God and His Word. What He says He will do, He will do. What He declares will come to pass does come to pass. These verses speak of the inviolate reliability of God's promises.

Isaiah 42:9

Behold, the former things have come to pass, and new things I now declare; before they spring forth I tell you of them."

God can declare things about future events before they come to pass. So, when He utters a promise about the future, we know it is 100% reliable. With God, past performance is a guarantee of future results!

We see the reliability of God's foreknowledge illustrated in the life of Joseph. According to the records in Genesis, God revealed to Joseph specific events that would occur in Egypt for the next 14 years.[3] Pharaoh asked Joseph to interpret a strange dream he had had, and God revealed the meaning to Joseph: there would be seven years of plenty followed by seven years of famine. Joseph relayed that information to Pharaoh, who believed the information. As a result, Pharaoh then appointed him second in command in Egypt. In his new position, Joseph was able to save Egypt and his family from starvation and bring immense wealth to Egypt. All this deliverance was based on God's foreknowledge and Joseph's acceptance of that information. This is but one example of the trustworthiness of God's revelation about the future.

In the Scriptures, God has revealed that Christ will come back.

Acts 1:9-11

[9]And when he had said these things, as they were looking on, he was lifted up, and a cloud took him out of their sight.

---

[3]   See Gen. 37-50.

¹⁰And while they were gazing into heaven as he went, behold, two men stood by them in white robes, ¹¹and said, "Men of Galilee, why do you stand looking into heaven? This Jesus, who was taken up from you into heaven, will come in the same way as you saw him go into heaven."

Immediately after his ascension, two men in white apparel told the apostles Christ would return. Just think of it: within moments of the ascension, God sent the promise that Christ would come back. Moreover, their message conveyed a sense of urgency. In other words, the apostles had no time to lose, for this was not the last time they would see Jesus Christ. He was coming back! This promise, given centuries ago, has not yet come to pass. But because of God's perfect track record revealing future events, we can be sure that Christ will return.

The First Coming of Christ

Jesus Christ has always been the hope for humanity, as far back as when man sinned in the Garden.

Genesis 3:15-19

¹⁵I will put enmity between you and the woman, and between your offspring and her offspring; he shall bruise your head, and you shall bruise his heel." ¹⁶To the woman he said, "I will surely multiply your pain in childbearing; in pain you shall bring forth children. Your desire shall be contrary to your husband, but he shall rule over you." ¹⁷And to Adam he said, "Because you have listened to the voice of your wife and have eaten of the tree of which I commanded you, 'You shall not eat of it,' cursed is the ground because of you; in pain you shall eat of it all the days of your life;

¹⁸thorns and thistles it shall bring forth for you; and you shall eat the plants of the field.

¹⁹By the sweat of your face you shall eat bread, till you return to the ground, for out of it you were taken; for you are dust, and to dust you shall return."

When man sinned in the garden, he brought such destruction and ruin that the effects are still felt today, as verses 16-19 indicate. As a result of man's disobedience, the ground became cursed, and cultivating it would require hard labor. In addition to producing food, the land would also produce thorns and thistles, indicating that there would be an increased amount of toil just to exist.

Despite the misery man brought upon himself, God immediately gave him hope. In verse 15, the woman's "offspring" refers to the promised Savior, Jesus Christ. The bruising of his heel indicates the suffering the Savior would endure while the bruising of the head refers to the ultimate destruction of the devil (see also Rev. 20:10). From the beginning, God gave man hope with His promise of the coming Savior, Jesus Christ.

God has always given humanity hope, and throughout the centuries, people such as Abraham, Moses, David and others looked forward to Christ's first coming.

Abraham

Abraham is a notable figure in the Scriptures. He is called the "friend of God" and the "father of all those who believe." In obedience to God's command, he left his homeland and traveled to Canaan. God revealed to Abraham that he would have a son, even though Sarah was barren. Abraham clung to this promise for many, many years before it came to pass. God fulfilled His promise to Abraham, and Isaac was born. Sometime after Isaac's birth, God further revealed to Abraham that the Savior would come through Isaac.⁴ Not surprisingly,

---

4   Compare Gen. 21:12 and Gal. 3:16

this information made Abraham rejoice (John 8:56). Who wouldn't be delighted to receive such joyful news? But then, God asked him to do the unthinkable:

> **Genesis 22:1-2**
> ¹After these things God tested Abraham and said to him, "Abraham!" And he said, "Here I am."
> ²He said, "Take your son, your only son Isaac, whom you love, and go to the land of Moriah, and offer him there as a burnt offering on one of the mountains of which I shall tell you."

How difficult would it have been for him to sacrifice his beloved son? What enabled him to obey such a command? The book of Hebrews tells us:

> **Hebrews 11:17-19**
> ¹⁷By faith Abraham, when he was tested, offered up Isaac, and he who had received the promises was in the act of offering up his only son,
> ¹⁸of whom it was said, "Through Isaac shall your offspring be named."
> ¹⁹He considered that God was able even to raise him from the dead, from which, figuratively speaking, he did receive him back.

Abraham was convinced of the veracity of God's promise that the Christ would come through Isaac. If Isaac died at Abraham's hand, how would God's promise be fulfilled? Verse 19 gives us the answer: Abraham was willing to sacrifice his son because he fully believed that God would raise Isaac from the dead! Further, verse 17 tells us that Abraham did this "by faith," meaning that he was obeying God's directives in offering up Isaac. This wasn't something Abraham decided to do on his own. Abraham was so sure about the promise that the Christ would come through Isaac that he was willing to do the unspeakable. No wonder

Abraham is called "the father of all those who believe." In this record, we see that the hope of Christ's first coming was living and real to Abraham to an astonishing level. Abraham certainly believed God's promise about the coming Christ and look how it impacted his life!

Moses

Like Abraham, Moses also looked forward to the first coming of Christ. The book of Hebrews gives us more insight into Moses' decisions based on this hope.

> **Hebrews 11:24-26**
> [24]By faith Moses, when he was grown up, refused to be called the son of Pharaoh's daughter,
> [25]choosing rather to be mistreated with the people of God than to enjoy the fleeting pleasures of sin.
> [26]He considered the reproach of Christ greater wealth than the treasures of Egypt, for he was looking to the reward.

Moses was the adopted son of Pharaoh's daughter. He grew up in the king's court and had all the privileges a prince might have. Egypt was perhaps the most powerful and wealthiest nation at that time in history, partly because of the prosperity brought to the land by Joseph's walk with God. And Moses had these resources at his disposal. He could easily have lived in luxury with a fine palace, hundreds of servants, and all the other trappings that come with prestige and power. Yet Moses gave it all up! For what? "To be mistreated along with the people of God." Why exchange pleasure for mistreatment?

Moses' actions would be judged reckless, short-sighted, or maybe even delusional by most people. Yet he made this decision because "He considered the reproach of Christ greater wealth than the treasures of Egypt, for he was looking to the reward." Moses wasn't only thinking about the present, his eyes were on the future: the coming of Christ and the reward! At some point, Moses must have weighed the two options: 1) a life of pleasure enjoying the treasures of Egypt spread out before him, or 2) mistreatment with God's people and an unseen promise. Moses chose the intangible *promise* over the material realities.

Verse 24 says that Moses made this decision by faith or believing. He must have been convinced about the information from God to make such a radical choice. It is easy for us to read about Moses's sacrifice, but how difficult would it have been to give up all that wealth and privilege? As the NIV puts it, "He regarded disgrace for the sake of Christ as of greater value than the treasures of Egypt, because he was looking ahead to his reward" (Heb. 11:26). Moses valued the eternal riches of Christ more than Egypt's temporary riches. Like Abraham, Moses had enough confidence in the promise of the coming Savior to make a *life-altering* decision. That certainly speaks to the reliability of God's promises!

David

David also looked forward to the coming Savior, which greatly impacted his life.

> **Acts 2:25-28**
> ²⁵For David says concerning him, "'I saw the Lord always before me, for he is at my right hand that I may not be shaken;
> ²⁶therefore my heart was glad, and my tongue rejoiced; my flesh also will dwell in hope.
> ²⁷For you will not abandon my soul to Hades, or let your Holy One see corruption.
> ²⁸You have made known to me the paths of life; you will make me full of gladness with your presence.'

In this passage, Peter quotes from Psalm 16. When David wrote that he "saw the Lord always before me," he was referring to the coming Savior. Having this knowledge always in mind helped David not to be shaken.

Furthermore, this knowledge caused David to be glad and rejoice. The word "dwell" in verse 26 can also mean "to encamp, pitch one's tent."[5] Today, we might say, David "camped out" in hope; that's where he lived, so to speak. If you are familiar with the records of David, you know that he did not lead an easy, carefree life. He was frequently in danger. Saul pursued him for years, trying to kill him. Two of David's sons rebelled against him, one bent on killing him. David fought fierce foreign enemies and faced many obstacles as a soldier and king. But if you read his Psalms, you learn that David continually looked to God for deliverance and kept the promise of the coming Savior in the forefront of his mind. The hope of Christ's first coming was not a passing thought to David. He camped out in hope. As a result, he was able to rejoice and not be moved, despite many hardships. For David, the hope of the coming Messiah was a source of stability and comfort.

Simeon

In the Gospel of Luke, we read about a wonderful man named Simeon who had been given a promise from God that he would see the Christ before he died.

> **Luke 2:25-32**
> [25]Now there was a man in Jerusalem, whose name was Simeon, and this man was righteous and devout, waiting for the consolation of Israel, and the Holy Spirit was upon him.
> [26]And it had been revealed to him by the Holy Spirit that he would not see death before he had seen the Lord's Christ.
> [27]And he came in the Spirit into the temple, and when the parents brought in the child Jesus, to do for him according to the custom of the Law,
> [28]he took him up in his arms and blessed God and said,

---

5   Strong, *The New Strong's Expanded*, s.v. "*kataskēnoō*."

> [29]"Lord, now you are letting your servant depart in peace, according to your word;
> [30]for my eyes have seen your salvation
> [31]that you have prepared in the presence of all peoples,
> [32]a light for revelation to the Gentiles, and for glory to your people Israel."

At God's instructions, Simeon went to the Temple at precisely the same time Mary and Joseph were there "to do for him according to the custom of the Law." Simeon had been waiting for the coming Savior, and that day, he had the privilege of beholding him as a young child. When Simeon saw the child, he knew that this was the promised Messiah. He took the child up in his arms and blessed God. His joy overflowed, for Simeon knew that the coming of Christ meant salvation for all people, light to the Gentiles, and glory for Israel. Simeon had looked forward to the first coming of Christ, but now his wait was over! How thrilled and thankful do you think Simeon was as he held the child in his arms, the one upon whom God's plan of salvation depended?

Magi

In the gospel of Matthew, we read about the wise men (Magi) from the East who came seeking the King of the Judeans that had been born.

Matthew 2:1-5
[1]Now after Jesus was born in Bethlehem of Judea in the days of Herod the king, behold, wise men from the east came to Jerusalem,
[2]saying, "Where is he who has been born king of the Jews? For we saw his star when it rose and have come to worship him."
[3]When Herod the king heard this, he was troubled, and all Jerusalem with him;

⁴and assembling all the chief priests and scribes of the people, he inquired of them where the Christ was to be born.

⁵They told him, "In Bethlehem of Judea, for so it is written by the prophet:

Although the background and origins of the Magi are unclear, most historians agree that they were a religious sect, likely from Persia and Media, who had special training in interpreting celestial signs.⁶ When the wise men saw "his star when it rose," they knew this was a phenomenon of tremendous significance. They knew this meant the king of the Jews had been born. So, they embarked on a journey to the capital city, Jerusalem, to find the child. In the lands and times of the Bible, this would be no small undertaking. The Magi would have likely traveled in a caravan for safety, Jerusalem being a great distance away. When Herod heard about their arrival, he and all of Jerusalem were troubled. After asking the chief priests for more information about where this child was to be born, Herod then told the Magi to go to Bethlehem and search there. Herod commanded them to report back to him, pretending that he too wanted to go and worship this king.

Matthew 2:9-12
⁹After listening to the king, they went on their way. And behold, the star that they had seen when it rose went before them until it came to rest over the place where the child was.
¹⁰When they saw the star, they rejoiced exceedingly with great joy.
¹¹And going into the house, they saw the child with Mary his mother, and they fell down and worshiped him. Then, opening their treasures, they offered him gifts, gold and frankincense and myrrh.
¹²And being warned in a dream not to return to Herod, they departed to their own country by another way.

---

⁶ Freeman, *Manners and Customs of the Bible*, 332. Wierwille, *Jesus Christ Our Promised Seed*, 13-21

The wise men who visited the Savior in Bethlehem had recognized the meaning of the astronomical events that announced the birth of Christ, and they traveled a long way to see and honor him. The people of Jerusalem were unaware of the celestial signs, but these Magi of a Gentile background, had faithfully observed the heavens for generations. They had perhaps waited centuries for the first coming of Christ, and now they saw the long-awaited Messiah. Anticipating his coming had no small impact on their lives.

The hope of Christ's first coming had a profound, life-altering effect on people like Abraham, Moses, David, and others. Abraham was willing to sacrifice his own son because he was convinced of the promise of Christ's first coming. Moses was willing to give up all of Egypt's riches because he believed in the promise of future reward. David derived strength and comfort anticipating the coming Savior. All rejoiced, knowing that he would come! From the beginning, God gave humanity hope with the promise of Jesus Christ. Just as these Old Testament believers hoped in the first coming of Christ, so we can hope in his promised return. Since we know that God's promises are true, we can unreservedly invest in this information.

If you recall our opening story about XYZ stock, you remember that having knowledge of the future, even 90 days in advance, could profoundly impact your life. In that scenario, the more a person believed the information, the more it showed in his actions, and the greater the payoff. What benefit might there be when we understand what God reveals about the future, not just for 90 days, but for ages to come?

Practicality of the Hope

For the born-again one, there is only one hope, Christ Jesus:

> **Ephesians 4:4**
> There is one body and one Spirit—just as you were called to the one hope that belongs to your call—

1 Timothy 1:1
Paul, an apostle of Christ Jesus by command of God
our Savior and of **Christ Jesus our hope**, [7]

A Christian's hope does not rest in material goods, financial security,
the promise of a dream retirement, or other things the world may value.
For the Christian, there is one hope—Christ Jesus.

However, it's possible to think of the hope of Christ's return as
something that will impact us *only* in the future. But the Scriptures are
full of exhortations to walk in light of that hope, to abound in hope, be
steadfast in hope, and rejoice in hope. Rather than think about Christ's
return once in a blue moon, we are to be rooted and anchored in hope
and live as if his return is imminent. Here are some Scriptural appeals
regarding the Hope:

- "Rejoice in hope." (Rom. 5:2)
- "Abound in hope." (Rom. 15:13)
- "Know the hope of His calling." (Eph. 1:18)
- "Put on as a helmet, the hope of salvation." (1 Thess. 5:8)
- "Be joyful in hope." (Rom. 12:12)
- "Wait for our blessed hope." (Titus 2:13)
- "Hold fast the confession of our hope." (Heb. 10:23)
- "Be ready to give an answer to every man of the hope that
  we have." (1 Pet. 3:15)

Before we move on, let's take a moment to discuss the meaning of
the word "hope." In modern usage, hope often means something vague
that is wished for. For instance, we say, "I *hope* I get that job" or "I *hope*
she calls soon." What we mean is we aren't sure we will get the job but
wish we would, or we aren't sure she will call but wish she would. But
we find a different meaning of this word in the Bible. Romans 8:24-25

---

[7] Throughout this book, bolded type in Bible quotations is used by the authors
to add emphasis or to draw attention to particular words or phrases that are under
discussion.

reads, "For in this hope we were saved. Now hope that is seen is not hope. For who hopes for what he sees? But if we hope for what we do not see, we wait for it with patience." In these verses, the same truth is expressed three different ways:

- Hope that is seen is not hope.
- Who hopes for what he sees?
- We hope for what we do not see.

In other words, to hope is to look for something *not seen*. From this, we conclude that hope is a) based on the reliability of the Scriptures and b) something not seen. Hope means having a clear and confident expectation based on Scripture; it is not wishful thinking based on imagination or whim.

> Hope means having a clear and confident
> expectation based on Scripture; it is not wishful
> thinking based on imagination or whim.

The apostle Paul, by revelation, often advised the saints to conduct their lives in a particular way not only because it would profit them in this lifetime but also because Christ would return.

Colossians 3:1-5
¹If then you have been raised with Christ, seek the things that are above, where Christ is, seated at the right hand of God.
²Set your minds on things that are above, not on things that are on earth.
³For you have died, and your life is hidden with Christ in God.
⁴When Christ who is your life appears, then you also will appear **with him in glory**.

[5]Put to death **therefore** what is earthly in you: sexual immorality, impurity, passion, evil desire, and covetousness, which is idolatry.

In verse 1, the word "if" should be translated as "since." Since they have been raised with Christ, born again ones are to seek and set their thinking on things above, not on temporal, earthly matters.[8] In verse 5, the word "therefore" indicates purpose. Christians are to put to death what is earthly because Christ will appear, and they will appear with him in glory. Note how believers are encouraged to walk in this manner *because* Christ will return.

In 1 Corinthians 15, we see more exhortations in view of the Hope.

1 Corinthians 15:51-58

[51]Behold! I tell you a mystery. We shall not all sleep, but we shall all be changed,

[52]in a moment, in the twinkling of an eye, at the last trumpet. For the trumpet will sound, and the dead will be raised imperishable, and we shall be changed.

[53]For this perishable body must put on the imperishable, and this mortal body must put on immortality.

[54]When the perishable puts on the imperishable, and the mortal puts on immortality, then shall come to pass the saying that is written: "Death is swallowed up in victory."

[55]"O death, where is your victory? O death, where is your sting?"

[56]The sting of death is sin, and the power of sin is the law.

[57]But thanks be to God, who gives us the victory through our Lord Jesus Christ.

---

[8] Being raised with Christ is an accomplished reality as Col. 2:12-13 already stated. This word in Greek can also be translated as "since." Given the context, the word "if" in verse 1 might better be understood as "since."

58Therefore, my beloved brothers, be steadfast, immovable, always abounding in the work of the Lord, knowing that in the Lord your labor is not in vain.

In verse 58, we see the word "therefore." Christians are to be steadfast, immovable, and always abounding in the work of the Lord because Christ will return, and one's labor will not be in vain. Such work in the lord is not in vain because it will profit in this life *and* in the one to come.[9]

In the book of Galatians, we read:

Galatians 6:7-9
7Do not be deceived: God is not mocked, for whatever one sows, that will he also reap.
8For the one who sows to his own flesh will from the flesh reap corruption, but the one who sows to the Spirit will from the Spirit reap eternal life.
9And let us not grow weary of doing good, for in due season we will reap, if we do not give up.

Paul exhorts the saints not to grow tired of doing good because they would reap in due season, meaning they would be blessed and rewarded in the future. Once again, we see that this exhortation to live a certain way is given in consideration of the Hope.

When Paul initially went to Thessalonica, he was there for approximately three weeks.[10] In that short time, Paul taught many things and set the hope of Christ's return before them.

1 Thessalonians 1:6-10
6And you became imitators of us and of the Lord, for you received the word in much affliction, with the joy of the Holy Spirit,

---

9   To learn more about this phrase, "not in vain," please see Chapter 4: "The Reward."
10   For Paul's visit to Thessalonica, see Acts 17:1-10.

⁷so that you became an example to all the believers in Macedonia and in Achaia.

⁸For not only has the word of the Lord sounded forth from you in Macedonia and Achaia, but your faith in God has gone forth everywhere, so that we need not say anything.

⁹For they themselves report concerning us the kind of reception we had among you, and how you turned to God from idols to serve the living and true God,

¹⁰and to wait for his Son from heaven, whom he raised from the dead, Jesus who delivers us from the wrath to come.

In verse 6, we read that the Thessalonians were examples to the Macedonian and Achaian churches because they received the Word despite many afflictions and made known the Gospel. Further, they turned to God from idols and *waited for Jesus Christ to return from heaven.* As the Thessalonians were waiting for the Lord to return, they were not sitting idly by, focused only on this life. They were making known the Gospel and serving the living, true God.

Indeed, the hope of Christ's return is a central theme in the Thessalonian epistles.[11] For example, in chapter 4, Paul writes about how this hope of Christ's return brings unparalleled encouragement and comfort to the Christian.

1 Thessalonians 4:13-18

¹³But we do not want you to be uninformed, brothers, about those who are asleep, that you may not grieve as others do who have no hope.

¹⁴For since we believe that Jesus died and rose again, even so, through Jesus, God will bring with him those who have fallen asleep.

---

[11]   For instance, Paul writes about the hope of Christ's return in 1 Thess. 1:3, 10; 2:19; 3:13; 4:13-18; 5:8-11, 23; and 2 Thess. 1:7-10; 2:1-12, 15.

¹⁵For this we declare to you by a word from the Lord, that we who are alive, who are left until the coming of the Lord, will not precede those who have fallen asleep. ¹⁶For the Lord himself will descend from heaven with a cry of command, with the voice of an archangel, and with the sound of the trumpet of God. And the dead in Christ will rise first.

¹⁷Then we who are alive, who are left, will be caught up together with them in the clouds to meet the Lord in the air, and so we will always be with the Lord.

¹⁸Therefore encourage one another with these words.

Perhaps the greatest sorrow in life is losing a loved one. Death is a sting, and stings are painful. Even though Christians grieve, they do not have to sorrow as unbelievers do, for they can look forward to Christ's return when the dead in Christ rise first. Then, those alive in Christ will be caught up in the clouds, and all will always be together with the Lord. Truly this knowledge brings great comfort to those who are grieving. While the separation death brings is painful, it is *temporary*. At Christ's return, the reunion is *eternal*. Wouldn't that bring comfort to those grieving?

The Hope is given as one of the key motivators for Christians to live a godly life.

1 Timothy 4:7-8

⁷Have nothing to do with irreverent, silly myths. Rather train yourself for godliness;

⁸for while bodily training is of some value, godliness is of value in every way, as it holds promise for the present life and also for the life to come.

We train ourselves in godliness not only because it profits us in this life but also because it will profit us in the life to come. We might do things for many reasons: duty, personal welfare, desire for approval, etc. But the Scriptures often encourage the saints to live in a particular way, not because it's expedient, not because it's popular, but because Christ is coming back. Perhaps E. W. Bullinger sums it up best when he writes, "There is scarcely a duty or a responsibility connected with Christian living that is not immediately linked on to, and thus bound up with, the hope of our Lord's return."[12]

Impact of Christ's Return

So great is this hope, it impacts all creation.

Romans 8:19-25
[19]For the **creation** waits with eager longing for the revealing of the sons of God.
[20]For the **creation** was subjected to futility, not willingly, but because of him who subjected it, in hope
[21]that the **creation** itself will be set free from its bondage to corruption and obtain the freedom of the glory of the children of God.
[22]For we know that the whole **creation** has been groaning together in the pains of childbirth until now.
[23]And not only the **creation**, but we ourselves, who have the firstfruits of the Spirit, groan inwardly as we wait eagerly for adoption as sons, the redemption of our bodies.
[24]For in this hope we were saved. Now hope that is seen is not hope. For who hopes for what he sees?
[25]But if we hope for what we do not see, we wait for it with patience.

Verse 19 describes a startling reality: the creation is waiting for the revealing of the sons of God, which takes place in the future. In verse 19, "eager longing" means "to watch with head erect or outstretched,

---

12   Bullinger, "The Practical Power of our Hope," 31.

to direct attention to anything, to wait for in suspense."[13] If you've ever witnessed someone waiting for a train to arrive at the station, you have seen this very act—with head outstretched, the person peers down the track for the train to arrive. The Scriptures declare that all creation is waiting with outstretched necks for the revealing of the sons of God to take place. Why? Because it will be set free from the bondage of corruption. The hope of Christ's return is so momentous that all creation will be impacted.

Angels are, of course, part of creation, and they also eagerly look forward to the future glory associated with Christ.

> **1 Peter 1:10-12**
> [10]Concerning this salvation, the prophets who prophesied about the grace that was to be yours searched and inquired carefully,
> [11]inquiring what person or time the Spirit of Christ in them was indicating when he predicted the sufferings of Christ and the subsequent glories.
> [12]It was revealed to them that they were serving not themselves but you, in the things that have now been announced to you through those who preached the good news to you by the Holy Spirit sent from heaven, things into which angels long to look.

Angels long to investigate certain things about the Gospel. Contextually, the "things" in verse 12 refer to future salvation (v. 5) and future glories (v. 11). Angels long to know more about what's coming in the future! The hope of Christ's return and all that takes place in the coming ages are so far-reaching that all creation, including angels, eagerly look forward to it. The fulfillment of the Christian's hope is not a mere blip in the timeline of the ages. It is a monumental occurrence which brings deliverance to all creation.

---

[13]   Thayer, *A Greek-English Lexicon*, s.v. "*apokaradokia*."

> The fulfillment of the Christian's hope is not a mere
> blip in the timeline of the ages. It is a monumental
> occurrence which brings deliverance to all creation.

Summary and Conclusion

In this chapter, we have seen that God's promises regarding the future are dependable. In contrast, man's words and forecasts are often unreliable, if not downright deceptive. But when God tells us in His Word that Christ is coming back, we can take that knowledge to the bank.

Time and again, the Scriptures remind us that Christ *is coming back*. This was the first message given to the apostles immediately after Christ's ascension and, therefore, is of utmost importance. The Scriptures tell us that we are to *abound* in hope and to *rejoice* in hope, not to put it on the back burner, so to speak. Far from ignoring the Hope, Christians are to pray for understanding of this vital topic.

Ephesians 1:16-20

[16]I do not cease to give thanks for you, remembering you in my prayers,

[17]that the God of our Lord Jesus Christ, the Father of glory, may give you the Spirit of wisdom and of revelation in the knowledge of him,

[18]having the eyes of your hearts enlightened, that you may know what is the hope to which he has called you, what are the riches of his glorious inheritance in the saints,

[19]and what is the immeasurable greatness of his power toward us who believe, according to the working of his great might

[20]that he worked in Christ when he raised him from the dead and seated him at his right hand in the heavenly places,

God desires that His children understand their hope. Paul prayed this for the Ephesians, and we can pray this for ourselves today. Jesus Christ has always been the hope of humanity, and today Christ Jesus is our One Hope.

Chapter 2

The Return of Christ

Having seen some of the momentous significance of the Hope, we now will consider what the Scriptures say about Christ's return. The Bible speaks about Christ coming for the Church, which is often called the Gathering Together. But it also speaks about Christ coming during the Day of the Lord, which occurs at a different time. Conflating these two comings of Christ has caused untold confusion. In this chapter, we first cover the clear Scriptures that speak about Christ's return for the Church and then address some common passages that are often misconstrued regarding his return. We will also cover some Scriptures that describe the Day of the Lord.

Today, people may have heard that Jesus Christ is coming back, but controversy and speculation tend to pervade this field. To compound matters, there has been a failure to appreciate what Christ's return means for the Christian because of the erroneous teaching of life after death, meaning that people immediately ascend into heaven or enter some alternate realm after dying. After all, why would Christ's return be such a momentous occasion if the dead are already alive, enjoying themselves in heaven?

The Scriptures tell us that when a person dies, he no longer has conscious thought. All his plans and ideas end on the day of his death. His body goes back to the earth, meaning that it corrupts and decomposes (Ps. 6:5, 146:4). The Scriptures also tell us that the dead know nothing and have no memory or other human capability and that there is no work, thought, knowledge, or wisdom in death (Eccles. 9:5-6, 10).[14] The soul of man does not live eternally, and there is no life after death apart from the resurrection of the dead. Man does not

---

[14] For a detailed discussion of this topic, see the book *Are the Dead Alive Now?* listed in the bibliography.

immediately go to heaven after he dies. In fact, the Scriptures declare that no man has gone to heaven except the Lord Jesus Christ (John 3:13). Moreover, the Bible tells us that at his return, the dead in Christ will rise first (1 Thess. 4:16). If the dead are already in heaven, why would they need to be raised? That is one reason why the return of Christ is necessary—to raise the dead!

Another erroneous teaching says that Christ's coming is a single event when, in truth, his return encompasses many events. The first coming of Christ involved his birth in Bethlehem, his family's move to Egypt, and then to Nazareth. Jesus began his ministry when he was about thirty years old. He was crucified, died, buried, and then God raised him from the dead. Sometime later, he ascended into heaven. All these events and more were part of his *first* coming. Just as his first coming involved numerous events and spanned a period of time, so too will his return involve a series of events and span a period of time. Assuming that Christ's return is a *single* event results in much confusion.

Here are some of the things that the Scriptures say will take place in the future:[15]

- Coming of the Lord for the Church, Gathering Together (1 Cor. 15:51-58; 1 Thess. 4:13-18; 2 Thess. 2:1)
- The Abomination of Desolation (Dan. 9:27, 11:31; Matt. 24:15; Mark 13:14)
- The Revealing of the Man of Lawlessness (2 Thess. 2:3-10)
- The Great Tribulation (Matt. 24:21; Mark 13:24; Rev. 7:14)
- The Day of the Lord and the wrath of God (Isa. 14)
- Darkening of Sun and Moon and Shaking of the Powers of Heaven (Isa. 13:10-13; Joel 2:10, 31; Matt. 24:29; Mark 13:24; Acts 2:20; Rev. 6:12-14)

---

[15] This is not an exhaustive list of future events, nor is it intended to indicate a particular order. While we can ascertain some information as to the relative placement of future events, it is impossible to know their precise timing. As Jesus Christ warned, "It is not for you to know times or seasons that the Father has fixed by his own authority" (Acts 1:7).

- The Coming of the Son of Man (Matt. 24:30; Mark 13:26, 14:62; Luke 21:27; Rev. 1:7)
- The Gathering of the Elect (Matt. 24:31; Mark 13:27)
- Binding of Satan for 1000 years (Rev. 20:1-3)
- The First Resurrection (Rev. 20:4-5)
- The Reign of Christ and Others for a 1000 Years on Earth (Rev. 20:4)
- The Great White Throne Judgment (Matt. 19:28, 25:31; Rev. 20:11-15)
- Lake of Fire and the Second Death (Rev. 20:10ff)
- The New Heavens and Earth (Isa. 51:6, 65:17; 2 Pet. 3:5-13; Rev. 21:1)
- The Administration of the Fullness of Times (Eph. 1:9-10)
- The End (1 Cor. 15:24-28)

Note how several future events speak of Christ's coming: the coming of the Lord for the Church, the Day of the Lord, the Coming of the Son of Man. As we will see, these are not the same event. The coming of the Lord for the Church is one event, while his coming during the Day of the Lord is another.

Christ's Return for the Church: The Gathering Together

In this section, we will cover two very clear passages about Christ's return: 1 Corinthians 15:51-58 and 1 Thessalonians 4:13-18. In these verses, we will learn about what takes place when Christ returns to gather the Church.

1 Corinthians 15:51-58
[51]Behold! I tell you a mystery. We shall not all sleep, but we shall all be changed,
[52]in a moment, in the twinkling of an eye, at the last trumpet. For the trumpet will sound, and the dead will be raised imperishable, and we shall be changed.

⁵³For this perishable body must put on the imperishable, and this mortal body must put on immortality.

⁵⁴When the perishable puts on the imperishable, and the mortal puts on immortality, then shall come to pass the saying that is written: "Death is swallowed up in victory."

⁵⁵"O death, where is your victory? O death, where is your sting?"

⁵⁶The sting of death is sin, and the power of sin is the law.

⁵⁷But thanks be to God, who gives us the victory through our Lord Jesus Christ.

⁵⁸Therefore, my beloved brothers, be steadfast, immovable, always abounding in the work of the Lord, knowing that in the Lord your labor is not in vain.

These verses are quite clear about what occurs when Christ returns for the Church. First, we note that this passage refers to believers, born again ones, and not to every person.[16] Second, we note that Paul is revealing a mystery, meaning that this information was previously unknown. Third, we see that not all believers will die before Christ's return, but all will be changed. The dead in Christ will be raised and given imperishable bodies, and those alive at Christ's coming will put on immortality. Finally, this change occurs instantly, beautifully expressed in the phrase "in the twinkling of an eye." Both the living and the dead go through this miraculous change. Not every saint will be dead at Christ's return, but every saint will be transformed!

God's Word describes the sequence of events in slow motion, so to speak, but all of this happens quickly. Those Christians who are alive when Christ returns will put on immortality; those who have died will put on new, imperishable bodies. What a thrilling reality! In view of these great truths, the believers are encouraged to be steadfast, immovable, and always abounding in the work of the lord.

---

[16]   1 Cor. 15:23 reads, "But each in his own order: Christ the firstfruits, then at his coming those who belong to Christ."

The return of Christ for the Church is also described in 1 Thessalonians 4.

1 Thessalonians 4:13-18

[13]But we do not want you to be uninformed, brothers, about those who are asleep, that you may not grieve as others do who have no hope.

[14]For since we believe that Jesus died and rose again, even so, through Jesus, God will bring with him those who have fallen asleep.

[15]For this we declare to you by a word from the Lord, that we who are alive, who are left until the coming of the Lord, will not precede those who have fallen asleep.

[16]For the Lord himself will descend from heaven with a cry of command, with the voice of an archangel, and with the sound of the trumpet of God. And the dead in Christ will rise first.

[17]Then we who are alive, who are left, will be caught up together with them in the clouds to meet the Lord in the air, and so we will always be with the Lord.

[18]Therefore encourage one another with these words.

In verses 13, 14, and 15, "asleep" is a euphemism meaning those who had died. These verses have important information regarding those believers who had died. God did not want the Thessalonians to be uninformed about what was in store for them. They were told that when Christ returns, the dead in Christ would be raised first! Then, those Christians who are still alive when Christ returns would be caught up in the air with their raised brethren, and together they would meet the lord in the air. No wonder these are such encouraging words!

Incidentally, this meeting together with the lord is referred to as our being "gathered together" to him (2 Thess. 2:1). As such, in many Christian circles, Christ's return for the Church is often called the "Gathering Together." So, in this book when we speak of the

Gathering Together, we are speaking about the event described here in 1 Thessalonians 4:13-18.

In verse 16 of this same passage, we read that "the Lord himself will descend from heaven with a cry of command, with the voice of an archangel, and with the sound of the trumpet of God." The phrase "cry of command" is a translation of one Greek word *keleusma,* meaning "an order, command, specifically, a stimulating cry."[17] According to Thayer, the word was used in profane Greek literature to refer to a ship's captain urging on his rowers. In other words, this cry of command is a summoning shout that signals *something significant* is about to take place: the dead in Christ are raised, and the alive in Christ are caught up in the air. Then all sons of God will always be with the lord.[18]

We should carefully note that 1 Thessalonians 4:13-18 did not say that the dead in Christ are already in heaven with Jesus. Neither does the passage mention anything about Christ coming *on the earth,* for the Gathering Together takes place *in the air.* Finally, there is no directive to look for any signs leading up to Christ's coming for the Church.

> The return of Christ for the Church is referred to as
> the Gathering Together
> (2 Thess. 2:1).

---

[17]   Thayer, *A Greek-English Lexicon,* s.v. *"keleusma."*

[18]   The phrase "always be with the Lord" does not necessarily mean the Church will always be exactly where the lord is at all times in the future. According to Greek syntax, the last phrase of this verse reads, "always with the Lord we shall be," which draws emphasis to the word "we." The phrase, occurring at the end of the sentence emphasizes that the dead and the living will no longer be separated from one another, nor will they be separated from their lord. This would bring comfort to those who were grieving. In other words, those who had been separated from their loved ones by death would now be reunited. For the Christian, Christ's return destroys that separation forever. Right before he ascended, Christ declared, "Behold, I am with you always to the end of the age" (Matt. 28:20), and yet he ascended into heaven, leaving his followers on earth. So, the phrase "always be with" does not necessarily mean to literally be with someone in the same place. Essentially, it means no more separation by death.

So far, we have seen from the Scriptures that:

- The dead in Christ shall be raised first and put on imperishable bodies.
- Those that are alive in Christ will put on immortal bodies.
- When Christ comes, he will descend with a cry of command and the voice of an archangel, and there will be the sound of the trumpet of God.
- The dead in Christ who are raised and the alive in Christ will be caught up together in the clouds to meet the lord in the air.
- All this will happen "in a moment, in the twinkling of an eye."
- All Christians will always be with the lord.
- These words bring great comfort and encouragement!

The two clear passages we have read, 1 Corinthians 15:51-58 and 1 Thessalonians 4:13-18, tell us what will take place when Christ returns for the Church. These are records of great comfort and victory. There is nothing to suggest that his return is something to fear or dread, nor is there any directive to look for signs of his coming. Whether Christians are dead or alive, when Christ returns, all will be changed, all will have new bodies, and all will meet the lord in the air. And thereafter, we all will be forever with our lord! Such knowledge is cause for great joy and rejoicing.

The Day of the Lord

Having opened with two very clear sections of Scripture that describe Christ's coming for the Church, the Gathering Together, we now turn our attention to some passages that are often misconstrued or misunderstood. These passages speak about Christ's coming, but they refer to his coming during the Day of the Lord, which is not the same event as his coming for the Church. [19]

---

[19] For more details on this topic see Appendix A: "The Day of the Lord."

To begin, let's recall that 1 Thessalonians 4:13-18 describes that glorious, joyous event, the Gathering Together of the Church. However, in the very next verse, 1 Thessalonians 5:1, Paul introduces a *new* topic keyed by the word "now":

1 Thessalonians 5:1-3

[1]**Now** concerning the times and the seasons, brothers, you have no need to have anything written to you.
[2]For you yourselves are fully aware that the **day of the Lord** will come like a thief in the night.
[3]While people are saying, "There is peace and security," then sudden destruction will come upon them as labor pains come upon a pregnant woman, and they will not escape.

Paul shifts from writing about the return of Christ for the Church to the Day of the Lord. You may recall that the information Paul gave the Thessalonians about the Gathering Together was *new* information. Indeed, this was called a "mystery" (1 Cor. 15:51). In contrast, Paul says that the Thessalonians already knew about the Day of the Lord.

How did they know about the Day of the Lord? Perhaps Paul and others had taught them, or perhaps they learned about it from reading or hearing references to it in the Old Testament.[20] No matter how they learned it, the Thessalonians were completely aware that the Day of the Lord "would come like a thief in the night," meaning by surprise and without warning. So, while the Thessalonians had just learned about the return of Christ and the Gathering Together, they had been "fully aware" about the Day of the Lord. Whereas the Gathering Together meant comfort for the saints, the Day of the Lord meant "sudden destruction" for those caught by it. What contrasting events!

---

[20] It's likely that Paul did teach them some things about the Day of the Lord. In 2 Thess. 2:5, in referring to the things related to the Day of the Lord, Paul says, "Do you not remember that when I was with you I told you these things?"

The Day of the Lord: Old Testament Records

The Day of the Lord is not the same as the Gathering Together. Christ returns for the Church—this is the Gathering Together—but Christ also comes during the Day of the Lord, as we will see. People confuse these two comings of Christ. Therefore, at this point in the chapter, we will need to digress to learn some truths about the Day of the Lord. [21] (The reader may wish to read Appendix A: "The Day of the Lord"). Let's turn to one section from the book of Isaiah.

Isaiah 13:6-9

[6]Wail, for the **day of the LORD** is near; as destruction from the Almighty it will come!
[7]Therefore all hands will be feeble, and every human heart will melt.
[8]They will be dismayed: pangs and agony will seize them; they will be in anguish like a woman in labor. They will look aghast at one another; their faces will be aflame.
[9]Behold, the **day of the LORD** comes, cruel, with wrath and fierce anger, to make the land a desolation and to destroy its sinners from it.

Note that the Day of the Lord comes suddenly, bringing destruction, fear, pain, agony, and anguish. It comes with wrath and fierce anger. It goes without saying that no one would be comforted by these words!

Let's continue reading about the Day of the Lord from Isaiah 13:

Isaiah 13:10-16

[10]For the stars of the heavens and their constellations will not give their light; the sun will be dark at its rising, and the moon will not shed its light.

---

[21] The Day of the Lord spans a period of time. It is not literally a day, a 24-hour period.

[11]I will punish the world for its evil, and the wicked for their iniquity; I will put an end to the pomp of the arrogant, and lay low the pompous pride of the ruthless. [12]I will make people more rare than fine gold, and mankind than the gold of Ophir. [13]Therefore I will make the heavens tremble, and the earth will be shaken out of its place, at the **wrath of the LORD of hosts in the day of his fierce anger.** [14]And like a hunted gazelle, or like sheep with none to gather them, each will turn to his own people, and each will flee to his own land. [15]Whoever is found will be thrust through, and whoever is caught will fall by the sword. [16]Their infants will be dashed in pieces before their eyes; their houses will be plundered and their wives ravished.

From this record, we see that the Day of the Lord is not a desirable time, for it brings "destruction from the Almighty" (v. 7). People's hands will be weak, and their hearts will melt, which are allusions to pain and dismay. People will experience agony like a woman going into labor. During the Day of the Lord, the ground will become a wasteland. Sinners will be destroyed. Note how God's intense wrath and anger are associated with the Day of the Lord.

Let's also note the cataclysmic celestial events that take place during the Day of the Lord. The stars of heaven and the constellations will not give light; the sun will be darkened, and the moon will not shine. The world will be punished for its evil and the wicked for their iniquity. During this period, there will be so much destruction that man will be "more rare than fine gold." Gold is precious or costly because of its relative rarity, so the implication is that few people will survive. What a dramatic, unforgettable way to describe utter ruin. Can we begin to see that the Day of the Lord is *not* the same joyous, comforting event as the Gathering Together?

Day of the Lord: 1 Thessalonians 5

Having briefly looked at one passage from the Old Testament about the Day of the Lord, let's return to 1 Thessalonians 5:1-5, remembering that these verses are speaking about the *Day of the Lord*.

1 Thessalonians 5:1-5

¹Now concerning the times and the seasons, brothers, you have no need to have anything written to you.
²For you yourselves are fully aware that the **day of the Lord** will come like a thief in the night.
³While people are saying, "There is peace and security," then sudden destruction will come upon **them** as labor pains come upon a pregnant woman, and **they** will not escape.
⁴But **you** are not in darkness, brothers, for that day to surprise [overtake] **you** like a thief.
⁵For **you** are all children of light, children of the day. **We** are not of the night or of the darkness.

This passage refers to the Day of the Lord, *not* to the return of Christ for the Church. The "labor pains" in verse 3 is the same comparison used in Isaiah 13:8. Isaiah told us that this destruction would be sudden, just as verse 3 describes it. Even though they occur back-to-back in the printed Bible, 1 Thessalonians 4:13-18 and 1 Thessalonians 5:1-5 do not speak about the same subject! The first passage describes the Gathering Together, and the second describes events of the Day of the Lord. Keeping these two passages straight is tantamount to rightly handling the Word of truth and letting the Scripture interpret itself.

| 1 Thessalonians 4:13-18 | The Gathering Together |
| 1 Thessalonians 5:1-5 | The Day of the Lord |

Further, if we pay close attention to the pronouns in 1 Thessalonians 5:1-5, we see that they signify two different groups of people. The word "they" in verse 3 refers to those who would go through the Day of the Lord. In contrast, "you" in verses 4 and 5 refers to the saints, those who would be gathered together. In addition, the word "but" in verse 4 contrasts these two groups of people. Finally, the word "surprise" in verse 4 might also be translated as "to lay hold of, seize, overtake."[22] Why wouldn't the saints be overtaken by the Day of the Lord? Because they would already be gathered together before the events of the Day of the Lord unfolded.

In 1 Thessalonians 5:3-5, the pronouns "we" and "you" refer to those who are called "brothers, children of light, children of the day." In other words, the saints. The pronouns "they" and "them" refer to those who are called "people, [children] of the night, [children] of the darkness." In other words, unbelievers. Understanding to whom the pronouns refer shows us that the events spoken of in 1 Thessalonians 5:1-5 refer to the Day of the Lord, not Christ's coming to gather the Church.

We offer the following chart to help clarify these details regarding the pronouns.

Pronouns used in 1Thessalonians 5:3-5

Subject	We, you (those in Christ)	They, them (those not in Christ)
Who is being addressed	children of the light, children of the day,	children of darkness, children of the night,
As to their knowledge of the Day of the Lord	fully aware/not in darkness	surprised by it/in darkness
As to the effect of the Day of the Lord	not overtaken by it (gathered together before the Day of the Lord occurs), appointed to salvation	sudden destruction/they will not escape, appointed to wrath

---

[22] Strong, *The New Strong's Expanded Exhaustive*, s.v. "*katalambanō*."

In the next five verses, Paul leaves off speaking about the Day of the Lord and gives some appeals to the Church.

1 Thessalonians 5:6-11

⁶So then let **us** not sleep, as others do, but let **us** keep awake and be sober.

⁷For those who sleep, sleep at night, and those who get drunk, are drunk at night.

⁸But since we belong to the day, let us be sober, having put on the breastplate of faith and love, and for a helmet the hope of salvation.

⁹For God has not destined us for wrath, but to obtain salvation through our Lord Jesus Christ,

¹⁰who died for us so that whether we are awake or asleep we might live with him.

¹¹Therefore encourage one another and build one another up, just as you are doing.

In verse 6, "us" refers to the children of light who await the return of Christ. Paul has now shifted back to speaking about matters pertaining to the Church, not matters that take place during the Day of the Lord. The Thessalonians are encouraged not to "sleep" while waiting for Christ to return. In this context, "sleep" is used figuratively to mean yielding to indifference or apathy concerning one's spiritual state.[23] Indeed, Christians are not to become complacent while waiting for Christ's return but to keep awake and sober because he could return at any moment.

In this section, we have seen that information about the return of Christ is encouraging and comforting. In contrast, the events of the Day of the Lord are fearsome and dreadful. It is a great comfort for Christians to recognize that Christ will come for them *before* the Day of the Lord and that they are delivered from the coming wrath!

The first epistle to the Thessalonians has made this abundantly

---

[23]   Thayer, *A Greek-English Lexicon*, s.v. "*katheudō*."

clear: Christ's coming for the Church takes place *before* the Day of the Lord. Therefore, meeting the lord in the air must take place before the events of the Day of the Lord start to unfold. Only those in darkness will be subject to the destruction and wrath that accompanies the Day of the Lord, and this cannot refer to any in the Church because we are delivered from the wrath to come.

Romans 5:9
Since, therefore, we have now been justified by his blood, much more shall we be saved by him from the wrath of God.

1 Thessalonians 1:10
and to wait for his Son from heaven, whom he raised from the dead, Jesus who delivers us from the wrath to come.

Could these verses be any clearer? Christians are saved from the wrath of God to come, which takes place during the Day of the Lord.

In the records we have studied, there is no mention of precisely *when* Christ will return for the Church. We only know that the Gathering Together *precedes* the Day of the Lord. One might say the Gathering Together is the triggering event for the end times to start to unfold. Furthermore, there is no directive to look for signs of Christ's return. Instead, Christians are to be alert, looking for his return because it may happen at any time.

> The Gathering Together of the Church is the triggering event for the end times to start to unfold.

Deceptive Teaching about the Day of the Lord

Having looked at key passages from the Pauline epistles, we understand that Christ's return for the Church *precedes* the Day of the Lord. We also understand that the Day of the Lord is associated with the wrath of God, fearsome celestial events, and the pride of man being humbled. Finally, we know that the Church has been *delivered* from this wrath to come.

However, some wrongly teach that Christians must go through the fearsome events of the Day of the Lord, or they conflate the Day of the Lord with the Gathering Together. These doctrinal errors have caused great confusion and discouragement.

It turns out that this confusion is not unique to our time. Deceptive teaching about the Day of the Lord had already become a serious concern in the first-century Church, as we see from the following passage:

> **2 Thessalonians 2:1-6**
> ¹Now concerning the coming of our Lord Jesus Christ and our being gathered together to him, we ask you, brothers,
> ²not to be quickly shaken in mind or alarmed, either by a spirit or a spoken word, or a letter seeming to be from us, to the effect that the **day of the Lord** has come.
> ³Let no one deceive you in any way. For that day will not come, unless the rebellion (*apostasia*) comes first, and the man of lawlessness is revealed, the son of destruction,
> ⁴who opposes and exalts himself against every so-called god or object of worship, so that he takes his seat in the temple of God, proclaiming himself to be God.
> ⁵Do you not remember that when I was still with you I told you these things?
> ⁶And you know what is restraining him now so that he may be revealed in his time.

In verse 1, Paul speaks about the Gathering Together, and yet in the same breath, he asks them not to be shaken up or alarmed. How can this be? We know that information concerning the Gathering Together was given for encouragement and comfort, so why would they have been disturbed? According to verses 2 and 3, someone was trying to deceive the Thessalonian saints by teaching them that the Day of the Lord had already come.

Knowing about some of the dreadful events accompanying the Day of the Lord, we can appreciate why these saints would be deeply unsettled. They had been taught that the Day of the Lord would not overtake them as a thief, but now someone was teaching them otherwise. Paul told the Thessalonians they were not to allow themselves to be deceived by such false information, whether by "a spirit or a spoken word, or a letter seeming to be from us." They must not allow anyone to deceive them with this false teaching, which said the Day of the Lord had already come.

In verse 3, Paul rightly reminds them that the Day of the Lord would not come unless the "rebellion" (*apostasia*) comes first. What does this mean? Some English Bibles translate rebellion as "departure" or "departing":

> **2 Thessalonians 2:3** (WEB)
> Let no one deceive you in any way. For it will not be, unless the **departure** (*apostasia*) comes first, and the man of sin is revealed, the son of destruction,

> **2 Thessalonians 2:3** (HNV)
> Let no one deceive you in any way. For it will not be, unless the **departure** (*apostasia*) comes first, and the man of sin is revealed, the son of destruction,

> **2 Thessalonians 2:3** (GEN)
> Let no man deceive you by any means: for *that day shall not come*, except there come a **departing** (*apostasia*) first,

and that that man of sin be disclosed, *even* the son of perdition.

2 Thessalonians 2:3 (WT)

Do not let anyone deceive you in any way, *for that day will not be present* unless there first comes the **departure** (*apostasia*) and the man of /lawlessness {Or/ sin} is revealed, the son of destruction,

The "departure" in verse 3 is the Gathering Together of verse 1. Paul again assures the Thessalonians that the Day of the Lord *would not come* until after the departure of the Church. That is, the Church would be gathered together *before* the Day of the Lord. This is important for all Christians to remember, so they are not deceived. Once the Church has been gathered together and has departed, many future events described in the Scriptures will start to unfold. The Gathering Together of the Church and the Day of the Lord are not the same, nor does the Gathering Together come during the Day of the Lord.

> Gathering Together of the Church
> *then*
> the Day of the Lord

Unfortunately, some versions of the Bible translate *apostasia* as "rebellion" or "apostasy." "Apostasy" means to turn away from the truth. Based on this translation, there would have to be a significant turning away from the truth before the Day of the Lord took place. Let's assume for a moment that *apostasia* does refer to a turning away from the truth. Would that bring comfort to any Christian? Would knowing that Christians are to expect a great departure from the truth help them to not be "shaken in mind or alarmed"? The idea is preposterous. The thought of many fellow Christians forsaking the truth would cause *even more* alarm.

We should recognize that during Paul's lifetime, there *was* a significant turning away from the truth (2 Tim. 1:15). Yet Paul did not say this departing from the truth was a source of rejoicing or that it indicated the Day of the Lord was just around the corner.

As any student of Church history knows, throughout the centuries, there have been great revivals of the truth of God's Word and significant departures from the truth, yet the Day of the Lord still has not come. Suggesting to the Thessalonians that a rebellion from the truth needed to happen before the Day of the Lord would be no basis for comfort. Furthermore, if the saints were now to look for apostasy to take place, wouldn't that be a "sign" that the Day of the Lord was imminent? How then would it come "like a thief in the night"? Taking all of this into account, we understand that "rebellion" and "apostasy" are not legitimate translations of the word *apostasia* in 2 Thessalonians 2:3. Instead, this word should be translated as "departure."

> **2 Thessalonians 2:3** (WT)
> Do not let anyone deceive you in any way, *for that day will not be present* unless there first comes the **departure** *(apostasia)* and the man of /lawlessness {Or/ sin} is revealed, the son of destruction,

Christians are not to let *anyone* deceive them in *any* way! They are to know that the departure of the Church—the Gathering Together— comes *first* and then the events of the Day of the Lord take place.

Christ's Coming during the Day of the Lord

Hopefully, we have cleared up some potentially confusing Scriptures and have shown that Christ comes for the Church *before* the Day of the Lord. To conclude this section, we now consider two passages that are often used to say the Day of the Lord is the same thing as the Gathering Together of the Church.

Matthew 24:29-31

[29]"Immediately after the tribulation of those days the sun will be darkened, and the moon will not give its light, and the stars will fall from heaven, and the powers of the heavens will be shaken.

[30]Then will appear in heaven the sign of the Son of Man, and then all the tribes of the earth will mourn, and they will see the Son of Man coming on the clouds of heaven with power and great glory.

[31]And he will send out his angels with a loud trumpet call, and they will gather his elect from the four winds, from one end of heaven to the other.

Revelation 1:7

Behold, he is coming with the clouds, and every eye will see him, even those who pierced him, and all tribes of the earth will wail on account of him. Even so. Amen.

Even though there are similarities between these verses and those that describe the return of Christ for the Church—they mention clouds, angels, a trumpet, and the bodily presence of Christ—there are stark differences. First, the events recorded in these verses take place *after* the tribulation. Second, there is mourning on the part of all the tribes of the earth, not rejoicing. Third, there is no mention of the dead in Christ being raised. Fourth, there is no mention of people meeting Christ in the air, but angels are sent out to gather the elect. Finally, there are notable celestial events such as the sun being darkened, the stars falling, the moon not giving light, and the powers of heaven being shaken. (Indeed, if we continued reading Matthew 24, we would see even more differences.)[24]

Recall that when we read Isaiah 13, we saw that these fearsome celestial events took place during the Day of the Lord. Let's reread just two verses:

---

[24] For a more detailed discussion of the comparisons, please see Appendix A: "The Day of the Lord."

Isaiah 13:9-10

⁹Behold, the **day of the LORD** comes, cruel, with wrath and fierce anger, to make the land a desolation and to destroy its sinners from it.

¹⁰For the stars of the heavens and their constellations will not give their light; the sun will be dark at its rising, and the moon will not shed its light.

The stars, moon, and sun being darkened are not everyday occurrences! These strange and wondrous events take place during the Day of the Lord.

The prophet Joel also wrote about these alarming celestial events:

Joel 2:10-11

¹⁰The earth quakes before them; the heavens tremble. The sun and the moon are darkened, and the stars withdraw their shining.

¹¹The LORD utters his voice before his army, for his camp is exceedingly great; he who executes his word is powerful. For the **day of the LORD** is great and very awesome; who can endure it?

Joel 3:14-15

¹⁴Multitudes, multitudes, in the valley of decision! For **the day of the LORD** is near in the valley of decision.

¹⁵The sun and the moon are darkened, and the stars withdraw their shining.

Like Isaiah, the prophet Joel also wrote about the sun, moon, and stars being darkened and that this takes place during the Day of the Lord. So, when Jesus Christ speaks of his coming in Matthew 24:29-31, and when the apostle John wrote about Christ's coming on the clouds in Revelation 1:7, they are referring to his coming *during the Day of the Lord.*

The sun, moon, and stars will be darkened during the Day of

the Lord, and then Jesus Christ will appear, coming on the clouds of heaven. But for our purposes in this chapter, let us repeat: Christ's coming for the Church and his coming during the Day of the Lord are *not* the same event!

Christ's coming to gather the Church
*is **not** the same as*
Christ's coming during the Day of the Lord.

The Lord's Return Brings Comfort

Let's close this chapter by looking at some final passages which speak of that blessed event, the Gathering Together.

James 5:7-11

[7]Be patient, therefore, brothers, until the coming of the Lord. See how the farmer waits for the precious fruit of the earth, being patient about it, until it receives the early and the late rains.

[8]You also, be patient. Establish your hearts, for the coming of the Lord is at hand.

[9]Do not grumble against one another, brothers, so that you may not be judged; behold, the Judge is standing at the door.

[10]As an example of suffering and patience, brothers, take the prophets who spoke in the name of the Lord.

[11]Behold, we consider those blessed who remained steadfast. You have heard of the steadfastness of Job, and you have seen the purpose of the Lord, how the Lord is compassionate and merciful.

Here, the saints were encouraged to patiently wait for the lord's coming, like a farmer waits for his harvest. In verse 8, "at hand" is an idiom meaning near in time. James encouraged the saints to be patient and to establish their hearts because the coming of Christ was near—he could return at any moment! Note how the word "patient" occurs four times in this passage. Patient means "to be of a long spirit, not to lose heart, to persevere patiently in enduring misfortunes and troubles, to be patient in bearing the offenses and injuries of others."[25] Knowing that the Lord can appear at any moment, the believers are enabled to be patient and to persevere, especially in the face of suffering.

And in 1 Peter, we read:

1 Peter 1:3-9, 13
[3]Blessed be the God and Father of our Lord Jesus Christ! According to his great mercy, he has caused us to be born again to a living hope through the resurrection of Jesus Christ from the dead,
[4]to an inheritance that is imperishable, undefiled, and unfading, kept in heaven for you,
[5]who by God's power are being guarded through faith for a salvation ready to be revealed in the last time.
[6]In this you rejoice, though now for a little while, if necessary, you have been grieved by various trials,
[7]so that the tested genuineness of your faith—more precious than gold that perishes though it is tested by fire—may be found to result in praise and glory and honor at the revelation of Jesus Christ.
[8]Though you have not seen him, you love him. Though you do not now see him, you believe in him and rejoice with joy that is inexpressible and filled with glory,
[9]obtaining the outcome of your faith, the salvation of your souls.

---

[25] Strong, *The New Strong's Exhaustive*, s.v. *"makrothymeō."*

Verse 13
Therefore, preparing your minds for action, and being sober-minded, set your hope fully on the grace that will be brought to you at the revelation of Jesus Christ.

The hope of Christ's return is a source of great joy and rejoicing, not fear or sorrow, especially during trials. Here, Peter reminds the saints that continuing to believe through these trials would result in "praise and glory and honor at the revelation of Jesus Christ," meaning they would receive recognition when Christ came back. They were to set their expectation fully on the grace that would be brought to them at the revelation of Christ. Christ's return for the Church is to be anticipated with joy; this hope is put forth as one source of motivation and encouragement for believers, especially during trying times.

Summary and Conclusion

In this chapter, we have seen that Christ is coming back for the Church and that this blessed event—the Gathering Together—is to be anticipated with great joy and rejoicing. The hope of Christ's return is an unparalleled source of comfort for the believer, not a source of fear or dread. In contrast, the Day of the Lord is a fearsome time associated with the wrath of God. Catastrophic celestial events will occur, such as stars falling from the sky and the sun and moon being darkened. There will be great mourning upon the earth during the Day of the Lord.

Sadly, many conflate Christ's return for the Church and Christ's coming during the Day of the Lord. Because both of these comings mention clouds, angels, a trumpet, and the bodily presence of Christ, many assume they are the same event. However, we must also acknowledge that there are *stark differences* between Christ's coming for the Church and Christ's coming during the Day of the Lord, as we have seen.

It's essential to recall that Christ's return for the Church, our gathering together unto him, takes place *before* the Day of the Lord.

On this, God's Word is very clear. By God's abundant love, mercy, and grace, the Church has been saved from the wrath to come. Knowledge of these truths brought comfort to the first-century Church, just as it brings great comfort to us today. We look forward to Christ's return with joyous anticipation.

Chapter 3

The Inheritance

If you've ever read a novel by Charles Dickens, you are familiar with the ending where a poor orphan suddenly inherits a large sum of money, and all his woes vanish. In the novel *Oliver Twist*, the titular character begins his life as a destitute child, cast out of an orphanage only to be swept up into a life of crime on the streets of London. By the end of the story, Oliver's identity is revealed: He is a rich man's son. Finally, Oliver inherits a fortune, and his troubles are resolved. It's a classic Dickens ending.

In our western culture, when we think of an inheritance, we may think of someone inheriting money, much like Oliver. Or we may think of inheriting valuable heirlooms or antiques, which are bequeathed to us in a will. But in the lands and times of the Bible, receiving an inheritance often meant something different. For Israel, the inheritance meant receiving land.

Israel's Inheritance

In the book of Joshua, chapters 13-22, we read about the conquest and subsequent dividing up of the inheritance amongst the twelve tribes of Israel.[26] In these chapters, God details the amount, location, and allotment of inheritance given to each tribe. The tribes of Reuben, Gad, and the half-tribe of Manasseh received their inheritance (land) east of the Jordan River, while the other nine-and-a-half tribes received their inheritance (land) west of the river. Note what each tribe of Israel inherited.

---

[26] The tribe of Levi did not inherit land, leaving eleven tribes. However, the tribe of Joseph was divided between his sons, Manasseh and Ephraim, thereby making a total of twelve who inherited the land.

Joshua 13:15-16

¹⁵And Moses gave an **inheritance** to the tribe of the people of Reuben according to their clans.

¹⁶So their **territory** was from Aroer, which is on the edge of the Valley of the Arnon, and the city that is in the middle of the valley, and all the tableland by Medeba;

For the tribe of Reuben, their inheritance was a specific territory.

Joshua 13:24-25

²⁴Moses gave an **inheritance** also to the tribe of Gad, to the people of Gad, according to their clans.

²⁵Their **territory** was Jazer, and all the cities of Gilead, and half the land of the Ammonites, to Aroer, which is east of Rabbah,

For the tribe of Gad, their inheritance was a specific territory.

Joshua 13:29-30

²⁹And Moses gave an **inheritance** to the half-tribe of Manasseh. It was allotted to the half-tribe of the people of Manasseh according to their clans.

³⁰Their **region** extended from Mahanaim, through all Bashan, the whole kingdom of Og king of Bashan, and all the towns of Jair, which are in Bashan, sixty cities,

For the half-tribe of Manasseh, their inheritance was a specific region.

Joshua 15:1, 20

The allotment for the tribe of the people of Judah according to their clans reached southward to the boundary of Edom, to the wilderness of Zin at the farthest south.

Verse 20

This is the **inheritance** of the tribe of the people of Judah according to their clans.

For the tribe of Judah, their inheritance was land.

Joshua 16:4-5
⁴The people of Joseph, Manasseh and Ephraim, received their **inheritance**.

⁵The **territory** of the people of Ephraim by their clans was as follows: the boundary of their **inheritance** on the east was Ataroth-addar as far as Upper Beth-horon,

Ephraim's inheritance was a specific territory. The book of Joshua continues in this fashion, describing the geographic limits and boundaries of each tribe's inheritance. Benjamin's inheritance was land (Josh. 18:11-20), as was Simeon's (Josh. 19:1); Zebulun's (Josh. 19:10); Issachar's (Josh. 19:17-23); Asher's (Josh.19:24-31); Naphtali's (Josh. 19:32-39); and Dan's (Josh. 19:40-48).

In a place and time when land might indicate wealth, status, and protection, as well as family lineage, it's understandable how important the inheritance of land would be. But, more significantly, God gave each tribe (except for the Levites) a specific portion of land as an inheritance, and they were to honor and respect that inheritance accordingly.

Deuteronomy 19:14
"You shall not move your neighbor's landmark, which the men of old have set, in the inheritance that you will hold in the land that the LORD your God is giving you to possess.

In his book on biblical culture and customs, Richard Gower writes the following about Israel's inheritance:

Once allocated, inheritances were marked by landmarks —a heap of stones, a natural feature, or a double furrow of ploughed land—and the landmark could never be moved because to do so was to alter the gift of God (Deut. 19:14). For the same reason, it was dishonouring to God to sell one's inheritance. Naboth refused to sell his vineyard to King Ahab for this reason (1 Kings 21:3).[27]

Gower's point is that because Israel's inheritance was given to them by God, they were to respect and honor their inheritance.

The Inheritance of the Levites

As we have just seen, the records in Joshua tell us that the inheritance for the tribes of Israel was a territory, a region, cities, or other land designations. Only the Levites did not inherit land.

Joshua 13:32-33

[32]These are the inheritances that Moses distributed in the plains of Moab, beyond the Jordan east of Jericho. [33]But to the tribe of Levi Moses gave no inheritance; the LORD God of Israel is their inheritance, just as he said to them.

Numbers 18:20-24

[20]And the LORD said to Aaron, "You shall have no inheritance in their land, neither shall you have any portion among them. I am your portion and your inheritance among the people of Israel. [21]"To the Levites I have given every tithe in Israel for an inheritance, in return for their service that they do, their service in the tent of meeting, [22]so that the people of Israel do not come near the tent of meeting, lest they bear sin and die. [23]But the Levites shall do the service of the tent of meeting, and they shall bear their iniquity. It shall be a perpetual statute throughout your generations, and among the people of Israel they shall have no inheritance.

---

27   Gower, *The New Manners and Customs*, 22-23.

> [24]For the tithe of the people of Israel, which they present as a contribution to the LORD, I have given to the Levites for an inheritance. Therefore I have said of them that they shall have no inheritance among the people of Israel."

The Levites did not inherit the land, but their inheritance was the Lord God of Israel (Deut. 10:9; Num. 18:20). As such, they lived off the tithes and offerings of the people in return for their service in the Tabernacle.[28] The Levites did not lose out in any way because, in addition to the tithes and offerings, they were allotted land to live on even though they did not own the land. The Levites were the tribe set apart by God to minister before Him in the Tabernacle and later in the Temple. Even though the Levites did not inherit the land, their inheritance was more significant because it gave them access to God as they ministered in the Tabernacle. Their inheritance was not physical but spiritual and, therefore, more valuable. When the Levites entered the Tabernacle, this was as close as any person could approach unto the presence of God.

The Approach unto God

In this section, we will consider what the Scriptures say about the approach unto God. This will have a bearing on the significance of the Christian's inheritance, as we will see later in the chapter.

In the Old Testament, God was particular about who might approach Him, how they might approach Him, and what conditions they were to fulfill before approaching Him. God is *holy* and cannot be approached by someone in a manner of their own choosing. The approach to God is on *His* terms alone. Because of this, before they could carry out their priestly functions, the Levites had to follow strict

---

[28] The ESV uses "tent" rather than "tabernacle" in most places. In order to make sure readers know this refers to the special tent that God had Moses make in the wilderness, and not just any tent, we will use the word "Tabernacle" (capital "T") throughout this chapter. The ESV retains the word "tent" or "tent of meeting."

procedures, such as going through a seven-day purification ceremony (Lev. 8:35) and wearing certain garments while in the Tabernacle (Exod. 28:3ff). These and many other directions were given to the Levites concerning how they were to carry out their priestly service.

In addition, God gave solemn warnings about how the Levites were to go into the Tabernacle and carry out the sacrifices.

Exodus 30:20-21

[20]When they go into the tent of meeting, or when they come near the altar to minister, to burn a food offering to the LORD, they shall wash with water, **so that they may not die**.

[21]They shall wash their hands and their feet, **so that they may not die**. It shall be a statute forever to them, even to him and to his offspring throughout their generations."

The Levites were to approach the altar to offer sacrifices as God directed and specified. If the Levites failed to do so, they would die. God lovingly set forth these rules so that the approach could be made unto Him.

In addition to following strict rules regarding their conduct inside and outside the Tabernacle, the Levites who ministered in the Tabernacle also had to be without physical blemish.

Leviticus 21:17-23

[17]"Speak to Aaron, saying, None of your offspring throughout their generations who has a blemish may approach to offer the bread of his God.

[18]For no one who has a blemish shall draw near, a man blind or lame, or one who has a mutilated face or a limb too long,

[19]or a man who has an injured foot or an injured hand,

[20]or a hunchback or a dwarf or a man with a defect in his sight or an itching disease or scabs or crushed testicles.

²¹No man of the offspring of Aaron the priest who has a blemish shall come near to offer the LORD's food offerings; since he has a blemish, he shall not come near to offer the bread of his God.

²²He may eat the bread of his God, both of the most holy and of the holy things,

²³but he shall not go through the veil or approach the altar, because he has a blemish, that he may not profane my sanctuaries, for I am the LORD who sanctifies them."

If a Levite had a blemish or a physical defect, he could partake of the holy things, but he could not enter behind the veil or approach the altar, meaning he could not enter the Holy Place. The Levite's approach unto God in their service in the Tabernacle was not haphazard or casual. It was on His terms and was to be carried out according to His specific directions.

Even the high priest was given specific directives on how he would approach God in the Most Holy Place. For instance, note the detailed instruction regarding the high priest's robe:

Exodus 28:33-35

³³On its hem you shall make pomegranates of blue and purple and scarlet yarns, around its hem, with bells of gold between them,

³⁴a golden bell and a pomegranate, a golden bell and a pomegranate, around the hem of the robe.

³⁵And it shall be on Aaron when he ministers, and its sound shall be heard when he goes into the Holy Place before the LORD, and when he comes out, **so that he does not die.**

God laid out strict rules regarding how even the high priests were to conduct themselves in the Tabernacle. If they failed to follow God's commands, they would die. God's rules regarding the approach unto Him in the Tabernacle were not to be trifled with.

Indeed, the consequences were swift if a Levite violated the terms God laid out for the approach unto Him. Note what happened to Aaron's sons, Nadab and Abihu, when they took the matter of approaching God into their own hands.

Leviticus 10:1-11

[1]Now Nadab and Abihu, the sons of Aaron, each took his censer and put fire in it and laid incense on it and offered unauthorized fire before the LORD, which he had not commanded them.

[2]And fire came out from before the LORD and consumed them, and they died before the LORD.

[3]Then Moses said to Aaron, "This is what the LORD has said: 'Among those who are near me I will be sanctified, and before all the people I will be glorified.' " And Aaron held his peace.

[4]And Moses called Mishael and Elzaphan, the sons of Uzziel the uncle of Aaron, and said to them, "Come near; carry your brothers away from the front of the sanctuary and out of the camp."

[5]So they came near and carried them in their coats out of the camp, as Moses had said.

[6]And Moses said to Aaron and to Eleazar and Ithamar his sons, "Do not let the hair of your heads hang loose, and do not tear your clothes, lest you die, and wrath come upon all the congregation; but let your brothers, the whole house of Israel, bewail the burning that the LORD has kindled.

[7]And do not go outside the entrance of the tent of meeting, lest you die, for the anointing oil of the LORD is upon you." And they did according to the word of Moses.

[8]And the LORD spoke to Aaron, saying,

[9]"Drink no wine or strong drink, you or your sons with you, when you go into the tent of meeting, lest you die. It shall be a statute forever throughout your generations.

¹⁰You are to distinguish between the holy and the
common, and between the unclean and the clean,
¹¹and you are to teach the people of Israel all the statutes
that the LORD has spoken to them by Moses."

Nadab and Abihu offered "unauthorized" fire before the Lord, which
He did not command. The Lord responded with fire of His own and
consumed them. In a word, they died. Why? Because as verse 3 says,
God was to be set apart among those who came near Him. He was
to be honored (glorified) before all people, approached on His terms.
Even though they were Levites and had been sanctified to serve in the
Tabernacle, Nadab and Abihu still had to obey what God had specified.
They could not make up their own way of approaching God. He is
holy and must not be treated as common or ordinary. In this instance,
Nadab and Abihu died because of their disobedience to what God
had commanded regarding the Tabernacle service. They knew the
conditions yet chose to disregard them.

God made it clear that there was a difference between what is "holy"
and what is "common." God is the One Who decides who approaches
unto Him and how He is to be approached. God is the One Who
decides what the conditions are to be in His presence.[29]

One of the privileges of the Levite's inheritance was having
an approach unto God. We will pick up the thread of the Levite's
inheritance later in the chapter, but for now, let's proceed to what the
Scriptures say about the Christian's inheritance.

---

[29] Likewise, if you know the record of King Uzziah from 2 Chronicles 26, you
know that he had decided to approach God on his own terms. The Scriptures declare
that Uzziah had grown prideful and had become unfaithful to God (2 Chron.
26:16). He entered the temple in order to burn incense, which was strictly the
priests' responsibility. Azariah, the priest, along with 80 of the priests of the Lord,
confronted Uzziah (v. 18). Uzziah became angry at the priests and did not heed their
instruction. Consequently, he became a leper for the rest of his life, having to live
sequestered because of the disease. God determines who will approach Him. As in
the case of Uzziah, just because you're the king doesn't mean you are exempt from
God's requirements regarding the services and sacrifices of the Temple.

The Christian's Inheritance: Some Characteristics

If Israel's inheritance was land and the Levite's inheritance was the Lord Himself, what is the Christian believer's inheritance? How is it received, and what are its characteristics? This section seeks to answer these questions.

In the following record, Paul gives his defense before King Agrippa and recounts when the Lord Jesus Christ appeared to him on the road to Damascus. Note what the lord said about how a Christian receives an inheritance.

> **Acts 26:15-18**
> [15]And I said, 'Who are you, Lord?' And the Lord said, 'I am Jesus whom you are persecuting.
> [16]But rise and stand upon your feet, for I have appeared to you for this purpose, to appoint you as a servant and witness to the things in which you have seen me and to those in which I will appear to you,
> [17]delivering you from your people and from the Gentiles—to whom I am sending you
> [18]to open their eyes, so that they may turn from darkness to light and from the power of Satan to God, that they may receive forgiveness of sins and a **place** [inheritance] among those who are sanctified by faith in me.'

In the Greek New Testament, the word "place" in verse 18 is *klēros*, which can also be translated as "inheritance," as it is in some English Bibles:

> **Acts 26:18** (KJV)
> To open their eyes, and to turn them from darkness to light, and from the power of Satan unto God, that they may receive forgiveness of sins, and **inheritance** among them which are sanctified by faith that is in me.

Acts 26:18 (NASB95)
to open their eyes so that they may turn from darkness to light and from the dominion of Satan to God, that they may receive forgiveness of sins and an **inheritance** among those who have been sanctified by faith in Me.'

The inheritance is for all those who have been sanctified by believing in Jesus Christ. Earlier in the book of Acts, Paul spoke to the elders at Ephesus about the inheritance: "And now I commend you to God and to the word of his grace, which is able to build you up and to give you the inheritance among all those who are sanctified" (Acts 20:32). From these verses, we see that the inheritance is for all the sanctified ones, meaning those who have believed concerning Jesus Christ and are set apart by the new birth spirit.

The book of Hebrews gives more insight into the saints' inheritance:

Hebrews 9:15
Therefore he [Jesus Christ] is the mediator of a new covenant, so that those who are called may receive the promised eternal **inheritance**, since a death has occurred that redeems them from the transgressions committed under the first covenant.

The inheritance is eternal, meaning that it will not have an end. How unlike an earthly inheritance.

The inheritance is further described in 1 Peter:

1 Peter 1:3-4
³Blessed be the God and Father of our Lord Jesus Christ! According to his great mercy, he has caused us to be born again to a living hope through the resurrection of Jesus Christ from the dead,
⁴to an **inheritance** that is imperishable, undefiled, and unfading, kept in heaven for you,

The saints' inheritance will not perish, it is undefiled, meaning pure, and will not fade away. If the inheritance cannot fade away, it's not something a believer can lose. If it cannot perish, then the believer's inheritance is permanent. So far, we have not read any Scripture that suggests the inheritance is received by merit or works or that it can be lost, removed, or changed. But we have read that it is eternal, imperishable, undefiled, and unfading. What's more, the Christian's inheritance is kept in heaven for us, as verse 4 indicates. Note that our inheritance is *in heaven*, not on earth.

We see another aspect of the inheritance in the book of Colossians:

Colossians 1:12-14
[12]giving thanks to the Father, who has qualified you to share in the **inheritance** of the saints in light.
[13]He has delivered us from the domain of darkness and transferred us to the kingdom of his beloved Son,
[14]in whom we have redemption, the forgiveness of sins.

Here we learn that the Father has qualified the born-again ones to share in the saints' inheritance in the light. The Christian doesn't qualify himself to share in this inheritance: he is qualified by God through His Son Jesus Christ. This point cannot be stressed enough. It is by the finished work of Jesus Christ, all that he accomplished for man's complete redemption and salvation, that has qualified the saints to share in this eternal inheritance.

> The Christian doesn't qualify himself to share in this inheritance; God qualifies him through His Son Jesus Christ.

We see the same truth expressed in the following passage:

Ephesians 1:7-14

[7]**In him** [Christ] we have redemption through his blood, the forgiveness of our trespasses, according to the riches of his grace,

[8]which he lavished upon us, in all wisdom and insight

[9]making known to us the mystery of his will, according to his purpose, which he set forth **in Christ**

[10]as a plan for the fullness of time, to unite all things in him, things in heaven and things on earth.

[11]**In him** [Christ] we have obtained an **inheritance**, having been predestined according to the purpose of him who works all things according to the counsel of his will,

[12]so that we who were the first to hope **in Christ** might be to the praise of his glory.

[13]**In him** you also, when you heard the word of truth, the gospel of your salvation, and believed in him, were sealed with the promised Holy Spirit,

[14]who is the guarantee (*arrabōn*) of our **inheritance** until we acquire possession of it, to the praise of his glory.

Verses 7, 9, 10, 11, 12, and 13 all have the phrase "in him" or "in Christ." This repetition drives home the point that all the blessings, rights, and privileges spoken of in this passage, including the inheritance, are *in Christ*, not in any individual's work or worth. It is *in Christ* that we have redemption. It is *in Christ* that we were sealed with the promised holy spirit. It is *in Christ* that we have obtained an inheritance. The Christian's inheritance is given *in Christ*, not because of one's merits or worth. And it is God who qualified each one of us to share in this eternal, imperishable inheritance!

What's more, God has given the saints an inheritance guarantee. In the Greek New Testament, "guarantee" in verse 14 is the word *arrabōn*, which means "money which in purchases is given as a pledge that the full amount will subsequently be paid."[30] Today, we would call this a down payment. For instance, when you buy a house, mortgage companies will not finance the purchase without the buyers first making a down payment, a percentage of the total cost of the house. This guarantees the bank that you will make good on the rest of the amount owed. God has given His sons a *guarantee* of the inheritance, and that is the gift of holy spirit. What a blessed reality. God promised that the Christian will receive an inheritance, and He has not only qualified each Christian to receive the inheritance, but God has also given His children a guarantee of that promise.

In sum, we have learned the following about the Christian's inheritance:

- It is for those who are set apart (sanctified) by the new birth.
- It is eternal, imperishable, undefiled, and unfading.
- It is kept in heaven.
- God has qualified the saints for the inheritance.
- It is given on the merits of Christ.
- God has given us a down payment on the inheritance, the gift of holy spirit.

Finally, the Scriptures tell us when the inheritance will be received.

1 Corinthians 15:48-54
[48]As was the man of dust, so also are those who are of the dust, and as is the man of heaven, so also are those who are of heaven.

[49]Just as we have borne the image of the man of dust, we shall also bear the image of the man of heaven.

[50]I tell you this, brothers: flesh and blood cannot inherit the kingdom of God, nor does the perishable inherit the imperishable.

[51]Behold! I tell you a mystery. We shall not all sleep, but we shall all be changed,

---

[30] Thayer, *A Greek-English Lexicon*, s.v. "arrabōn."

⁵²in a moment, in the twinkling of an eye, at the last trumpet. For the trumpet will sound, and the dead will be raised imperishable, and we shall be changed.

⁵³For this perishable body must put on the imperishable, and this mortal body must put on immortality.

⁵⁴When the perishable puts on the imperishable, and the mortal puts on immortality, then shall come to pass the saying that is written: "Death is swallowed up in victory."

The saints' inheritance cannot be realized in all its fullness until they have received their new bodies, which will take place at the Gathering Together.[31] This is because perishable, mortal bodies cannot inherit the imperishable kingdom of God and receive the promised inheritance. The saints, therefore, patiently wait for God's Son from heaven to return, knowing that when they receive their new bodies, they will be able to receive the inheritance that is kept for them in heaven. Meanwhile, they can rest assured of their inheritance because they have a down payment, the gift of holy spirit.

What the Tabernacle Signified

As we saw earlier in this chapter, the Levite's inheritance was the Lord Himself, and as such, they were given the privilege of being able to approach unto Him. The Scriptures tell us that the Tabernacle and everything associated with it was a shadow and copy of heavenly things.

Hebrews 8:1-5

¹Now the point in what we are saying is this: we have such a high priest, one who is seated at the right hand of the throne of the Majesty in heaven,

²a minister in the holy places, in the true tent that the Lord set up, not man.

---

31   See Chapter 2: "The Return of Christ."

³For every high priest is appointed to offer gifts and sacrifices; thus it is necessary for this priest also to have something to offer.

⁴Now if he were on earth, he would not be a priest at all, since there are priests who offer gifts according to the law. ⁵They serve **a copy and shadow of the heavenly things**. For when Moses was about to erect the tent, he was instructed by God, saying, "See that you make everything according to the pattern that was shown you on the mountain."

The earthly Tabernacle was a physical tent, but the "true tent" (v. 2) refers to something heavenly. Moses set up the earthly Tabernacle by God's direction, but God Himself set up the true tent. The earthly Tabernacle, along with the priest's functions and ministry, was a copy and shadow—a representation—of the heavenly. In other words, the tent and the priesthood served as a *representation of heavenly things*. Copies are not the true original, and shadows do not have the substance of the original, but copies and shadows may represent the original. This was one of the functions of the Tabernacle—to serve as a symbol of the true tent in heaven.

> The earthly Tabernacle, along with the priest's function and ministry, was a copy and shadow—a representation— of the heavenly. In other words, the tent and the priesthood served as a *representation of heavenly things*.

In Hebrews 9, we read more about what the earthly Tabernacle signified:

Hebrews 9:2-8

²For a tent was prepared, the first section, in which were the lampstand and the table and the bread of the Presence. It is called the Holy Place.

³Behind the second curtain was a second section called the Most Holy Place,

⁴having the golden altar of incense and the ark of the covenant covered on all sides with gold, in which was a golden urn holding the manna, and Aaron's staff that budded, and the tablets of the covenant.

⁵Above it were the cherubim of glory overshadowing the mercy seat. Of these things we cannot now speak in detail.

⁶These preparations having thus been made, the priests go regularly into the first section, performing their ritual duties,

⁷but into the second only the high priest goes, and he but once a year, and not without taking blood, which he offers for himself and for the unintentional sins of the people.

⁸By this the **Holy Spirit indicates that the way into the holy places is not yet opened** as long as the first section is still standing[32]

The earthly Tabernacle had two parts: 1) the Holy Place and 2) the Most Holy Place. A curtain or veil separated the two sections. All priests could minister in the first part (the Holy Place), but only the high priest could enter the second part (the Most Holy Place) once a year on the Day of Atonement.[33] He went in once a year with a blood sacrifice to make atonement for himself and the people.

Then verse 8 tells us one of the things that God, the Holy Spirit, was indicating or signifying when He set up the Tabernacle: "the way into the holy places is not yet opened." Under the Old Covenant, access to the Most Holy Place was highly restricted. Only once a year and only the high priest could enter the Most Holy Place. This limited access to

---

[32] In verse 8, "holy places" is a figurative way of saying "the holiest place" or "the most holy place." In other words, there aren't several holy places, but one Holy Place that is the holiest of all.

[33] See for example Lev. 23:26ff.

the Most Holy Place in the earthly Tabernacle illustrated that the way into *the* holy place, heaven itself, was not yet opened. In other words, full and open access to God was not yet available.

The earthly Tabernacle showed that the way into heaven was *not yet open*. It took the coming of Christ to make the approach unto God available.

Hebrews 4:14-16

[14]Since then we have a great high priest who has passed through the heavens, Jesus, the Son of God, let us hold fast our confession.

[15]For we do not have a high priest who is unable to sympathize with our weaknesses, but one who in every respect has been tempted as we are, yet without sin.

[16]Let us then with confidence draw near to the throne of grace, that we may receive mercy and find grace to help in time of need.

Because of Jesus Christ, we can draw near to God's throne of grace.

Hebrews 9:24

For Christ has entered, not into holy places made with hands, which are copies of the true things, but into heaven itself, now to appear in the presence of God on our behalf.

Jesus Christ came to make the approach unto God possible. He never entered the most holy place in the earthly Tabernacle because his ministry as high priest is in heaven itself, The Holy Place.

Ephesians 3:11-12

[11]This was according to the eternal purpose that he has realized in Christ Jesus our Lord,

[12]in whom we have boldness and access with confidence through our faith in him.

Today, we may take for granted that we have free access to God's throne of grace and that we can boldly come before Him. But before Christ accomplished man's redemption and salvation, such an approach unto God was impossible. The earthly Tabernacle served to remind Israel that the way into the very presence of God was not yet available! Recall how strict and exact the standards were for priests to be allowed into the Holy Place. And then, for the high priest, his entrance into the Most Holy Place was even more restricted. Approach unto God was on His terms, and the conditions were not to be trifled with, as Nadab and Abihu discovered.

Because of all that Jesus Christ accomplished, Christian believers now have an inheritance in the very presence of God Himself, in the holy of holies. The Christian believer's inheritance is in heaven, in God's presence. The Levite's inheritance was the Lord Himself, being in God's presence as they served in the Tabernacle, the earthly tent. The Church's inheritance is in heaven, the true tent, being directly in God's magnificent presence! Perhaps now we can begin to see the immensity of this inheritance. It took the coming of Christ and all that he accomplished for man's redemption and salvation to make the way into the Most Holy Place, heaven itself, available.

Summary and Conclusion

The practice of presenting someone to a dignitary may be foreign to those of us from democratic and casual cultures. But throughout history, people were routinely presented before kings or potentates, which was a high honor. A commoner wouldn't dream of walking up to a king or standing in his court uninvited. He would first have to be invited and then follow the correct protocol of being presented to the king. Even today, individuals are presented to kings, queens, and presidents, something that is still an honor.

In a similar vein, born-again ones have been reconciled by the work of Christ and, therefore, can be presented to God.

Colossians 1:21-22

²¹And you, who once were alienated and hostile in mind, doing evil deeds,

²²he has now reconciled in his body of flesh by his death, in order to present you holy and blameless and above reproach before him,

Jesus Christ will present the Church as holy, blameless, and above reproach to God. The word "blameless" in verse 22 means "without blemish." Recall that the Levites could not approach unto God in the earthly Tabernacle if they had any blemish whatsoever! And yet, Christ will present the Church as holy, above reproach, and without blemish before God. This access to God is not something we could have achieved on our own; it is all thanks to the finished work of Christ.

While we have access to God now, the Church is going to be presented to God in the future and will be in the *presence of His glory*.

Jude 24-25

²⁴Now to him who is able to keep you from stumbling and to present you blameless before the **presence of his glory** with great joy,

²⁵to the only God, our Savior, through Jesus Christ our Lord, be glory, majesty, dominion, and authority, before all time and now and forever. Amen.

These verses speak of all saints being presented to God and thereafter being in His glorious presence. Our presentation is still in the future. In the Old Testament, when the glory of the Lord filled the Tabernacle, no one could stand in its presence, so great and overpowering was this glory.[34] But in the ages to come, the Church will be presented to God and will be in His glorious presence, a glory so magnificent and all-encompassing it is difficult to take in.

Thanks to the perfect sacrifice of the Lord Jesus Christ, the Church has a spectacular inheritance—heaven itself, in the presence of God.

---

[34]   See Exod. 40:34-35.

Under the Old Covenant, God's people inherited the Promised Land, a physical place where they were to dwell. The Christian believer's inheritance is also a place where they will dwell—in heaven itself in God's presence. This inheritance is eternal and pure, cannot perish or fade away, and is reserved in heaven for us. The inheritance, received by grace, is where the saints will abide once Christ returns. It follows that they would need their new, incorruptible bodies before taking possession of the promised eternal inheritance. This is the Christian believer's inheritance—heaven itself—made possible by the finished work of the Lord Jesus Christ.

Chapter 4

The Reward

In the book of Hebrews, we read about the saints facing hardships and growing weary. Notice how the writer, by revelation, encourages them:

> **Hebrews 10:32-35**
> [32]But recall the former days when, after you were enlightened, you endured a hard struggle with sufferings, [33]sometimes being publicly exposed to reproach and affliction, and sometimes being partners with those so treated.
> [34]For you had compassion on those in prison, and you joyfully accepted the plundering of your property, since you knew that you yourselves had a better possession and an abiding one.
> [35]Therefore do not throw away your confidence, which has a **great reward**.

These saints had been publicly disgraced or were partners with those who had been. Just imagine the emotional pain of public disgrace. In addition, their personal property had been confiscated by force—another attack that must have been difficult to bear. Yet the Scriptures say that these saints had put up with this injustice *with joy* because they knew they "had a better possession and an abiding one" coming, meaning future reward. The writer encouraged them not to "throw away" their confidence. What was the incentive for them to persevere during these trials? Great reward. As we move through this chapter, we will see this recurring theme: God's people are encouraged to persevere despite hardships because of future reward.

What does the word "reward" mean biblically? When will Christians be rewarded? What is rewarded? This chapter answers these and other questions about the Christian's reward.

Jesus Christ: Treasure in Heaven

No one taught more about future reward than Jesus Christ. His teachings provide unparalleled understanding in this field.[35] Time and again, we see that Jesus Christ taught his *disciples* about reward.

Luke 6:20-36
20And he lifted up his eyes on his **disciples**, and said: "Blessed are you who are poor, for yours is the kingdom of God.

21"Blessed are you who are hungry now, for you shall be satisfied. "Blessed are you who weep now, for you shall laugh.

22"Blessed are you when people hate you and when they exclude you and revile you and spurn your name as evil, on account of the Son of Man!

23Rejoice in that day, and leap for joy, for behold, your **reward is great in heaven**; for so their fathers did to the prophets.

24"But woe to you who are rich, for you have received your consolation.

25"Woe to you who are full now, for you shall be hungry. "Woe to you who laugh now, for you shall mourn and weep.

26"Woe to you, when all people speak well of you, for so their fathers did to the false prophets.

27"But I say to you who hear, Love your enemies, do good to those who hate you,

28bless those who curse you, pray for those who abuse you.

---

35   See Appendix E: "Jesus Christ's Teachings on Reward."

²⁹To one who strikes you on the cheek, offer the other also, and from one who takes away your cloak do not withhold your tunic either.

³⁰Give to everyone who begs from you, and from one who takes away your goods do not demand them back.

³¹And as you wish that others would do to you, do so to them.

³²"If you love those who love you, what benefit is that to you? For even sinners love those who love them.

³³And if you do good to those who do good to you, what benefit is that to you? For even sinners do the same.

³⁴And if you lend to those from whom you expect to receive, what credit is that to you? Even sinners lend to sinners, to get back the same amount.

³⁵But love your enemies, and do good, and lend, expecting nothing in return, and your **reward will be great**, and you will be sons of the Most High, for he is kind to the ungrateful and the evil.

³⁶Be merciful, even as your Father is merciful.

In this record, Jesus Christ addressed his *disciples*, not the multitudes. Biblically speaking, a disciple abides in the teacher's words: "Jesus said to the Jews who had believed him, If you abide in my word, you are truly my disciples" (John 8:31). E. W. Bullinger describes a disciple as one who "follows both the teacher and his teaching."³⁶ In this record, Jesus Christ is addressing disciples, *not* casual spectators who were mildly interested in his teachings.

He taught them some startling truths: he told them to rejoice and leap for joy in the face of being excluded and reviled. Why? Because their reward in heaven would be great. He also taught them to love their enemies, do good to those who hated them, bless those that cursed them, and pray for those who abused them, and their reward would be great. Jesus didn't encourage his disciples to do these things because

---

³⁶   Bullinger, *A Critical Lexicon and Concordance.* s.v. "disciple."

they were nice maxims to live by but because their reward in heaven would be great. In doing so, they would be like their Heavenly Father.

Generally speaking, one expects to be paid back for a good deed. One expects to receive an act of kindness in response to the kindness given. One loves, expecting to be loved in return; one lends, expecting to be paid back, and so forth. Yet, in his teaching, Jesus Christ introduced a radical departure from a *quid pro quo* way of thinking when he spoke about expecting nothing in return. Instead, he taught his disciples that such actions *now* would yield great reward in heaven *later*.

Let's look at another record where Jesus Christ spoke to his disciples about future reward.

Matthew 5:1, 10-12
¹Seeing the crowds, he went up on the mountain, and when he sat down, his **disciples** came to him.

Verses 10-12
¹⁰"Blessed are those who are persecuted for righteousness' sake, for theirs is the kingdom of heaven.
¹¹"Blessed are you when others revile you and persecute you and utter all kinds of evil against you falsely on my account.
¹²Rejoice and be glad, for your **reward** is great in heaven, for so they persecuted the prophets who were before you.

Normally, to be persecuted, reviled, or falsely accused would not be cause for celebration. However, Jesus Christ taught his disciples they should rejoice when persecuted and reviled because their reward in heaven would be great. Jesus Christ was clear about the cost of discipleship: they would endure hardship. Yet, the disciples were not to be deterred by these injustices because of the promise of great future reward.

Let's consider a second record from the gospel of Matthew.

Matthew 16:21-27

²¹From that time Jesus began to show his disciples that he must go to Jerusalem and suffer many things from the elders and chief priests and scribes, and be killed, and on the third day be raised.

²²And Peter took him aside and began to rebuke him, saying, "Far be it from you, Lord! This shall never happen to you."

²³But he turned and said to Peter, "Get behind me, Satan! You are a hindrance to me. For you are not setting your mind on the things of God, but on the things of man."

²⁴Then Jesus told his disciples, "If anyone would come after me, let him deny himself and take up his cross and follow me.

²⁵For whoever would save his life will lose it, but whoever loses his life for my sake will find it.

²⁶For what will it profit a man if he gains the whole world and forfeits his soul? Or what shall a man give in return for his soul?

²⁷For the Son of Man is going to come with his angels in the glory of his Father, and then he will repay each person according to what he has done.

In response to Peter's outburst, Jesus Christ rebuked Peter and then said to his disciples, "if anyone would come after me, let him deny himself, and take up his cross, and follow me." The phrase "take up the cross" is an idiom that means to take on the responsibility to do the master's will rather than one's own will.[37] Then Jesus Christ added, "whoever would save his life will lose it: and whoever loses his life for my sake will find it." Literally, to lose one's life is to die. Is Jesus Christ asking his disciples to die for his sake? Of course not. In this verse, "to lose one's life" is figurative, meaning to give up one's self-interest and investment

---

[37] Wierwille, *Jesus Christ our Passover*, 222.

in the world. The disciples were to carry out their master's interests, to take on the responsibility of fully following him.

Jesus Christ was speaking about what someone did with their life, about the *profit* of that life. His rhetorical questions implied that a man who dedicated his whole life to gaining the world lost his life, meaning he wasted it. The lord was not talking about eternal life but reward. Those who committed to following and serving him would be rewarded, but those who committed to worldly pursuits would lose out. In other words, gaining everything the world has to offer is nothing compared to future reward. Jesus Christ assigned a very high value to the reward—greater than gaining the whole world.

In these records from Luke 6, Matthew 5, and Matthew 16, Jesus Christ was not talking about salvation but discipleship and future reward. He was addressing his disciples, not the multitudes. He taught that gaining the whole world was of less value than a life of sacrifice and commitment to Jesus Christ. According to these teachings, putting aside self-interest and becoming committed to following Christ would yield great future reward. Just from these three records alone, we can appreciate that Jesus Christ placed great value on future reward.

The Rich Young Ruler

There is a record in the gospel of Matthew where a man approached Jesus Christ to ask him about eternal life. If we read the parallel accounts, we learn that this man was a rich, young ruler.[38] Following the discussion with the man, Peter asked a question about future reward, and then Jesus Christ responded by teaching a parable. These passages all pertain to future realities, so we will consider them together.

Matthew 19:16
And behold, a man came up to him, saying, "Teacher, what good deed must I do to have eternal life?"

---

[38] See also Mark 10:17-22 and Luke 18:18-30.

Let's read the parallel verses to get a fuller picture of what's taking place.

Mark 10:17

And as he was setting out on his journey, a man ran up and knelt before him and asked him, "Good Teacher, what must I do to inherit eternal life?"

Luke 18:18

And a ruler asked him, "Good Teacher, what must I do to inherit eternal life?"

Reading these three verses together, we see that the man came running to Jesus and kneeled before him, addressing him as "Good Teacher." Given the culture of the lands and times of the Bible, we can appreciate that both this gesture and address signify the man's humility towards and respect for Jesus Christ. The young ruler then asked what he needed to do to inherit eternal life.

Matthew 19:17-21

[17]And he said to him, "Why do you ask me about what is good? There is only one who is good. If you would enter life, keep the commandments."

[18]He said to him, "Which ones?" And Jesus said, "You shall not murder, You shall not commit adultery, You shall not steal, You shall not bear false witness,

[19]Honor your father and mother, and, You shall love your neighbor as yourself."

[20]The young man said to him, "All these I have kept. What do I still lack?"

[21]Jesus said to him, "If you would be perfect, go, sell what you possess and give to the poor, and you will have treasure in heaven; and come, follow me."

After the initial discussion about eternal life and keeping the commandments, the young ruler wanted to know what he lacked. Jesus Christ answered that if he wanted to be perfect, meaning mature, he was to sell all he had and give the proceeds to the poor. In return for this sacrifice, he would have "treasure in heaven." Jesus Christ then asked the man to come and follow him. Notice how the discussion has shifted from inheriting eternal life to discipleship and reward. For this rich young ruler, there would be treasure in heaven, reward, for selling all and giving to the poor.[39]

How did the young man respond?

Matthew 19:22

When the young man heard this he went away sorrowful, for he had great possessions.

To go away is the opposite of following someone. His actions indicated that he did not obey Jesus Christ's directive to sell all and follow him. The lord asked the young man for a level of commitment and devotion and then said that this would yield treasure in heaven. But the young man did not obey the lord's directions and went away sad.

Peter was in the crowd while Jesus Christ was speaking to this rich young ruler and asked, "See, we have left everything and followed you. What then will we have?" (Matt. 19:27). The rich young ruler may not have been willing to forsake all and follow Jesus Christ, but Peter and the others *had* forsaken all and followed the lord.[40] Peter wanted to know what they would have in return for their commitment and sacrifice.

Matthew 19:28

Jesus said to them, "Truly, I say to you, in the new world, when the Son of Man will sit on his glorious throne, you who have followed me will also sit on twelve thrones, judging the twelve tribes of Israel.

---

[39] It's important to note that Jesus Christ's directive, given by revelation, was specifically addressed to this rich young ruler in response to his specific question and is not meant as a general directive for all people to follow, or even for all rich young rulers to follow. Regardless, it speaks to the value of future reward in comparison to earthly wealth.

[40] See Matt. 4:20-22; Mark 1:18-20; Luke 5:11.

Note that the lord did not scold Peter for asking such a question. In some Christian circles, asking for compensation for one's sacrifice would be scandalous. Yet, Jesus Christ did not rebuke Peter for asking such a question or having an expectation of compensation for his service and sacrifice. Peter asked—we've forsaken all to follow you, so what will we have in return? Jesus Christ answered that they would sit on twelve thrones, judging the twelve tribes of Israel. That is quite a reward! Their reward would include having positions of authority ("thrones") and having the responsibility of judgment over the twelve tribes of Israel. Note that Jesus did not say, "Nothing. You will have absolutely nothing for forsaking all and following me. How dare you ask!"

Jesus Christ continued to teach more about future reward.

Matthew 19:29-30
[29]And everyone who has left houses or brothers or sisters or father or mother or children or lands, for my name's sake, will receive a hundredfold and will inherit eternal life.
[30]But many who are first will be last, and the last first.

Let's read these verses from the parallel records to get a fuller picture of what Jesus Christ taught:

Mark 10:29-30
[29]Jesus said, "Truly, I say to you, there is no one who has left house or brothers or sisters or mother or father or children or lands, for my sake and for the gospel,
[30]who will not receive a hundredfold now in this time, houses and brothers and sisters and mothers and children and lands, with persecutions, and in the age to come eternal life.

Luke 18:29-30
[29]And he said to them, "Truly, I say to you, there is no one who has left house or wife or brothers or parents or children, for the sake of the kingdom of God,

³⁰who will not receive many times more in this time, and in the age to come eternal life."

At this point in the record, Jesus Christ was not only speaking about Peter and the other disciples; he was speaking of *anyone* who would sacrifice for the Gospel's sake. Taking these parallel records together, we learn that:

- People may forsake houses, parents, brethren, wives, children, and lands.
- Things forsaken are for Christ's name, for the Gospel's sake, and for the kingdom of God's sake (possibly the same thing said three different ways).
- Those who forsake these things now receive a hundredfold or many times more in this present time with persecutions *and* a hundredfold or many times more in the age to come.

In Matthew 19:29, Jesus Christ spoke of inheriting eternal life. In this context, the phrase "eternal life" is a metonymy put for the things that accompany eternal life, meaning the reward.[41] In other words, those who forsake all for the Gospel's sake would receive a hundredfold now and reward in the future. Though one can hardly undervalue eternal life, it is not the only thing that concerned Jesus Christ. He also taught about future reward. Earlier, we read that Jesus Christ asked his disciples to deny themselves, take up the cross, and follow him. Jesus Christ said he would repay them for what they had done (Matt. 16:27). And here, the lord again taught that there would be future compensation for such sacrifice, commitment, and devotion.

However, this did not end the discussion. Recognizing that chapter breaks are added by the editors and often interrupt the flow of thought, let's continue reading the record, understanding that the following parable is part of the lord's teaching on reward. [42]

---

41   A metonymy is a noun or name put for another related noun or name. Hans, *Go Figure!* 149.

42   Parable is an extended comparison in story form usually with one main point of comparison. Hans, *Go Figure!* 201.

Matthew 20:1-16

[1]"For the kingdom of heaven is like a master of a house who went out early in the morning to hire laborers for his vineyard.

[2]After agreeing with the laborers for a denarius a day, he sent them into his vineyard.

[3]And going out about the third hour he saw others standing idle in the marketplace,

[4]and to them he said, 'You go into the vineyard too, and whatever is right I will give you.'

[5]So they went. Going out again about the sixth hour and the ninth hour, he did the same.

[6]And about the eleventh hour he went out and found others standing. And he said to them, 'Why do you stand here idle all day?'

[7]They said to him, 'Because no one has hired us.' He said to them, 'You go into the vineyard too.'

[8]And when evening came, the owner of the vineyard said to his foreman, 'Call the laborers and pay them their wages, beginning with the last, up to the first.'

[9]And when those hired about the eleventh hour came, each of them received a denarius.

[10]Now when those hired first came, they thought they would receive more, but each of them also received a denarius.

[11]And on receiving it they grumbled at the master of the house,

[12]saying, 'These last worked only one hour, and you have made them equal to us who have borne the burden of the day and the scorching heat.'

[13]But he replied to one of them, 'Friend, I am doing you no wrong. Did you not agree with me for a denarius?

[14]Take what belongs to you and go. I choose to give to this last worker as I give to you.

¹⁵Am I not allowed to do what I choose with what belongs to me? Or do you begrudge my generosity?'
¹⁶So the last will be first, and the first last."⁴³

In the parable, the kingdom of heaven is compared to a master of a house who hires laborers to work in his vineyard. He employs the first group of workers early in the morning and promises to give them one denarius a day. They agree. He hires the second, third, and fourth groups later in the day (at the third, sixth, and ninth hours) and says regarding payment, "whatsoever is right I will give you." So far in the parable, no one has voiced any objections to the master's wages. Finally, the last group of laborers is hired (at the eleventh hour), and there is not even a promise of any wage for them. They simply agree to labor as the master requested. At the end of the day, the master of the house gives each laborer the *same* amount—one denarius.

Even though the laborers were hired at different times of the day and worked different amounts of time, the master gave each the same wage. This is startling to anyone who is paid by the hour. Most would not take too kindly to someone who worked for one hour getting the same paycheck as those who worked eight hours. So, it's understandable that those who labored all day were upset with the master of the house. The master of the house replied that he had done them no wrong, for he had paid them the agreed-upon wage. They all received what the master of the house deemed appropriate and just.

Remember that Jesus Christ is teaching this parable in response to Peter's question about what they would receive for their sacrifice. From this parable, we learn that some labored based on agreed-upon wages, others trusted the master of the house to give whatever was right, and others labored without asking for a wage. We can begin to appreciate how this relates to future reward. The master of the house is compared to the kingdom of God, and the parable highlights the

---

⁴³ In this context, the phrase "the last will be first and the first last" refers to the laborers in the parable. That is to say, the last ones to be hired were the first ones to be paid; the first ones to be hired were the last ones to be paid. They all got paid and received what the master of the house deemed appropriate and just.

generous compensation of the master. Parables generally illustrate one main point, and the focus of this parable is on the master and his generous compensation. In a word, Jesus Christ is saying to Peter and the others, trust in the good master's ability to give generously rather than *how much* you will get.

To close this section, let's read one more record where Jesus Christ speaks about future reward. In this account, the lord is eating dinner at the house of one of the chief Pharisees. While there, he teaches on several matters; but for our purposes, let's pick up the record in verse 12:

Luke 14:12-14

[12]He said also to the man who had invited him, "When you give a dinner or a banquet, do not invite your friends or your brothers or your relatives or rich neighbors, lest they also invite you in return and you be repaid.
[13]But when you give a feast, invite the poor, the crippled, the lame, the blind,
[14]and you will be blessed, because they cannot repay you. For you will be repaid at the resurrection of the just."

Jesus Christ told the Pharisee that he should strive to do something that he could not *possibly* be repaid for in this life. He taught the Pharisee to look forward to future compensation at the resurrection of the just. Recall how in Luke 6:35, Jesus Christ taught his disciples to give and serve, expecting nothing in return. Here, he takes it one step further, instructing them to give and serve those who couldn't possibly pay them back! Why? Because they would be repaid in the future. Once again, Jesus Christ directed people's attention to future reward for acts of service done in this lifetime.

In this section, we have seen that to his disciples, a certain rich young ruler, Peter, a Pharisee, and others, Jesus Christ spoke in numerous ways and in no uncertain terms about future reward. Jesus Christ taught his disciples that they could persevere in service, despite hindrances and hardships because their reward in heaven would be great. He taught Peter and the other disciples that they would receive reward in heaven for forsaking all and following him. By parable, Jesus taught that it is better to trust God's goodness to reward His laborers than to question the exact amount of one's reward. Certainly, these are not the only records where Jesus Christ taught about future reward, but they provide us with a rich understanding of this field.

Reward Means Wage

Having looked at some Gospel records about reward, we now seek to understand what the word "reward" means according to biblical usage. We start with a few verses from 1 Corinthians 3:

> ### 1 Corinthians 3:6-8, 14-15
> [6]I planted, Apollos watered, but God gave the growth.
> [7]So neither he who plants nor he who waters is anything, but only God who gives the growth.
> [8]He who plants and he who waters are one, and each will receive his **wages** (*misthos*) according to his labor.
>
> ### Verses 14-15
> [14]If the work that anyone has built on the foundation survives, he will receive a **reward** (*misthos*).
> [15]If anyone's work is burned up, he will suffer loss, though he himself will be saved, but only as through fire.

In the Greek New Testament, the word translated "wages" in verse 8 and "reward" in verse 14 is *misthos*, which means "dues paid for work, wages, hire, reward, compensation."[44] (This is the same word that is translated "reward" in all the Gospel records we've read so far in this chapter.)[45]

---

44 Thayer, *A Greek-English Lexicon*, s.v. "*misthos*."

45 Because in the Greek New Testament, the word *misthos* is always in the singular, we use the word "reward" not "rewards" when referring to what the individual receives. We only use the plural, "rewards," when referring to the reward that many people receive. The Scriptures never speak of one person receiving many rewards. They do speak of someone receiving "great reward," for example, but never many rewards.

In western culture, a reward is typically something you receive for doing a good deed, for turning in a bad guy to the authorities, or for finding a person's lost dog. But in its biblical usage, reward means wage or compensation. When you work at a company or business, you receive compensation for the work or service performed. An auto mechanic who fixes a faulty transmission receives a wage for his labor. A painter receives wages for a finished project. When it comes to our day-to-day lives, we understand the idea of receiving payment for work, service, and labor.[46] But somehow, we have difficulty carrying over this understanding when we read about reward in the Bible.

The Greek word *misthos* simply means wage or compensation. Romans 4 sheds more light on the meaning of this word:

Romans 4:4
Now to the one who works, his **wages** (*misthos*) are not counted as a gift but as his due.

Romans 4:4 (KJV)
Now to him that worketh is the **reward** (*misthos*) not reckoned of grace, but of debt.

Romans 4:4 is a declarative statement: one who works receives a wage, and a wage is not a gift. When someone works for something, he is compensated because a debt is owed for the work that was done. The auto mechanic and painter are paid for their work. This is a wage, not a gift. Romans 4:4 tells us that a wage is not given out of grace, meaning it isn't a gift. A wage is something you receive because it is due to you. As

---

[46] Our phrase "work, service, and labor" used throughout this book includes any and all of the works, deeds, services, actions, stewarding, believing, enduring, functioning, obeying, and so forth that will be judged for reward. This is not to be confused with the works of the Law or the works of the flesh. The Scriptures speak about workings, operations, activities, functions, work, service, labor, business, office, doing, action, practice, conduct, walk, stewarding, and more. However, for the sake of narrative simplicity, we use the phrase "work, service, and labor" to mean all the above-mentioned actions or doings, or any other possible actions or doings that will be judged for reward.

we will see later in this chapter, a Christian's reward is not a gift received by grace. The reward is received by merit. While one receives salvation by grace, the reward is dependent upon works done *after* one is saved.

> In its biblical usage, reward means wage or compensation.

What's more, reward does not mean "award." An award is generally given to some person or group for an outstanding accomplishment or achievement. In contrast, a wage is given for labor performed, work done, or service rendered. While we might conflate the words "reward" and "award," the biblical meaning of reward (*misthos*) is wage or compensation, not an award. It's important to keep this in mind.

We can see this definition of *misthos* from the Septuagint.[47] In Leviticus 19:13, we read, "You shall not oppress your neighbor or rob him. The **wages** (*misthos*) of a hired worker shall not remain with you all night until the morning." Here, *misthos* is a wage paid to a hired worker.

James 5:4 alludes to Leviticus 19:13:

James 5:4
Behold, the **wages** (*misthos*) of the laborers who mowed your fields, which you kept back by fraud, are crying out against you, and the cries of the harvesters have reached the ears of the Lord of hosts.

In the Greek New Testament, the word translated "wages" in this verse is *misthos*. Again, it's clear that *misthos* means a wage paid to a laborer. God hears the cries of those who are defrauded or robbed of their just wages. Man's standard of payment may be unjust or prejudicial, but God's standard for payment is just. The Scriptures attest that God would have a worker be paid the wages he deserves and not have those wages dishonestly withheld from him. From Romans 4:4, Leviticus 19:13, and James 5:4, we learn that reward (*misthos*) means wage given to a laborer.

---

[47] The Septuagint, the Greek translation of the Old Testament, is commonly abbreviated as the "LXX," the Roman numeral for 70.

Laborer Worthy of his Wages

We see the same meaning of *misthos* in the following passage:

> **Ezekiel 29:18-20**
> [18]"Son of Man, Nebuchadnezzar king of Babylon made his army labor hard against Tyre. Every head was made bald, and every shoulder was rubbed bare, yet neither he nor his army got anything from Tyre to **pay** (*misthos*) for the labor that he had performed against her.
> [19]Therefore thus says the Lord GOD: Behold, I will give the land of Egypt to Nebuchadnezzar king of Babylon; and he shall carry off its wealth and despoil it and plunder it; and it shall be the **wages** (*misthos*) for his army.
> [20]I have given him the land of Egypt as his payment for which he labored, because they worked for me, declares the Lord GOD.

In service to God, Nebuchadnezzar and his army fought against Tyre and were victorious in battle. However, he and his army did not receive wages for their labor. God told Ezekiel that He would reward Nebuchadnezzar by paying his wage (the spoils of war) because "they worked for me."[48] Once again, we see that *misthos* means wage or compensation for work done, or service rendered. We also see that God is concerned that wages be paid for service or labor rendered on His behalf.

Along the same lines, in Luke 10:1-9, Jesus Christ taught that a laborer should receive his wages. In the record, Jesus sent out 72 to labor by preaching the kingdom of God and healing the sick.[49] He told them their wage would be whatever people gave them, adding, "the laborer deserves his wages" (v. 7). Once again, we see that a wage (*misthos*) is something given to a laborer.

---

[48] See Jer. 27:6.

[49] The King James Version and other English Bibles have "70" rather than "72."

Later, the apostle Paul quotes this same phrase, "the laborer deserves his wages":

1 Timothy 5:17-18

[17]Let the elders who rule well be considered worthy of double honor, especially those who labor in preaching and teaching.

[18]For the Scripture says, "You shall not muzzle an ox when it treads out the grain," and, "The laborer deserves his **wages** (*misthos*)."

God considers those who labor in the Word worthy of double honor. Why? Because God has established that the laborer deserves to be compensated.

In 1 Corinthians 9, several illustrations highlight the truth that a laborer deserves his wages.

1 Corinthians 9:7-10

[7]Who serves as a soldier at his own expense? Who plants a vineyard without eating any of its fruit? Or who tends a flock without getting some of the milk?

[8]Do I say these things on human authority? Does not the Law say the same?

[9]For it is written in the Law of Moses, "You shall not muzzle an ox when it treads out the grain." Is it for oxen that God is concerned?

[10]Does he not certainly speak for our sake? It was written for our sake, because the plowman should plow in hope and the thresher thresh in hope of sharing in the crop.

Verse 7 contains three illustrations:

- A soldier doesn't go to war at his own expense; he is paid.
- A vintner doesn't plant a vineyard without eating some of the fruit.
- A shepherd doesn't care for his flock without taking sustenance from his animals.

God's Word uses this three-part illustration to underscore the truth that anyone who labors should expect a return for their labor. From God's perspective, a laborer deserves his wages.

Whether it was the hired man in Leviticus, Nebuchadnezzar's army in Ezekiel, the 72 commissioned by Jesus Christ in Luke, or the elders in 1 Timothy, God's Word makes it clear that the laborer deserves his wages. This is God's expressed will.

Yet, many Christians work and serve without expecting or even wanting to be repaid, which is commendable. That is fundamental to selfless service. Yet, we must acknowledge that from God's perspective, a laborer deserves his wages. What this means for the Christian is that from God's point of view, a Christian's work, service, and labor deserve to be compensated, and indeed will be compensated at the return of Christ.

The Christian's Reward

Having established that "reward" in the Bible means wage or compensation and that a laborer deserves his wages, we now turn our attention to 1 Corinthians 3. This chapter contains essential truths about the reward, so we will take the time to study it in detail.

One's Own Labor

1 Corinthians 3:5-15
⁵What then is Apollos? What is Paul? Servants through whom you believed, as the Lord assigned to each.
⁶I planted, Apollos watered, but God gave the growth.
⁷So neither he who plants nor he who waters is anything, but only God who gives the growth.
⁸He who plants and he who waters are one, and each will receive his **wages** (*misthos*) according to his labor.
⁹For we are God's fellow workers. You are God's field, God's building.

86

[10]According to the grace of God given to me, like a skilled master builder I laid a foundation, and someone else is building upon it. Let each one take care how he builds upon it.

[11]For no one can lay a foundation other than that which is laid, which is Jesus Christ.

[12]Now if anyone builds on the foundation with gold, silver, precious stones, wood, hay, straw—

[13]each one's work will become manifest, for the Day will disclose it, because it will be revealed by fire, and the fire will test what sort of work each one has done.

[14]If the work that anyone has built on the foundation survives, he will receive a **reward** (*misthos*).

[15]If anyone's work is burned up, he will suffer loss, though he himself will be saved, but only as through fire.

Here Paul writes about work built on the foundation of Jesus Christ, which is the work that will be rewarded. The passage is not speaking about receiving something by grace but by work and labor. Paul and Apollos were both laborers together. These verses mention planting, watering, and building, which are all types of work or labor.

This passage also highlights that each person who labors and works will receive compensation for their *own* labor or *own* work. Note how other English Bibles render verses 8 and 13:

1 Corinthians 3:8, 13 (NASB95)

Now he who plants and he who waters are one; but **each** will receive his **own** reward according to his **own** labor.

Verse 13

each man's work will become evident; for the day will show it because it is to be revealed with fire, and the fire itself will test the quality of **each** man's work.

1 Corinthians 3:8,13 (NKJV)
Now he who plants and he who waters are one, and
each one will receive his **own** reward according to his
own labor.

Verse 13
each one's work will become clear; for the Day will
declare it, because it will be revealed by fire; and the fire
will test **each one's** work, of what sort it is.

The repetition of the words "each," "each one," and "own" in verses 8
and 13 underscores the truth that *each* person will receive *their own*
reward according to *their own* labor. One believer will not receive
reward for another believer's labor, and vice-versa.

Furthermore, we see that not everyone does the same type of labor. In
the example from 1 Corinthians 3, Paul planted while Apollos watered.
When it comes to growing things, we all know that someone needs to
plant and that someone needs to water. But none of that is impressive
compared to God, who makes the plant grow. This illustration reminds
us that the recognition belongs to God alone, for He is the One Who
gives the increase. The passage also illustrates that there are different
kinds of labor, and that each person will be rewarded according to their
own labor.

In the Body of Christ, every member has a function.

Romans 12:4-8
[4]For as in one body we have many members, and the
members do not all have the same function,
[5]so we, though many, are one body in Christ, and
individually members one of another.
[6]Having gifts that differ according to the grace given
to us, let us use them: if prophecy, in proportion to our
faith;
[7]if service, in our serving; the one who teaches, in his
teaching;

[8]the one who exhorts, in his exhortation; the one who contributes, in generosity; the one who leads, with zeal; the one who does acts of mercy, with cheerfulness.

In the Greek New Testament, the word translated as "function" in verse 4 is *praxis*, which is "a doing, a mode of acting; a deed, act, transactions."[50] Verses 7-8 provide examples: serving, teaching, encouraging, contributing, leading, and showing acts of mercy. Just as each body part has a different function, so does each member of the Body of Christ have their own function. The exhortation in Romans 12 is to get busy doing whatever it is God has called you to do and to do it by believing.

This same truth is elaborated on in 1 Corinthians 12:12-27, where we learn that God has determined that *each* member in the body of Christ is indispensable. Indeed, God has arranged, composed, and appointed the different parts of the Body of Christ as it pleased Him. In the world, there are different wages based on the types of labor. A surgeon gets paid more than a store clerk, for instance. Not so in the Body of Christ. In the Body of Christ, one type of labor is not more important than another and will not be rewarded more than another. We need to keep this in mind as we continue studying the Christian believer's future reward.

Foundation of Jesus Christ

In 1 Corinthians 3:11, we read about the importance of building on the foundation of Jesus Christ.

1 Corinthians 3:10-11
[10]According to the grace of God given to me, like a skilled master builder I laid a foundation, and someone else is building upon it. Let each one take care how he builds upon it.

---

[50]   Thayer, *A Critical Greek Lexicon*, s.v. "*praxis*."

¹¹For no one can lay a foundation other than that which is laid, which is Jesus Christ.

A foundation is something one builds on, and we are to build on Jesus Christ, not on anything or anyone else. Note that it was Paul who laid this foundation, meaning that the Church Epistles, as revealed to the apostle Paul, form the basis of this foundation. Therefore, all preaching, teaching, and labor must be built on the Gospel of God concerning His Son Jesus Christ to be considered worthy of reward. For example, one may work to advance religious teaching based on something other than the Gospel of Christ. This work is not building on the foundation of Jesus Christ and is not the kind of work that is considered for reward, no matter how philanthropic, well-intentioned, or how much earthly good it may do. When it comes to future reward, there is no foundation other than Jesus Christ. God alone sets the criteria for the reward.

The next verses describe how works will be judged.

1 Corinthians 3:12-15

¹²Now if anyone builds on the foundation with gold, silver, precious stones, wood, hay, straw—
¹³each one's work will become manifest, for the Day will disclose it, because it will be revealed by fire, and the fire will test what sort of work each one has done.
¹⁴If the work that anyone has built on the foundation survives, he will receive a reward.
¹⁵If anyone's work is burned up, he will suffer loss, though he himself will be saved, but only as through fire.

Each one's work will be revealed by fire, and that fire will test what sort of work it is. What does this mean? Fire is a powerful agent used to test or purify materials. To have a work revealed and tested by fire is a figurative way of saying that work will be judged and found either acceptable or not. Those works founded on Jesus Christ will receive reward. That is what "gold, silver, precious stones" refers to, works that withstand the test by fire. In architectural terms, these are building materials that would survive fire. However, those works not founded on Jesus Christ will not receive reward. That is what "wood, hay, straw" refers to, materials that burn up quickly.

Furthermore, the loss mentioned in verse 15 is a loss of compensation, not a loss of eternal life:

1 Corinthians 3:15

If anyone's work is burned up, he will suffer **loss**, though he himself will be saved, but only as through fire.

The loss spoken of here is the loss suffered only regarding the reward, never salvation, because salvation is by grace and cannot be lost.

Note carefully that the Scriptures say every man's *work* will become manifest, not every man's *sin*. Salvation unto eternal life is by grace, whereas reward is given according to one's work, service, and labor. The sinner's salvation is *not* the topic of 1 Corinthians 3. The future reward is. The eternal salvation of born-again ones is never in question. It bears repeating that every man's *work* will be judged, not every man's sin. The individual believer has already been found blameless in Christ. It is his works that will be judged, not he, himself.

Evidently, some in Corinth were doing the wood, hay, and straw types of work. They were divisive and factious, causing others to stumble, and so forth. They were also trying to build on men as their foundation rather than on Jesus Christ. (Some other biblical examples of works that will be burned up include causing division, putting stumbling blocks in front of weak believers, presenting another gospel, teaching the wrong doctrine, preaching another Jesus, receiving another spirit, adulterating the Word of God, wrongly handling God's Word, and worshipping idols.) Remember that no punishment to the individual will ensue; instead, there will be a loss of reward because such works will be burned up.

Let's finish reading the rest of 1 Corinthians 3.

1 Corinthians 3:16-23

¹⁶Do you not know that you are God's **temple** [sanctuary] and that God's Spirit dwells in you?

¹⁷If anyone destroys God's **temple** [sanctuary], God will destroy him. For God's temple is holy, and you are that temple.

¹⁸Let no one deceive himself. If anyone among you thinks that he is wise in this age, let him become a fool that he may become wise.

¹⁹For the wisdom of this world is folly with God. For it is written, "He catches the wise in their craftiness,"

²⁰and again, "The Lord knows the thoughts of the wise, that they are futile."

²¹So let no one boast in men. For all things are yours,

²²whether Paul or Apollos or Cephas or the world or life or death or the present or the future—all are yours,

²³and you are Christ's, and Christ is God's.

At first, verse 17 seems unclear. What does it mean if a man "destroys God's temple, God will destroy him"? According to the Greek New Testament, "temple" should be the word "sanctuary," meaning the inner part of the Temple. This verse contains a figure of speech where "sanctuary" is a metaphor referring to the Church.[51] Considering the context, we are given to understand that destroying God's sanctuary means harming the Church. But who is the apostle speaking about in verse 17 when he writes "anyone"? Some say this refers to people *outside* the Church who cause harm. But, as we will see, the context indicates that this refers to those *within* the Church.

Verses 1-16 and 18-23 all speak about the saints, born-again ones. Why would the subject matter suddenly shift to unbelievers in verse 17 and then back to believers in the next verses? The context suggests that "anyone" in verse 17 refers to those *within* the Church. Such people destroy the Church by causing division, teaching the wrong doctrine, and being a stumbling block to others. By preaching another

---

51 Metaphor is a figure of comparison where one thing is declared to be another thing. Hans, Go *Figure!* 191.

Jesus or another gospel, they pervert the Gospel and cause some to be corrupted. [52]

Furthermore, when verse 17 says that God will "destroy" such a person, it is a figurative way (hyperbole or exaggeration) to say that that person will suffer loss: his works will be destroyed. It is not literally true that God will destroy a born-again one. It is a figurative way to say that this person will suffer a loss of reward. In using *hyperbole*, God draws attention to the gravity of the lost reward. Identifying the figures of speech and reading the context helps us to understand this potentially unclear verse.[53]

We can read about people in the Bible who adulterated the Word of God. We can read about those who taught God's Word intending to draw disciples after themselves or those who wrongly divided the Scriptures, teaching such things as "the resurrection is passed already." All these are works that will not stand the test of fire and will not be rewarded.

The saint's eternal salvation is never in question. The loss spoken of in 1 Corinthians 3:15 is the loss of *reward* for work that did not stand the test of fire. Though it is troubling to think that some of the Christian's works may be burned up in the fire on that Day, it is also comforting, for those things that one may be ashamed of will not be remembered. After the burning, God's recognition remains: "Then each one will receive his commendation from God" (1 Cor. 4:5).

---

[52]   See Rom. 14:13-15, 2 Cor. 11:4

[53]   We see the same figure of speech in 1 Corinthians 8, where Paul addresses the eating of food offered to idols. Weak ones who do not understand the freedom in Christ may be led to think that such idolatrous practices are acceptable. Paul says, "And so by your knowledge this weak person is destroyed, the brother for whom Christ died" (1 Cor. 8:11). Of course, no born again one will literally be destroyed by eating food offered to idols, but using hyperbole, the Scriptures emphasize the gravity of the matter.

Purposes of the Heart

The next passage contains important truths regarding the judging of a Christian's work.

1 Corinthians 4:1-5

¹This is how one should regard us, as servants of Christ and stewards of the mysteries of God.

²Moreover, it is required of stewards that they be found faithful.

³But with me it is a very small thing that I should be judged by you or by any human court. In fact, I do not even judge myself.

⁴For I am not aware of anything against myself, but I am not thereby acquitted. It is the Lord who judges me.

⁵Therefore do not pronounce judgment before the time, before the Lord comes, who will bring to light the things now hidden in darkness and will disclose the purposes of the heart. Then each one will receive his commendation from God.

Paul exhorts the saints to judge nothing until Christ returns rather than judging one minister better than another. Why? Because they cannot know the purposes of the heart, meaning what lies within a person's thinking or motives.

1 Corinthians 2:11

For who knows a person's thoughts except the spirit of that person, which is in him? So also no one comprehends the thoughts of God except the Spirit of God.

God alone knows what is in the depth of a person's heart, and therefore only He can judge accurately. Further, each Christian must stand before the judgment seat of Christ when he returns.

2 Corinthians 5:10

For we must all appear before the **judgment seat** (*bēma*) of Christ, so that each one may receive what is due for what he has done in the body, whether good or evil.

2 Corinthians 5:10 (NASB95)

For we must all appear before the **judgment seat** (*bēma*) of Christ, so that each one may be **recompensed** for his deeds in the body, according to what he has done, whether good or bad.

All Christians must appear before the judgment seat (*bēma*) of Christ.[54] It is before Christ's judgment seat where a believer's work will be judged and where the believer will be rewarded. Isn't it a comfort to know that when one's work, service, and labor are judged at the *bēma*, the purposes of the heart, and not just the actions, will also be considered?

However, 1 Corinthians 4:5 does not say that the purposes of the heart are the *only* thing taken into account at the judgment seat of Christ. That might lead some to erroneously think that so long as a person's "heart was in the right place," to borrow a common religious phrase, that person was exempt from building on the foundation of Jesus Christ. That sentiment is biblically groundless.

It is certain that no one is qualified to judge another believer's walk or service. Often, the counsels of the heart are hidden, and people misjudge based on appearance. There are several examples in the Scriptures where people misjudged others because they did not know the purposes of the heart. Samson's motive in marrying a Philistine, Moses' motive in killing the Egyptian, and Hannah's reason for crying while in prayer come to mind (see also Judg. 14:1-4; Acts 7:23-25, 35, 39; 1 Sam. 1:12-15).

Indeed, Jesus Christ taught that God, Who sees in secret, will reward.

---

54   For a detailed study of this topic, see Appendix C: "The Judgment Seat of Christ."

Matthew 6:1-6

[1]"Beware of practicing your righteousness before other people in order to be seen by them, for then you will have no reward from your Father who is in heaven.

[2]"Thus, when you give to the needy, sound no trumpet before you, as the hypocrites do in the synagogues and in the streets, that they may be praised by others. Truly, I say to you, they have received their reward.

[3]But when you give to the needy, do not let your left hand know what your right hand is doing,

[4]so that your giving may be in secret. And your **Father who sees in secret** will reward you.

[5]"And when you pray, you must not be like the hypocrites. For they love to stand and pray in the synagogues and at the street corners, that they may be seen by others. Truly, I say to you, they have received their reward.

[6]But when you pray, go into your room and shut the door and pray to your **Father who is in secret**. And your **Father who sees in secret** will reward you.

In this passage, the phrase "your Father who sees [or "is"] in secret" is repeated. Here, Jesus Christ taught that if they were to practice righteousness, give to the needy, and pray just so that they would look good in front of people, they would receive a reward, namely, recognition from people. They would not receive a heavenly reward. However, if they were to do these things in secret, God, who sees in secret, would reward them.

When Christ judges, it will be perfectly equitable.[55] In his earthly ministry, Jesus often knew what was in a person's heart when others didn't: the widow who cast in her mite, the woman with costly ointment, Zacchaeus the publican, the malefactor on the cross, and others. While other people judged from outward appearance, the lord did not. There

---

[55] For more on Christ judging at the *bēma*, see Appendix C: "The Judgement Seat of Christ."

can be no doubt that when the judgment of works takes place, Jesus Christ will take into account the purposes of the heart.

In this section, we have seen that 1 Corinthians 3 is an essential chapter regarding the Christian's future reward. The truths in this chapter do not address eternal salvation but a believer's work, service, labor, and corresponding reward. We learned that *each* person's work will be tested by fire and that *each* person will receive his *own* reward for his *own* work. Work that abides will receive reward. Work that does not remain will be burned up, meaning not rewarded. We also learned that for work, service, or labor to be rewarded, it must be built on the foundation of Jesus Christ. Finally, from 1 Corinthians 4:1-5, we learned we must not judge anyone's labor because only God knows the purposes of the heart. Christ alone is qualified to judge.

What is Rewarded?

We know that work, service, and labor built on the foundation of Jesus Christ will be rewarded, but what else does the Bible say on this topic?

> **1 Corinthians 15:58**
> Therefore, my beloved brothers, be steadfast, immovable, always abounding in the work **of the Lord**, knowing that **in the Lord** your labor is not in vain.

The Corinthians were encouraged to abound in the lord's work, knowing that such labor is not in vain, meaning empty. The saints were not to be idle as they waited for Christ to return. Instead, Paul exhorted the saints to always (not occasionally) abound (not a meager amount) in the work of the Lord. Why? Because such labor will not be empty: it would profit in this life and be rewarded in the future.

We learn more about what is rewarded in the epistle to the Ephesians:

Ephesians 6:5-8

[5]Bondservants, obey your earthly masters with fear and trembling, with a sincere heart, as you would Christ,

[6]not by the way of eye-service, as people-pleasers, but as bondservants of Christ, doing the will of God from the heart,

[7]rendering service with a good will as to the Lord and not to man,

[8]knowing that whatever good anyone does, this he will receive back from the Lord, whether he is a bondservant or is free.

Colossians 3:17, 22-25

And whatever you do, in word or deed, do everything in the name of the Lord Jesus, giving thanks to God the Father through him.

Verses 22-25

[22]Bondservants, obey in everything those who are your earthly masters, not by way of eye-service, as people-pleasers, but with sincerity of heart, fearing the Lord.

[23]Whatever you do, work heartily, as for the Lord and not for men,

[24]knowing that from the Lord you will receive the inheritance as your reward. You are serving the Lord Christ.

[25]For the wrongdoer will be paid back for the wrong he has done, and there is no partiality.

These passages describe a master-servant relationship. Ephesians speaks about bondservants of Christ doing the will of God from the heart. Such service will "receive back from the Lord," meaning it will be rewarded. Colossians indicates that whatever a believer does, he is to do it heartily "as for the Lord and not for men," knowing that he will receive the reward associated with the inheritance.[56] To work heartily is explained in the context: to work to please the lord, not men. (In verse 25, "the wrongdoer will be paid back for the wrong he has done," which means a loss of reward.)

These truths from Ephesians and Colossians offer tremendous encouragement. "Whatever you do" encompasses a lot of things, including one's secular job. At work, the saint is to work as if he is working for the lord, not his boss or superior. When we as Christians are mindful of this, work can take on a whole new meaning because we are looking for our ultimate compensation from the lord and not from men. Believing this truth can turn the most mundane task into joyful service in light of the return of Christ.

The following passage from the book of Hebrews sheds more light on what will be rewarded:

Hebrews 6:9-12
[9]Though we speak in this way, yet in your case, beloved, we feel sure of better things—things that belong to salvation.
[10]For God is not unjust so as to overlook your work and the love that you have shown for his name in serving the saints, as you still do.
[11]And we desire each one of you to show the same earnestness to have the full assurance of hope until the end,
[12]so that you may not be sluggish, but imitators of those who through faith and patience inherit the promises.

Work done out of love for God to serve the saints includes many things. People may forget or not appreciate the work done on their behalf, but God does not and indeed cannot forget because it would be unjust. In what way would God remember their work, service, and love? Reward. The Hebrew saints had been doing these things and now

---

[56]   See Appendix B: "Four Apparent Contradictions about the Inheritance" for more information about Col. 3:24.

were encouraged to remain faithful "to the end," knowing their reward in heaven would be sure.

Work, service, or labor done in love will also be rewarded:

> **1 Corinthians 13:3**
> If I give away all I have, and if I deliver up my body to be burned, but have not love, I gain nothing.

Even if I were to sacrifice in the extreme—give away all I had, including my life—it would still not be of any profit to me if it wasn't done in love. The apostle Paul is here using hyperbole to drive home just how essential love is when serving.

What God Commends

One way to approach an understanding of the kind of work, service, and labor that will be rewarded in heaven is to consider what God recognizes, values and commends in His Word. The following passages of Scripture are given as examples that illustrate this point. (The reader is kindly reminded that this is not an exhaustive study of the topic.)

> **1 Corinthians 16:15-16**
> [15]Now I urge you, brothers—you know that the household of Stephanas were the first converts in Achaia, and that they have devoted themselves to the service of the saints—
> [16]be subject to such as these, and to every fellow worker and laborer.

The household of Stephanas devoted themselves to serving the saints, and Paul exhorts the Corinthians to be subject to these believers. Why? Because of their dedicated service. Might not such dedication, commended by God in this life, merit reward in the life to come?

Another outstanding servant, Epaphras, is recognized in God's Word:

Colossians 4:12

Epaphras, who is one of you, a servant of Christ Jesus, greets you, always struggling on your behalf in his prayers, that you may stand mature and fully assured in all the will of God.

Epaphras served by intensive prayer on behalf of the Colossian Church. Other versions of Colossians 4:12 read that Epaphras was "wrestling in prayer for you" (NIV), "laboring earnestly for you in his prayers" (NASB), and "always labouring fervently for you in prayers" (KJV). His service to the saints in laboring fervently in prayer is recognized here, and assuredly, this type of labor will be rewarded at the return of Christ.

In the opening salutation in 1 Thessalonians, we see another instance of what God commends.

1 Thessalonians 1:1-3

[1]Paul, Silvanus, and Timothy, To the church of the Thessalonians in God the Father and the Lord Jesus Christ: Grace to you and peace.
[2]We give thanks to God always for all of you, constantly mentioning you in our prayers,
[3]remembering before our God and Father your work of faith and labor of love and steadfastness of hope in our Lord Jesus Christ.

The Thessalonians' labor was motivated by love, their work proceeded from believing, and they remained steadfast in the Hope. God, by Paul, commends the Thessalonians for this. Such labor and steadfastness, recognized today, will be rewarded in heaven.

Perhaps it goes without saying that a Christian will be rewarded for his obedience to God. We only have to look at the example of Jesus Christ to appreciate this truth.

Philippians 2:3-11

[3]Do nothing from selfish ambition or conceit, but in humility count others more significant than yourselves.
[4]Let each of you look not only to his own interests, but also to the interests of others.
[5]Have this mind among yourselves, which is yours in Christ Jesus,
[6]who, though he was in the form of God, did not count equality with God a thing to be grasped,
[7]but emptied himself, by taking the form of a servant, being born in the likeness of men.
[8]And being found in human form, he humbled himself by becoming obedient to the point of death, even death on a cross.
[9]Therefore God has highly exalted him and bestowed on him the name that is above every name,
[10]so that at the name of Jesus every knee should bow, in heaven and on earth and under the earth,
[11]and every tongue confess that Jesus Christ is Lord, to the glory of God the Father.

The word "therefore" in verse 9 indicates a reason. The reason Jesus Christ was highly exalted, given a name above every name, was because of his *obedience*. Because he was obedient even to the point of death, Jesus Christ was given a singular position of authority in the kingdom of God. He was rewarded for his obedience. Certainly, there is rich learning in his example.

We also see that material and financial giving is commended in the Scriptures:

Philippians 4:15-20

[15]And you Philippians yourselves know that in the beginning of the gospel, when I left Macedonia, no church entered into partnership with me in giving and receiving, except you only.

¹⁶Even in Thessalonica you sent me help for my needs once and again.

¹⁷Not that I seek the gift, but I seek the fruit that increases to your credit.

¹⁸I have received full payment, and more. I am well supplied, having received from Epaphroditus the gifts you sent, a fragrant offering, a sacrifice acceptable and pleasing to God.

¹⁹And my God will supply every need of yours according to his riches in glory in Christ Jesus.

²⁰To our God and Father be glory forever and ever. Amen.

The Philippian saints gave gifts to Paul to supply his need on more than one occasion. Not only was their giving acceptable and pleasing to God, but it also resulted in fruit being credited to their account. The "fruit credited to their account" mentioned in verse 17 has a double meaning: reward in this life and reward in the future.

And in 1 Timothy, we read:

1 Timothy 6:17-19

¹⁷As for the rich in this present age, charge them not to be haughty, nor to set their hopes on the uncertainty of riches, but on God, who richly provides us with everything to enjoy.

¹⁸They are to do good, to be rich in good works, to be generous and ready to share,

¹⁹thus storing up treasure for themselves as a good foundation for the future, so that they may take hold of that which is truly life.

Those in the Church who are wealthy are to be rich in good works, ready to share their abundance. In doing so, they are storing up future treasure for themselves—meaning reward.

In this section, we have looked at some examples of the type of work, service, and labor that will be rewarded. We also looked at some examples of the type of service that God's Word commends, such as ministering to the saints, praying for the saints, and financial giving. If God commends these things in this life, they will not be forgotten when the reward is given in the future. While this is not an exhaustive list of all the things God commends in His Word, it is a starting point for future study.

Summary and Conclusion

In this chapter, we learned that Jesus Christ taught many truths about the reward to his disciples and apostles and individuals like the rich young ruler. He taught his disciples that they could persevere in service, despite hindrances and hardships because their reward in heaven would be great. He taught Peter and the other apostles that they would receive reward in heaven for forsaking all and following him. By parable, he illustrated it is better to trust God's goodness to reward His laborers than to question the amount of one's reward. Jesus Christ taught that anyone who forsook things for the Gospel would be richly compensated both now and in the future.

We also learned that the biblical meaning of "reward" is wage or compensation. The Scriptures repeatedly teach us that a laborer deserves to be paid. From 1 Corinthians 3, we see that each Christian will be rewarded according to their own labor, not according to anyone else's service. Any labor built on the foundation of Jesus Christ will be rewarded.

In light of these truths about the Christian's reward, one might wonder: is our motivation to serve God so that we can receive a reward, or do we labor out of appreciation for all that God has done for us in Christ? Do we walk in love because we want a reward, or do we walk in love because He first loved us? Do we serve others because we expect compensation in heaven, or do we serve because we want to imitate our lord's example of service? Without a doubt, God is worthy of all our devotion, attention, love, talents, and abilities. We serve Him because we *love* Him and are *thankful* to Him for all He has done for us in Christ. While the reward does serve as *a* motivation to serve, it is not the *only* motivation. Love for and thanksgiving to God are also key motivators.

However, we can't deny that in the Scriptures, the reward is held up as motivation when service is *difficult,* when one is persecuted, reviled, and afflicted for Christ's sake. During such times, it's easy to see how some may want to quit. While the promise of future reward is not the only motivation to serve, it can certainly encourage one to persevere, especially in the face of affliction, apathy, or adversity. [57]

In addition to what we have already covered, note the following references where the reward is held up as a motivation:

- Christ spoke of the reward as an appeal to his disciples to pray in secret (Matt. 6:6).
- Paul spoke of the reward as an appeal to the saints to exercise self-control (1 Cor. 9:24-25).
- Paul spoke of the reward as an appeal to the saints to develop godliness (1 Tim. 4:7-8).
- Peter spoke of the reward as an appeal for the saints to conduct themselves with fear (1 Pet. 1:17).
- James spoke of the reward as an appeal for the saints to remain steadfast under trial (James 1:12).
- John spoke of the reward as an appeal to the saints to remain faithful (2 John 8).

So, while it would be misleading to say the reward is the only thing that motivates us to serve, it would also be misleading to say that the Bible never holds up reward as a source of motivation to serve.

It's instructive to consider what Jesus Christ *didn't* teach his disciples about reward. He didn't teach that the disciples were blessed when persecuted because they had the satisfaction of knowing they suffered for the lord. He didn't teach the rich young ruler that if he sold all his

---

[57] For more on this topic of the reward and motivation, see the answer to Question 10 in Appendix I: "Frequently Asked Questions."

possessions and gave the proceeds to the poor, he'd have a warm feeling of fulfillment afterward. He didn't teach Peter and the other apostles that the reward for their sacrifice would be the satisfaction of knowing they were his apostles and nothing more.

In contrast, Jesus Christ taught his disciples they could rejoice when persecuted, hated, and slandered because their reward in heaven was great. He taught a rich young ruler that if he sold all his possessions and gave the proceeds to the poor, he would have treasure in heaven. He taught Peter and the other apostles that they would be rewarded with positions of authority and responsibility for their sacrifice and service to him. Most of all, by his life and example, Jesus Christ taught that obedience to God brings great reward.

The grace of God that we have received is remarkable. No work of man can ever add to the redemptive work of Jesus Christ. Having received this grace, we now walk obediently with God, fulfilling whatever work, service, and labor He directs. Teaching the Gospel of Jesus Christ and all its associated labors requires effort and diligence. Though God could, by all rights, demand service in return for all He has done for us, He instead gives us the opportunity to be living sacrifices. Then He lovingly promises to reward us in heaven for that service.

Chapter 5

Reward and Grace

As we know, one is saved by grace through faith and not by works (Eph. 2:8). This is a foundational truth. So, when introduced to the idea of reward for work, service, or labor, some Christians are skeptical. They wonder if the reward somehow repudiates or contradicts God's grace. If one is saved by grace through faith and not by works, does reward, which is based on merit, negate this grace of God? In this chapter, we seek to answer that question.

Received by Grace

To start the discussion, let's distinguish between what the Scriptures say is received by grace and what is received by merit.

Ephesians 2:4-10
[4]But God, being rich in mercy, because of the great love with which he loved us,

[5]even when we were dead in our trespasses, made us alive together with Christ—by grace you have been saved—

[6]and raised us up with him and seated us with him in the heavenly places in Christ Jesus,

[7]so that in the coming ages he might show the immeasurable riches of his grace in kindness toward us in Christ Jesus.

[8]For by grace you have been saved through faith. And this is not your own doing; it is the gift of God,

[9]not a result of works, so that no one may boast.

¹⁰For we are his workmanship, created in Christ Jesus for good works, which God prepared beforehand, that we should walk in them.

From this passage, it is clear that salvation comes by the grace of God. The central idea that one is saved by grace is repeated five times in different ways:

- By grace, you have been saved
- By grace, you have been saved through faith
- Not of your own doing
- It is the gift of God
- Not a result of works

The repetition makes this truly emphatic. One might say, "for you are saved by GRACE and nothing but GRACE!" Referring to salvation as a "gift of God" makes it clear that no one earns salvation, for a gift is, by definition, something that is freely given. In addition, there are many other blessings that Christians have received by the grace of God, such as righteousness, redemption, sanctification, and so forth. The following chart offers examples of things that are received by grace.

Subject	Received By Grace Through Christ
Eternal Life	**Romans 6:23** For the wages of sin is death, but the free gift of God is eternal life in Christ Jesus our Lord.
Salvation	**Romans 10:9-10** ⁹because, if you confess with your mouth that Jesus is Lord and believe in your heart that God raised him from the dead, you will be saved. ¹⁰For with the heart one believes and is justified, and with the mouth one confesses and is saved. **Ephesians 2:8** For by grace you have been saved through faith. And this is not your own doing; it is the gift of God,

Subject	Received By Grace Through Christ
Sanctification	**1 Corinthians 1:2** To the church of God that is in Corinth, to those sanctified in Christ Jesus, called to be saints together with all those who in every place call upon the name of our Lord Jesus Christ, both their Lord and ours: **1 Corinthians 6:11** And such were some of you. But you were washed, you were sanctified, you were justified in the name of the Lord Jesus Christ and by the Spirit of our God.
Calling of God	**Romans 8:28** And we know that for those who love God all things work together for good, for those who are called according to his purpose. **2 Timothy 1:9** who saved us and called us to a holy calling, not because of our works but because of his own purpose and grace, which he gave us in Christ Jesus before the ages began,
Made holy and without blame	**Ephesians 1:4a** even as he chose us in him before the foundation of the world, that we should be holy and blameless before him. **Colossians 1:21-22** 21And you, who once were alienated and hostile in mind, doing evil deeds, 22he has now reconciled in his body of flesh by his death, in order to present you holy and blameless and above reproach before him,
Righteousness	**1 Corinthians 1:30** And because of him you are in Christ Jesus, who became to us wisdom from God, righteousness and sanctification and redemption, **2 Corinthians 5:21** For our sake he made him to be sin who knew no sin, so that in him we might become the righteousness of God.
Justification	**Romans 5:1** Therefore, since we have been justified by faith, we have peace with God through our Lord Jesus Christ.

Subject	Received By Grace Through Christ
Reconciliation	**Romans 5:10** For if while we were enemies we were reconciled to God by the death of his Son, much more, now that we are reconciled, shall we be saved by his life. **2 Corinthians 5:18** All this is from God, who through Christ reconciled us to himself and gave us the ministry of reconciliation; **Colossians 1:21-22** ^{21}And you, who once were alienated and hostile in mind, doing evil deeds, ^{22}he has now reconciled in his body of flesh by his death, in order to present you holy and blameless and above reproach before him,
Heirs	**Romans 8:16-17** ^{16}The Spirit himself bears witness with our spirit that we are children of God, ^{17}and if children, then heirs—heirs of God and fellow heirs with Christ, provided we suffer with him in order that we may also be glorified with him. **Titus 3:7** so that being justified by his grace we might become heirs according to the hope of eternal life.

As we can see from this brief list, many things are received by grace, a gift of God through the accomplished work of Jesus Christ. The reader may recall that the Christian's inheritance is received by grace, not merit. (See Chapter 3: "The Inheritance.")

Received by Merit

While the Scriptures are clear that sons of God have received many blessings by God's grace, the Scriptures are also clear that some things are received by merit, such as the reward.

1 Corinthians 3:13-15

[13]each one's work will become manifest, for the Day will disclose it, because it will be revealed by fire, and the fire will test what sort of work each one has done.
[14]If the work that anyone has built on the foundation survives, he will receive a reward.
[15]If anyone's work is burned up, he will suffer loss, though he himself will be saved, but only as through fire.

Each one's work will be tested by fire, and work that remains will be rewarded. Before moving on, we want to clarify a potential misunderstanding. The work that is rewarded, as stated in 1 Corinthians 3:13-15, is not the same as the works of the Law to bring about one's own righteousness, or some other work to gain righteousness.[58] Instead, the work that will be rewarded at the *bēma* of Christ is for service, labor, doings, functions, actions, giving, and so forth that a believer renders in service to God. Some might mistakenly conflate work that is rewarded with works done to achieve one's own righteousness. This is a grave mistake.

Put another way, works that will be judged are *not* works done to try to earn something from God that is already an accomplished reality. The reward is given based on the work, service, or labor done by the individual Christian *after* they have been saved by grace. It is essential to keep this in mind whenever considering the works that will be rewarded at the return of Christ. In some Christian circles, the word "work" is taboo, even though the Scriptures are clear that Christians will be rewarded for their *work*. One way to circumvent this anxiety is to substitute the word "service" for "work." The Scriptures are clear that born-again ones are called to serve.

---

58   Gal. 2:16: "Yet we know that a person is not justified by works of the law but through faith in Jesus Christ, so we also have believed in Christ Jesus, in order to be justified by faith in Christ and not by works of the law, because by works of the law no one will be justified."

Romans 12:1 (NKJV)
I beseech you therefore, brethren, by the mercies of God,
that you present your bodies a living sacrifice, holy,
acceptable to God, *which is* your reasonable **service**.

Galatians 5:13
For you were called to freedom, brothers. Only do not
use your freedom as an opportunity for the flesh, but
through love **serve** one another.

In Romans 12:1, giving one's life as a living sacrifice is deemed a logical
or reasonable service. Remembering all that God has done for us in
Christ, in consideration of all His mercy, it is only logical that we
would want to serve Him. Galatians 5:13 instructs us that we are to use
our liberty in Christ to serve one another through love. The believer's
salvation, justification, righteousness, and sanctification are assured,
for these are received by the grace of God, based on the sure and holy
merits of Jesus Christ.

Each believer is called to serve, but how the individual responds
will vary. Some will sacrifice all they have to serve God and the saints,
while others will refuse to lift a finger. Is it any wonder, then, that
their respective reward will differ? We see this in the Church today,
and we see this in the Scriptures. First, we read of men like Paul and
Epaphroditus who devoted themselves to the Gospel, even to the point
of imprisonment, life-threatening peril, and exhaustion. In contrast,
we read about those who did not serve the Lord Christ but "their own
appetites" (Rom. 16:18) and whose "god is their belly" (Phil. 3:19).[59]
These are Christians who serve themselves. Both types of Christians,
those who serve God and those who do not, are saved by grace. Both
have received the same righteousness, sanctification, redemption, and so
forth. But both will assuredly *not* receive the same reward at the return
of Christ. The reward is commensurate with one's service.

---

[59]   The word "bellies" is a synecdoche, a figure of exchange where a part is put for
the whole, or the whole is put for the part. Here, the belly is put for the whole person.
See Hans, *Go Figure!* 169.

The Pauline Epistles are filled with admonitions to serve. They provide us with outstanding examples of servants of Christ, such as the apostle Paul and Epaphroditus.

Colossians 1:24-29

[24]Now I rejoice in my sufferings for your sake, and in my flesh I am filling up what is lacking in Christ's afflictions for the sake of his body, that is, the church,

[25]of which I became a minister according to the stewardship from God that was given to me for you, to make the word of God fully known,

[26]the mystery hidden for ages and generations but now revealed to his saints.

[27]To them God chose to make known how great among the Gentiles are the riches of the glory of this mystery, which is Christ in you, the hope of glory.

[28]Him we proclaim, warning everyone and teaching everyone with all wisdom, that we may present everyone mature in Christ.

[29]For this I toil, struggling with all his energy that he powerfully works within me.

One of Paul's responsibilities as an apostle was to make the Word of God known so that the saints could be presented mature in Christ. That would include preaching, teaching, warning, praying, and so forth, according to the spirit of God at work in Paul. Besides being an apostle, Paul is referred to in the Scriptures as a "servant of Jesus Christ," a "minister," as well as a "preacher," and "teacher."[60] How could he fulfill these functions without work, service, or labor? Paul's functioning in the Body of Christ was not in name or title only but had accompanying action.

---

[60]   See for example, Rom. 1:1; 1 Cor. 1:1; 1 Cor. 3:5; 2 Cor. 1:1; Gal. 1:1; Eph. 1:1; Phil. 1:1, Col. 1:1; 1 Tim. 1:1; 2 Tim. 1:1; Col. 1:23; 1 Tim. 2:7; Tit. 1:1.

Paul, at the end of his life, wrote:

2 Timothy 4:6-8
⁶For I am already being poured out as a drink offering, and the time of my departure has come.
⁷I have fought the good fight, I have finished the race, I have kept the faith.
⁸Henceforth there is laid up for me the crown of righteousness, which the Lord, the righteous judge, will award to me on that day, and not only to me but also to all who have loved his appearing.

In verse 6, Paul said he was "being poured out as a drink offering." This is a powerful figure of speech, meaning that he poured out his life in service to God. Paul had not used grace as an excuse to sit around enjoying "me time." Instead, he spent his life in all-out service. In sports jargon, we might say, "He left it all on the field." Paul was saved by grace, and he certainly understood, better than most, what the grace of God signified in his life. But he also served God wholly and utterly. He labored and toiled night and day. Paul did not work to become saved; he worked because he was saved. We consider Paul's example in more detail in Chapter 9: "Running the Race to the Finish." But for now, let's note that as a servant of Christ, Paul worked, toiled, labored, pouring out his life in service. For Paul, grace did not mean that there was no work to be done.

We see the same commitment to serve in Epaphroditus.

Philippians 2:25-30
²⁵I have thought it necessary to send to you Epaphroditus my brother and fellow worker and fellow soldier, and your messenger and minister to my need,
²⁶for he has been longing for you all and has been distressed because you heard that he was ill.

²⁷Indeed he was ill, near to death. But God had mercy on him, and not only on him but on me also, lest I should have sorrow upon sorrow.

²⁸I am the more eager to send him, therefore, that you may rejoice at seeing him again, and that I may be less anxious.

²⁹So receive him in the Lord with all joy, and honor such men,

³⁰for he nearly died for the work of Christ, risking his life to complete what was lacking in your service to me.

Epaphroditus was Paul's brother in Christ, his fellow worker and fellow soldier. He nearly died because of his work for Christ. We do not read, "Epaphroditus simply worked too hard; he should have taken it easy. After all, he was saved by grace." Instead, the saints are encouraged to hold this man in honor because of his commitment and service. Did Epaphroditus risk his life for the work of Christ because he was trying to earn his salvation? Or did he expend himself in service because he was saved?

Note what Paul wrote about grace and work in his epistle to Titus.

Titus 2:11-14

¹¹For the **grace of God** has appeared, bringing salvation for all people,

¹²training us to renounce ungodliness and worldly passions, and to live self-controlled, upright, and godly lives in the present age,

¹³waiting for our blessed hope, the appearing of the glory of our great God and Savior Jesus Christ,

¹⁴who gave himself for us to redeem us from all lawlessness and to purify for himself a people for his own possession who are **zealous for good works**.

Verse 11 reminds us that God's grace made salvation available. The next verse tells us that the same grace *instructs* the saint to live a certain way:

to renounce ungodliness and worldly desire and to live self-controlled, upright, and godly. Further, as the saints wait for Christ's return, they are to be *zealous of good works*. These good works are not works done to achieve salvation but the service and labor to which every Christian is called. As we wait for Christ to return, we are not to sit idly by. We are to be zealous of good works. Past editor of *The Berean Expositor*, Stuart Allen, sums it up when he writes:

> In other words, 'good works' or Christian service and witness should flow from such free and unmerited salvation. The sinner has been saved to serve, and let us make no mistake, every true believer is called by the Lord to serve Him and to discover His will in this respect. It is only self-deception to refuse to recognize this. The words "servant" and "service" so permeate the epistles that it must be deliberate blindness that eliminates such service and responsibility to the Lord from the Christian life.[61]

Allen's point is that all believers are called by God to serve Him and to obey His will in this matter. One does good works, or Christian service and witness, not to *become* saved but because one *is* saved.

Called for a Work

In Acts 13, we read that God had called Paul and Barnabas for a specific work.

Acts 13:2
While they were worshiping the Lord and fasting, the Holy Spirit said, "Set apart for me Barnabas and Saul for the **work** to which I have called them."

---

[61]   Allen, "The Second Epistle to Timothy," 85.

If we read Acts 13 and 14, we see that these men obeyed God's directions and fulfilled the work. While we won't take the time here to recount all the rich details of this record, we note the following.

In Acts 13, Paul and Barnabas traveled to various locations, usually going to the local synagogue to preach the Gospel. Some believed, and some stood in opposition to the apostles. In Antioch of Pisidia, for instance, Paul spent a long time preaching and teaching. Many received the word of the Lord, and the Gospel spread throughout that region.

In Acts 14, we see a similar pattern. Paul and Barnabas continued their travels throughout the region, teaching and preaching in the synagogues. They faced opposition from those who did not believe. The power of God was in demonstration, including the healing of a man who was crippled from birth. Paul and Barnabas made many disciples in Derbe. As they made their way back home, Paul and Barnabas revisited the new disciples, to encourage them. They also appointed elders in each city.

At the end of their journey, we read:

Acts 14:26
and from there they sailed to Antioch, where they had been commended to the **grace of God** for the **work** that they had fulfilled.

Paul and Barnabas had been called, by God, to complete a particular work, and they *fulfilled* that work, meaning they left nothing undone. This work included preaching and teaching the Gospel, demonstrating signs, wonders, and miracles, encouraging the saints, withstanding Satanic opposition by the power of God, and setting up elders to oversee the disciples in these new areas. In this verse we also read that they had been "commended to the grace of God," meaning that they labored under God's grace.[62] Paul and Barnabas completed the work God gave them to do, and they did it within the framework of God's grace.

---

[62]   In Romans 6:14-15, we read, "For sin will have no dominion over you, since you are not under law but under grace. What then? Are we to sin because we are not under law but under grace? By no means!"

In his first epistle to the Corinthians, note what Paul wrote about grace and work.

1 Corinthians 15:10

But by the grace of God I am what I am, and his grace toward me was not in vain. On the contrary, I worked harder than any of them, though it was not I, but the grace of God that is with me.

Here Paul says that the grace extended to him was not in vain, meaning empty. What indicated that the grace was not in vain? His labor in response to that grace. He worked harder than the other apostles *because* of this grace. And so, we might think of the work we do as being under the umbrella of God's grace.

Rich in Good Works

As we have seen, all Christians are called to serve, and serving God does not negate or contradict the grace of God. The Bible sometimes refers to Christian service and witness as doing "good works." Because there may be some misunderstanding about this subject, in this section we will briefly consider what the Scriptures say regarding good works.

Titus 3:4-8

4But when the goodness and loving kindness of God our Savior appeared,
5he saved us, not because of works done by us in righteousness, but according to his own mercy, by the washing of regeneration and renewal of the Holy Spirit,
6whom he poured out on us richly through Jesus Christ our Savior,
7so that being justified by his **grace** we might become heirs according to the hope of eternal life.

[8]The saying is trustworthy, and I want you to insist on these things, so that those who have believed in God may be careful to **devote themselves to good works**. These things are excellent and profitable for people.

Because of God's goodness and loving-kindness, because He saved us according to His own mercy, because He made available the gift of holy spirit, because we are justified by His grace, and because we are heirs according to the hope of eternal life—we believers are to devote ourselves to good works.

The following verses shed interesting light on good works.

2 Timothy 3:16-17

[16]All Scripture is breathed out by God and profitable for teaching, for reproof, for correction, and for training in righteousness,
[17]that the man of God may be complete, equipped for every **good work**.

The Scriptures equip the man of God for every good work. In this context, a good work includes teaching, reproving, correcting, and training in righteousness.

Note what the following verses declare about Christian women and good works:

1 Timothy 2:9-10

[9]likewise also that women should adorn themselves in respectable apparel, with modesty and self-control, not with braided hair and gold or pearls or costly attire,
[10]but with what is proper for women who profess godliness—with **good works**.

1 Timothy 5:9-10

[9]Let a widow be enrolled if she is not less than sixty years of age, having been the wife of one husband,

[10]and having a reputation for **good works**: if she has brought up children, has shown hospitality, has washed the feet of the saints, has cared for the afflicted, and has devoted herself to every **good work**.

Women in the Church should "adorn themselves" with good works. In other words, their good works should be apparent. Further, widows in the Church are to have a reputation for good works. Some good works include raising children, being hospitable, serving the saints, and caring for the afflicted.

The Scriptures also have specific directives regarding those in the Church who are wealthy.

1 Timothy 6:17-18

[17]As for the rich in this present age, charge them not to be haughty, nor to set their hopes on the uncertainty of riches, but on God, who richly provides us with everything to enjoy.
[18]They are to do good, to be rich in **good works**, to be generous and ready to share,

Using a play on words, the Scriptures instruct rich believers to be rich in good works, which includes sharing their material abundance.

In the pastoral epistle of Titus, we read the following about good works.

Titus 2:7

Show yourself in all respects to be a model of **good works**, and in your teaching show integrity, dignity,

As a minister, Titus was not only to comport himself with dignity and teach with integrity but also to be a model of good works.

As we have already seen, all Christians are to devote themselves to good works (Titus 3:8). To devote oneself would require some concerted effort. We read something similar in the following verse:

Titus 3:1

Remind them to be submissive to rulers and authorities, to be obedient, to be ready for every **good work**,

All Christians are to be ready or prepared for every good work. Finally, we are to encourage one another to do these good works.

Hebrews 10:24

And let us consider how to stir up one another to love and **good works,**

In the Greek New Testament, the phrase translated as "stir up" means to stimulate or provoke.[63] Not only should the individual believer be devoted to good works, but they are also to stimulate other saints to love and good works. We can encourage one another to pursue good works because we know they benefit God's people, and they will be rewarded!

- Women in the Church are to adorn themselves with good works.
- Widows in the Church are to have a reputation for good works
- The wealthy in the Church are to be rich in good works.
- Ministers are to be a model of good works.
- All the saints are to be ready for every good work, devote themselves to good works, and stir up one another to love and good works.

In an attempt to avoid the error of promoting salvation by works, some gloss over clear verses that tell us to do good works. The Scriptures are clear: the believer is to *devote* himself to them.

---

63   Strong, *The New Strong's Expanded*, s.v. *"paroxusmos."*

The Basis of Good Works

When we think of good works in society, we may think of benevolent foundations, charities, or other organizations that seek to help the poor, the sick, or the disenfranchised. And without a doubt, these enterprises are commendable for the services they render. But let's learn what the Scriptures say about the basis of good works rather than rely on opinion or religious tradition.

> **John 5:36**
> But the testimony that I have is greater than that of John. For the **works** that the Father has given me to accomplish, the very **works** that I am doing, bear witness about me that the Father has sent me.

It's important to note that the works Jesus Christ accomplished were given to him by God. In other words, Jesus didn't make up his own plans. God directed these works and these works confirmed that God had sent him.

Next, we read about Jesus Christ's commitment to complete the work His Father gave him to do.

> **John 4:34**
> "My food is to do the will of him who sent me and to accomplish his **work**."

We all need food to live. Here, using a figure of speech, Jesus Christ says that doing God's will and accomplishing His work was his "food." It was what he lived on, so to speak. This highlights Jesus's commitment to God's will.

From the following verse, we learn how Jesus Christ was enabled to do these good works.

Acts 10:38
how God anointed Jesus of Nazareth with the Holy
Spirit and with power. He went about **doing good** and
healing all who were oppressed by the devil, for God
was with him.

Jesus was enabled to do the good works because of the powerful holy
spirit. Examples of good works Jesus did include teaching and preaching
the Kingdom of God and healing all who were oppressed by the devil.

In the following passage, let's note who is glorified as a result of a
God-directed good work.

Acts 4:9-10, 21
⁹if we are being examined today concerning a **good**
deed done to a crippled man, by what means this man
has been healed,
¹⁰let it be known to all of you and to all the people of
Israel that by the name of Jesus Christ of Nazareth,
whom you crucified, whom God raised from the dead—
by him this man is standing before you well.

Verse 21
And when they had further threatened them, they
let them go, finding no way to punish them, because
of the people, for all were praising God for what had
happened.

In verse 9, Peter and John's healing of a lame man is called a "good deed."
The outcome was that all praised God for this miraculous deliverance.

As we have seen in this section, biblical good works are those that
God directs a person to do, whether by the written revelation of the
Scriptures or by direct revelation from God. A believer is enabled
to do good works by the holy spirit born within. These good works
glorify God.

Conclusion

All Christians are saved by grace through faith, not according to works. And yet all Christians are called to serve. Each Christian will be rewarded for their work, service, and labor. Recall what Paul said about grace and work:

> **1 Corinthians 15:10**
> But by the grace of God I am what I am, and his **grace** toward me was **not in vain**. On the contrary, I worked harder than any of them, though it was not I, but the grace of God that is with me.

God had extended tremendous grace to Paul, and Paul's response was to work harder than any of the other apostles. This is referred to as not receiving the grace of God in vain. In other words, because of God's grace demonstrated to him as one who had previously persecuted the Church, Paul worked harder than others. We could say that Paul didn't do these works to be saved but because he was so incredibly thankful that he was saved.

Like Paul, we are to abound in the work of the Lord.

> **1 Corinthians 15:58**
> Therefore, my beloved brothers, be steadfast, immovable, always abounding in the work of the Lord, knowing that in the Lord your labor is not in vain.

Paul didn't write, "I know that you're saved by grace. So why not just take a long vacation until you hear the trumpet?" Instead, Paul admonished the brethren to always abound in the work of the Lord. Why? Because such labor would not be in vain, meaning empty. Work in the lord is profitable in this life and in the life to come.

Assuredly, we must now recognize that to "abound in the work of the Lord" does not mean we are trying to add to our redemption or salvation. By now, we know that this labor in the Lord refers to work, service, and labor directed by God to serve Him and benefit the Church. In this we are to abound.

The following is a chart of some examples of good works mentioned in the Gospels and New Covenant Writings.

Reference	Examples of Good Works
Matthew 26:10, Mark 14:6	Showing honor and respect to the lord Jesus Christ
John 3:21	Works carried out in God
John 6:28, 29	Works of God - believe in him whom He has sent
John 14:12	The works that Christ did and greater
Acts 9:36, 39	Tabitha was full of good works and acts of charity. These included making coats and garments to bless the saints.
Acts 13:2	Preaching the gospel
1 Corinthians 9:1	Saints won to Christ called "my workmanship in the Lord"
1 Corinthians 15:58, 16:10	Work of the Lord
Ephesians 4:12	Equipping the saints for the work of ministry, for building up the body of Christ
Philippians 2:30	The work of Christ
Colossians 1:10	Walk worthily bearing fruit in "every good work"
1 Thessalonians 1:3 2 Thessalonians 1:11 Hebrews 6:10	Work of believing, labor of love
1 Timothy 3:1	He that desires the office of a bishop (overseer) desires a "good work"

Reference	Examples of Good Works
1 Timothy 5:10	Brought up children, shown hospitality, washed the feet of the saints, cared for the afflicted, devoted to every good work
1 Timothy 6:18	Generous, sharing
2 Timothy 4:5	The work of an evangelist
Titus 3:1	Be ready for every good work
Hebrews 13:21	Doing God's will
1 Peter 2:12	Honorable conduct

Christians are to devote themselves to good works. And we know, a born again one will be rewarded for his work and labor as described in 1 Corinthians 3:13-15. The reward does not repudiate or deny the grace of God. If God, in addition to blessing His sons with all spiritual blessings in the heavenly places in Christ, chooses to further bless His sons by rewarding them in the future, that is His prerogative. God could have demanded service, but instead, He decided to reward His sons for their free will service. And so, we are led to conclude that rather than repudiate grace, the promise of future reward *magnifies* God's grace and His generous beneficence to His children.

Chapter 6

The Crown

Today, professional sports are a multi-billion-dollar industry. As a result, sports dominate the media, whether football, soccer, baseball, tennis, or basketball. Top athletes are glorified as cultural heroes, and major cities pride themselves on their professional sports teams. Because sports permeate our culture, it follows that our language and idioms are filled with sports jargon and sayings. How many of these sports idioms have you heard?

- Hit it out of the park.
- The ball is in your court.
- You call the shots.
- She's the front-runner.
- We are in the homestretch.

All these sayings come from the field of sports. Here's a chart that shows the origin and meaning of each idiom:

Idiom	Sport	Idiomatic Meaning
Hit it out of the park	baseball	tremendous success
The ball is in your court	tennis	your responsibility now
Call the shots	billiards	make the decisions
Front-runner	track	one who is expected to win
Homestretch	horse racing	near the end

Similarly, sports were a significant part of Greek and Roman culture, especially the public Games. Historians tell us that for the Greeks, the Games were an all-consuming passion, not just an amusement. One historian writes, "In every city throughout Asia Minor, and more especially at Ephesus, the stadium, and the training for the stadium, were among the chief subjects of interest to the whole population. These busy amusements were well known even in Palestine and at Jerusalem itself."[64] In other words, the athletic competitions during the public Games were integral to the culture, especially for city dwellers. And so, when we read about the prize and crown in 1 Corinthians 9:24-25, it helps to realize that these are athletic terms drawn from the world of ancient sport.

1 Corinthians 9:24-25

[24]Do you not know that in a race all the runners run, but only one receives the **prize**? So run that you may obtain it.
[25]Every athlete exercises self-control in all things. They do it to receive a perishable **wreath** (*stephanos*), but we an imperishable.

While the ESV renders the word *stephanos* as "wreath," most English Bibles translate it as "crown."

1 Corinthians 9:24-25(NIV)

[24]Do you not know that in a race all the runners run, but only one gets the **prize**? Run in such a way as to get the **prize**.
[25]Everyone who competes in the games goes into strict training. They do it to get a **crown** (*stephanos*) that will not last, but we do it to get a **crown** that will last forever.

The words "prize" and "crown" come directly from the public Games. Because the Games were part of life, readers of that time would likely have understood that the prize and crown were athletic terms. Today, we may attach different meanings to the words "prize" and "crown," so it's essential to understand these terms taking into account the culture in which they were written. Indeed, athletic imagery occurs frequently in

---

64   Coneybeare and Howson, *The Life and Epistles*, 539.

the Pauline Epistles: running a race, boxing, wrestling, contending in the contest, playing according to the rules, training, contending for the prize, and so forth. Moreover, the culture of Paul's time, particularly in places like Ephesus and Corinth, was steeped in athletic ritual and pageantry, so athletic allusions would have been well known to first-century readers.

The Public Games

The Greek public Games were held regularly: the Olympian and Pythian Games took place every four years, while the Nemean and Isthmian every two years. The Olympian Games took place in Athens, the Pythian Games were at Delphi, and the Isthmian Games were held outside Corinth. Thousands of visitors—athletes, delegates, merchants, spectators—gathered in the host city to attend the Games.[65] During the Games, the winner of an event would be given a crown to wear, which was an outward symbol of the highest victory and achievement. One historian writes, "The greatest achievement for an athlete in the ancient world was to win the Olympic crown. The material prizes offered at other athletic festivals were insignificant compared to the fame and glory earned by the Olympic victor."[66]

The crown itself was made from leaves. At the Olympic Games, the crown was woven from olive leaves; at the Pythian Games, the crown was made from laurel; the Nemean, from wild celery.[67] Because the crown (wreath) was made from leaves, it had no monetary value. But a victorious athlete would also receive prizes such as sums of money, free food and tax exemption for life, gold and other valuables, a pension, a statue made in his likeness, and so forth.[68] Crowned athletes enjoyed elevated social status and would be treated like celebrities. Although the crown had no monetary value, it symbolized the highest honor and achievement.

---

[65] Broneer, "The Apostle Paul and the Isthmian Games," 4-5.
[66] Swaddling, *The Ancient Olympic Games,* 90.
[67] Broneer, "The Apostle Paul and the Isthmian Games," 16.
[68] Broneer, "The Apostle Paul and the Isthmian Games," 16.

Isthmian Games

Because it will shed light on the prize and crown, it is helpful to learn about the Isthmian Games held outside Corinth. The Isthmian Games took place from 582 BC to about 53 AD, so historians consider it "highly probable" that Paul was in Corinth during one of the Isthmian festivals, likely the one held in 51 AD.[69] Moreover, because Paul was a tentmaker and there were so many out-of-town visitors to accommodate, a tent maker like Paul would have been in demand whenever the public Games were held.[70]

The Isthmian Games took place every two years at the end of spring and were generally organized into three parts: horse racing, athletics, and, later, musical contests. Special buildings were erected to host the event, including stadiums, a theatre, and a hippodrome for chariot and horse racing. The facilities were situated near a temple dedicated to the Greek god Poseidon. Next to or below the temple was another small building where the athletes went to take the mandatory oath. The oath, which was rigorously enforced, stated that competitors vowed to play the Games according to the rules.[71] Breaking this oath would result in disqualification, so the rules for contending in the Games were strict. For instance, if a boxer accidentally made contact with his opponent during warm-up and inflicted bodily injury, that boxer would be disqualified from the event.[72]

As one can imagine, training for the Games required singular commitment and discipline. A competitor might train for a year or more, avoiding excess of any kind for the entire training period. Consider this

---

[69]   Coneybeare and Howson, *The Life and Epistles*, 540.

[70]   Broneer, "The Apostle Paul and the Isthmian Games," 16.

[71]   It should be noted that paganism was an integral part of the athletic Games. In addition to the buildings which housed the athletic events, temples to pagan gods were also erected on the site. Outside of these temples, animal sacrifices took place, and cult priests officiated over the oaths and other particulars. Modern excavations of one site revealed hundreds of small lamps, which were evidently carried by worshippers at night as they participated in nightly mystery rites. Broneer, "The Apostle Paul and the Isthmian Games," 11-16.

[72]   Broneer, "The Apostle Paul and the Isthmian Games," 24-25.

passage from the Greek philosopher Epictetus (55 AD-135 AD), who had firsthand knowledge of the training process:

> Would you be a victor in the Olympic games? So in good truth would I, for it is a glorious thing; but pray consider what must go before, and what may follow, and so proceed to the attempt. You must then live by rule, eat what will be disagreeable, refrain from delicacies; you must oblige yourself to constant exercises at the appointed hour, in heat and cold; you must abstain from wine and cold liquors; in a word, you must be as submissive to all the directions of your master as to those of a physician.[73]

Epictetus is saying that athletes in ancient times, like their modern-day counterparts, demonstrated all-out commitment to training to compete and win in the Games. With this background in mind, we now turn to the subject of the prize.

The Prize

As we have stated, "prize" and "crown" in the Pauline Epistles are athletic terms. There are only two occurrences of the word "prize," (*brabeion*) meaning "the award to the victor in the games, a prize."[74]

1 Corinthians 9:24
Do you not know that in a race all the runners run, but only one receives the **prize** (*brabeion*)? So run that you may obtain it.

Philippians 3:14
I press on toward the goal for the **prize** (*brabeion*) of the upward call of God in Christ Jesus.

---

[73] Qtd. in Freeman, *Manners and Customs*, 457.
[74] Thayer, *A Greek-English Lexicon*, s.v. "*brabeion*."

In both verses, the prize is something a runner seeks to obtain, something one presses on towards as a goal.

Let's read the context of the first occurrence of prize. First Corinthians 9:1-14 addresses the right of those who preach the Gospel to live off the Gospel, meaning that they have the right to live from the donations and financial giving of the Church. We pick up the record in verse 15.

1 Corinthians 9:15-23

[15]But I have made no use of any of these rights, nor am I writing these things to secure any such provision. For I would rather die than have anyone deprive me of my ground for boasting.

[16]For if I preach the gospel, that gives me no ground for boasting. For necessity is laid upon me. Woe to me if I do not preach the gospel!

[17]For if I do this of my own will, I have a reward, but if not of my own will, I am still entrusted with a stewardship.

[18]What then is my reward? That in my preaching I may present the gospel free of charge, so as not to make full use of my right in the gospel.

[19]For though I am free from all, I have made myself a servant to all, that I might win more of them.

[20]To the Jews I became as a Jew, in order to win Jews. To those under the law I became as one under the law (though not being myself under the law) that I might win those under the law.

[21]To those outside the law I became as one outside the law (not being outside the law of God but under the law of Christ) that I might win those outside the law.

[22]To the weak I became weak, that I might win the weak. I have become all things to all people, that by all means I might save some.

²³I do it all for the sake of the gospel, that I may share with them in its blessings.

According to some translators, all of verse 18 should be a question.[75]

1 Corinthians 9:18 (WT)

Then what is my compensation so that when I proclaim the gospel, I may make the gospel without expense so as not to make full use of my authority in the gospel?

Paul is asking, "If I'm not charging anyone for preaching the gospel, and I'm not exercising my God-given right to live off of the Church's gifts and offerings, then how will I be compensated?" The answer occurs in verses 24 and 25.

1 Corinthians 9:24-25

²⁴Do you not know that in a race all the runners run, but only one receives the **prize** (*brabeion*)? So run that you may obtain it.
²⁵Every athlete exercises self-control in all things. They do it to receive a perishable wreath, but we an imperishable.

The answer to how Paul would be compensated is the prize. Paul then encouraged the Corinthians to run so that they, too, may obtain the prize.

The prize in verse 24 is the wreath (crown) in verse 25. Paul wrote to the Corinthians that athletes exercise self-control in all things to receive a perishable wreath. He then urged his readers to exercise self-control in all things so they might obtain an imperishable wreath, meaning an eternal reward. Unlike the wreath made of leaves placed on the victor's head at the Games, this wreath is imperishable. In the Panhellenic Games, when athletes competed in a race, only one received the prize,

---

75 Ellicott asserts that this entire verse should be a question. Ellicott, *A New Testament Commentary*, n.p.

though many competed. However, all believers are encouraged to run the race to obtain the prize.

The passage continues:

1 Corinthians 9:26-27

[26]So I do not run aimlessly; I do not box as one beating the air.

[27]But I discipline my body and keep it under control, lest after preaching to others I myself should be disqualified.

Note the athletic imagery: running, boxing, disciplining the body, being disqualified. These athletic terms would have been very familiar to the Corinthians, who hosted the public Games every two years. What's more, the figurative language draws attention to how Christians are to conduct their lives to receive the prize. They are to run so that they *may* obtain it. In other words, although available to all Christians, receiving the prize is dependent upon how one runs the race. First, they are to exercise self-control in all things the way an athlete does. Second, they are to run with certainty, unlike someone with no aim or who shadow boxes. Third, they must contend according to the rules, lest they be disqualified. We will come back to these verses (1 Cor. 9:24-27) later, but for now, let's keep in mind that the prize of verse 24 refers to the wreath in verse 25.

---

prize = crown (wreath)

The biblical researcher and author Charles H. Welch explains that in 1 Corinthians 9:26-27, the prize is the genus while the crown is the species.[76] Put another way, the prize is the *general* term, while the crown is the *specific* term. In our own culture, we use the word "prize" similarly.

Emblazoned on the front of a children's cereal box or Cracker Jack box are the words "Prize Inside!" In past generations, the prize would

---

[76]   Welch, *An Alphabetical Analysis Part 1,* 205.

be a tiny car, a puzzle, a plastic ring, and so forth. Today, the prize might be a card with a hyperlink to a game app. The prize is a *general* term, while the toy is specific, whether it's a card, a puzzle, or a ring. They refer to the same thing. Or consider the top prize in sports. Each sports team strives for the top prize in their field: the Stanley Cup in the National Hockey League, the Vince Lombardi Trophy in the National Football League, and the FIFA World Cup in Football (soccer). Ask any American ice hockey team if they are striving to win the ultimate prize, and they will say, "Yes, we want to bring home the Stanley Cup." The prize is the general term, while Stanley Cup is specific.

In sum, having studied the first occurrence of "prize" (*brabeion*) in its context, we learned that the prize is the crown, the prize is general while the crown is specific, and receiving the prize (crown) is dependent upon how one runs the race.

The prize is the *general* term, while the crown is the *specific* term.

Now let's consider the second occurrence of prize (*brabeion*) in its context.

Philippians 3:8-16
[8]Indeed, I count everything as loss because of the surpassing worth of knowing Christ Jesus my Lord. For his sake I have suffered the loss of all things and count them as rubbish, in order that I may gain Christ [9]and be found in him, not having a righteousness of my own that comes from the law, but that which comes through faith in Christ, the righteousness from God that depends on faith—
[10]that I may know him and the power of his resurrection, and may share his sufferings, becoming like him in his death,
[11]that by any means possible I may attain the resurrection from the dead.

[12]Not that I have already obtained this or am already perfect, but I press on to make it my own, because Christ Jesus has made me his own.

[13]Brothers, I do not consider that I have made it my own. But one thing I do: forgetting what lies behind and straining forward to what lies ahead,

[14]I press on toward the goal for the **prize** (*brabeion*) of the upward call of God in Christ Jesus.

[15]Let those of us who are mature think this way, and if in anything you think otherwise, God will reveal that also to you.

[16]Only let us hold true to what we have attained.

Paul said that he had not yet finished the race (v. 12). So, it stands to reason that he had not yet received the prize (v. 13). In fact, Paul was still pressing on towards the prize (v. 14). One cannot receive the prize until one finishes the race.

Further, in verse 14, "press on" is an athletic term meaning "to run swiftly in order to catch some person or thing, to run after."[77] It connotes intense effort. In a race, a runner pursues other runners so that he may overtake them and finish first. He would not look back over his shoulder and lose precious time. Verses 13 and 14 allude to a runner in a foot race pursuing the prize. (Of course, Christians are not in competition with one another for the prize, but they are to exhibit some of the drive and determination of a runner intent on winning a race.)

The word "goal" in verse 14 is also an athletic term meaning "the distant mark looked at, the goal or end one has in view."[78] It refers to a post that marks the end of the race. In the public Games, the end of a foot race was generally marked with a post, not a finish line like in modern sports. Imagine a long-distance runner nearing the end of his grueling race. He enters the stadium, where the crowd rises to its feet. He can see the end post up in the distance. Keeping that end post

---

77   Thayer, *A Greek-English Lexicon*, s.v. "*diokō*."

78   Thayer, *A Greek-English Lexicon*, s.v. "*skopos*."

in sight, he kicks up his heels with even more intensity as he pushes himself to final victory. He presses on towards the goalpost with the prize in mind.

In verse 14, the "prize of the upward call" is the prize associated with the upward call of God in Christ Jesus.[79] Just as a runner had his eyes set on the end post so he could win the prize, so did Paul have his sights set on the heavenly prize. Paul encouraged all mature believers to think the same way—to keep their eyes fixed on the end prize.[80] What a vivid, emotionally charged image, and how it would have communicated to first-century saints.

While we have looked at both occurrences of *brabeion*, it may prove helpful to look at a form of this word, *katabrabeuō*, which only occurs once.

Colossians 2:18

Let no one **disqualify** (*katabrabeuō*) you, insisting on asceticism and worship of angels, going on in detail about visions, puffed up without reason by his sensuous mind,

The word *katabrabeuō* means "to decide as umpire against one, to declare him unworthy of the prize; to defraud of the prize of victory."[81] In classical Greek, the word usually meant to deprive someone of something he would have otherwise possessed.[82] It, too, is an athletic term. Note how other English Bibles render this phrase:

Colossians 2:18 (NASB95)

Let no one keep defrauding you of your prize...

Colossians 2:18 (KJV)

Let no man beguile you of your reward...

---

[79]   This is the genitive of relation.

[80]   Note also the directional words of verse 14: "press on," "towards," "goal," "prize," "upward." These all point the reader's attention upward, towards the prize.

[81]   Thayer, *A Greek-English Lexicon*, s.v. "*katabrabeuō*."

[82]   Allen, *Letters from Prison*, 152.

Colossians 2:18 (NKJV)

Let no one cheat you out of your reward...

Colossians 2:18 (WT)

Let no one rob you of your prize...

This verse says that one could be robbed of the prize if they turned aside unto worshipping of angels and other such practices. No Christian would lose his eternal life or inheritance, but he could be robbed of the prize. As we recall, obtaining the prize is conditional, based on how one runs the race (1 Cor. 9:24). Therefore, it is possible to be robbed of the prize, meaning to be cheated out of it. In the next section, we will explore in more detail what this means, but for now, let's note that the prize *can be forfeited*.[83] How significant that Paul writes to the faithful in Christ (Col. 1:2) not to be defrauded out of the prize.

In this section, we have learned the following about the prize:

- The answer to Paul's question, "What will my compensation be," is the prize.
- The prize in 1 Corinthians 9:24 is the crown in 1 Corinthians 9:25.
- One may be robbed of the prize.
- In Philippians 3:14, Paul pressed on towards the goal of the prize. He had not yet obtained the prize.
- Paul encouraged all who were mature to think the same way.

Unlike military terminology, which often draws attention to the gravity of spiritual warfare, athletic terminology draws attention to other aspects of the Christian life, such as the need for endurance, the need to play according to the rules, the need to exercise self-control in all things, the need to keep one's eyes on the goal, and so forth. As one writer puts it, Paul uses this athletic language "when he wishes to enforce the zeal and the patience with which a Christian ought to strain after his heavenly

---

[83] See also 2 Tim. 2:5: An athlete is not crowned unless he competes according to the rules.

reward."[84] Such language would have resonated with those in the first century who lived in a culture steeped in athletic ritual.

The CROWN

Having studied the two occurrences of the prize in the New Testament, we now turn our attention to what the Scriptures say about the crown.

Before we delve into a study of the crown in the New Testament, we will take a brief look at some Old Testament passages that speak of crowns.

> **2 Samuel 12:30**
> And he took the **crown** of their king from his head. The weight of it was a talent of gold, and in it was a precious stone, and it was placed on David's head. And he brought out the spoil of the city, a very great amount.

> **2 Kings 11:12**
> Then he brought out the king's son and put the **crown** on him and gave him the testimony. And they proclaimed him king and anointed him, and they clapped their hands and said, "Long live the king!"

> **Esther 1:11**
> to bring Queen Vashti before the king with her royal **crown**, in order to show the peoples and the princes her beauty, for she was lovely to look at.

> **Zechariah 6:11**
> Take from them silver and gold, and make a **crown**, and set it on the head of Joshua, the son of Jehozadak, the high priest.

---

[84]   Coneybeare and Howson, *The Life and Epistles*, 538.

Leviticus 8:9
And he set the turban on his head, and on the turban, in front, he set the golden plate, the holy **crown**, as the LORD commanded Moses.

From these verses, we see that royalty wore crowns to signify the monarchy, and priests wore crowns to signify consecration. The crown was an outward symbol of a position of authority or consecration.

A crown might also be part of the bride's wedding ensemble. Historians tell us that a bride in biblical times might dress up to resemble a queen. She would be adorned with family jewels and wear a decorative crown on her head as a symbol of joy. The following passage from Ezekiel describes a bride's wedding gifts. (In this record, God, by Ezekiel, addresses Jerusalem figuratively as a bride.)

Ezekiel 16:9-14
⁹Then I bathed you with water and washed off your blood from you and anointed you with oil.
¹⁰I clothed you also with embroidered cloth and shod you with fine leather. I wrapped you in fine linen and covered you with silk.
¹¹And I adorned you with ornaments and put bracelets on your wrists and a chain on your neck.
¹²And I put a ring on your nose and earrings in your ears and a beautiful **crown** on your head.
¹³Thus you were adorned with gold and silver, and your clothing was of fine linen and silk and embroidered cloth. You ate fine flour and honey and oil. You grew exceedingly beautiful and advanced to royalty.
¹⁴And your renown went forth among the nations because of your beauty, for it was perfect through the splendor that I had bestowed on you, declares the Lord GOD.

Note how the marriage gifts included a crown (v. 12) in addition to ornaments, jewelry, and fine clothing. Indeed, this is a picture of love and joy.

So, when we consider the culture of the Old Testament, we see that the crown was something that royalty, a high priest, or a bride might wear. It might signify rulership, authority, consecration, joy, honor, and glory. With that brief background, we now turn our attention to the crown spoken of in the New Testament.

In the Greek New Testament, the word translated as "crown" is *stephanos*. It occurs four times in the Gospels, referring exclusively to the crown of thorns Roman soldiers put on Jesus Christ's head before his crucifixion. In these occurrences, *stephanos* is a literal wreath made of thorns placed on Jesus Christ's head in mockery of his being referred to as "the king of the Jews."

Matthew 27:29
and twisting together a **crown** (*stephanos*) of thorns, they put it on his head and put a reed in his right hand. And kneeling before him, they mocked him, saying, "Hail, King of the Jews!"

Mark 15:17
And they clothed him in a purple cloak, and twisting together a **crown** (*stephanos*) of thorns, they put it on him.

John 19:2, 5
And the soldiers twisted together a **crown** (*stephanos*) of thorns and put it on his head and arrayed him in a purple robe.

Verse 5
So Jesus came out, wearing the **crown** (*stephanos*) of thorns and the purple robe. Pilate said to them, "Behold the man!"

Excluding the book of Revelation, *stephanos* occurs six more times in the Greek New Testament.[85]

1 Corinthians 9:25
Every athlete exercises self-control in all things. They do it to receive a perishable **wreath** (*stephanos*), but we an imperishable.

Philippians 4:1
Therefore, my brothers, whom I love and long for, my joy and **crown** (*stephanos*), stand firm thus in the Lord, my beloved.

1 Thessalonians 2:19
For what is our hope or joy or **crown** (*stephanos*) of boasting before our Lord Jesus at his coming? Is it not you?

2 Timothy 4:8
Henceforth there is laid up for me the **crown** (*stephanos*) of righteousness, which the Lord, the righteous judge, will award to me on that day, and not only to me but also to all who have loved his appearing.

James 1:12
Blessed is the man who remains steadfast under trial, for when he has stood the test he will receive the **crown** (*stephanos*) of life, which God has promised to those who love him.

---

[85] Because the occurrences of *stephanos* in the book of Revelation do not refer to the crown available to those of the Church of the One Body of Christ, a discussion of the meaning of "crown(s)" in the book of Revelation is outside the scope of this book. For interested readers, *stephanos* in the book of Revelation occurs in 2:10, 3:11, 4:4, 4:10, 6:2, 9:7, 12:1, 14:14.

1 Peter 5:4
And when the chief Shepherd appears, you will receive
the unfading **crown** (*stephanos*) of glory.

To understand the Christian's crown, we will study each occurrence of
stephanos in detail.

Crown as Metaphor: Two Local Churches

In his letter to the Philippians, note how Paul addressed his readers:

Philippians 4:1
Therefore, my brothers, whom I love and long for, my
joy and **crown** (*stephanos*), stand firm thus in the Lord,
my beloved.

Here, *stephanos* is a metaphor where Paul compares the Philippians to
a crown.[86] A metaphor is a figure of comparison where one thing is
said to be another thing. A metaphor may be understood in light of a
simple equation:

$$noun = noun$$

In its most basic usage, a metaphor states one thing as being another
thing.[87] When we say, "that linebacker is a beast," we use a metaphor.
We don't mean that the linebacker is a green-skinned creature with
horns but that he is fierce and strong like a beast. Other examples of

---

[86] There is some debate as to whether this figure is metaphor or *hypocatastasis*.
Modern scholars refer to an implied comparison as metaphor whereas older sources
consider *hypocatastasis* to be an implied comparison. According to the Oxford English
Dictionary, *hypocatastasis* is an obsolete word, and its meaning and use is virtually
lost to contemporary rhetoricians. For this reason, we choose to refer to an implied
comparison as a metaphor.

[87] The authors are aware that metaphor can include other parts of speech such as
verbs, but for our purposes, this simple equation of "noun=noun" helps to illustrate
this particular use of metaphor.

metaphor include saying someone is a "peach" if they are sweet-tempered or a "pill" if they have a sour disposition. Metaphors are common in most languages, and the reader usually understands the comparison immediately. Based on these examples, here's the simple equation:

Beast = linebacker
Peach = nice person
Pill = bitter person

In Philippians 4:1, when Paul addresses the Philippian saints as his "crown," he uses a metaphor to convey the joy and elation of a victorious athlete. It is a vivid way of communicating Paul's love for and joy in the Philippians. (Not coincidentally, joy and rejoicing are dominant themes in Paul's epistle to the Philippians.)

Philippians = crown

Paul uses metaphor in the same manner in the following verse:

1 Corinthians 9:2
If to others I am not an apostle, at least I am to you, for you are the **seal** of my apostleship in the Lord.

Here Paul compares the Corinthians with a seal. He doesn't say they are *like* a seal; he uses metaphor and states that they *are* a seal. Does he mean that they are made from hot wax like seals? Of course not; this is metaphoric language. A seal is used, amongst other things, to authenticate a document or a mandate. This means the Corinthians were proof or authentication of Paul's apostleship in the lord. This is a metaphor used to describe the Corinthians. And our simple equation would read:

Corinthians = seal

In a subsequent epistle, Paul again refers metaphorically to the Corinthians.

2 Corinthians 3:2
You yourselves are our **letter** of recommendation,
written on our hearts, to be known and read by all.

Paul could have written, "You are like our letter of recommendation,"
but again, he uses a metaphor stating that the Corinthians were his
letter of recommendation. Does he mean they were a roll of parchment
with writing on it? Of course not. He refers to them metaphorically as
his "letter of recommendation" because the Corinthians were proof of
Paul's genuine ministry. And here's that equation again:

Corinthians = letter

So, when Paul wrote of the Philippians as his "joy and crown," he
was using a metaphor, meaning that they were an achievement of his
ministry, so to speak. They brought Paul joy and a sense of victory. To
refer to someone as a "joy and crown" is similar to our expression "pride
and joy" or "crowning achievement." Moreover, note that Paul spoke
of the Philippians as his crown in the present. He did not refer to this
crown as something to be received in the future, nor did he say that he
would receive a crown for or because of the Philippians.

Paul uses "crown" in the same way in the following verse:

1 Thessalonians 2:19
For what is our hope or joy or **crown** of boasting before
our Lord Jesus at his coming? Is it not you?

Here Paul refers to the Thessalonians as his "crown of boasting." In this
verse, a crown is a metaphor used to describe the Thessalonian church.
Once more, the equation:

Thessalonians = crown

Paul called the Thessalonians his "crown of boasting," but he did not
say he would receive a crown for them in the future. In this verse, the
crown is not referring to a specific reward that Paul would receive in

the future for having brought about the salvation of the Thessalonian church. Rather, it is a figurative way of saying that at Christ's return, one of Paul's reasons for boasting would be the Thessalonians. When Paul said they are his "crown of boasting," it is a figurative, emphatic way of conveying his joy in and love for them and his pride in their faithfulness. Note how other versions render verse 19:

> **1 Thessalonians 2:19** (ISV)
> "After all, who is our hope, joy, or reason for rejoicing in the presence of our Lord Jesus at his coming? It is you, isn't it?"

> **1 Thessalonians 2:19** (GNT)
> After all, it is you—you, no less than others!—who are our hope, our joy, and our reason for boasting of our victory in the presence of our Lord Jesus when he comes.

In sum, in Philippians 4:1 and 1 Thessalonians 2:19, the word "crown" is a metaphor used to describe a local church.

Crown as Metaphor: A Specific Reward

We now move on to consider passages where the crown is a specific type of reward. In these instances, the word "crown" is a metaphor to signify a specific reward, and not a local church.

Crown of Righteousness

> **2 Timothy 4:6-8**
> [6]For I am already being poured out as a drink offering, and the time of my departure has come.
> [7]I have fought the good fight, I have finished the race, I have kept the faith.

146

⁸Henceforth there is laid up for me the **crown of righteousness**, which the Lord, the righteous judge, will award (*apodidōmi*) to me on that day, and not only to me but also to all who have loved his appearing. [88]

At the time of this writing, Paul was near the end of his life and ministry. Because Paul had finished the race, he would receive the crown of righteousness, which Jesus Christ, the righteous judge, would give him.

Earlier in his life, Paul had said he had not yet attained the prize (crown). But at the end of his life, Paul had been shown that the crown now awaited him. In the ancient Games, the victor's crown was customarily given out on the last day of the Games. Paul's race had ended, and he would receive the crown of righteousness on that day, referring to the return of Christ. (The "righteous judge" and the word "Lord" in verse 8 both refer to Jesus Christ.) This crown is given to all who love his appearing. What does this mean?

We must first understand that the verb in 2 Timothy 4:8 is in the perfect tense and should be translated as "have loved" his appearing. It isn't a sudden love for Christ's appearance but love that someone has shown throughout his life. Second, if we read the context, we see that to love his appearing is explained by means of a contrast:

2 Timothy 4:1-10
¹I charge you in the presence of God and of Christ Jesus, who is to judge the living and the dead, and by his appearing and his kingdom:
²preach the word; be ready in season and out of season; reprove, rebuke, and exhort, with complete patience and teaching.

---

[88]   The word "award" is an unfortunate rendering for *apodidōmi*. According to Bullinger, this word means "to give in full, render, pay over *or* off, render." Bullinger, *A Critical Lexicon,* s.v. "reward." So, a better rendering of the phrase would be "will repay or give me on that day."

³For the time is coming when people will not endure sound teaching, but having itching ears they will accumulate for themselves teachers to suit their own passions,

⁴and will turn away from listening to the truth and wander off into myths.

⁵As for you, always be sober-minded, endure suffering, do the work of an evangelist, fulfill your ministry.

⁶For I am already being poured out as a drink offering, and the time of my departure has come.

⁷I have fought the good fight, I have finished the race, I have kept the faith.

⁸Henceforth there is laid up for me the crown of righteousness, which the Lord, the righteous judge, will award to me on that day, and not only to me but also to all who have **loved his appearing.**

⁹Do your best to come to me soon.

¹⁰For Demas, in **love with this present world** [age], has deserted me and gone to Thessalonica. Crescens has gone to Galatia, Titus to Dalmatia.[89]

To love his appearing is contrasted with loving this present world or present age. The Scriptures explain why Demas forsook Paul: because he loved this present age, which the Scriptures call an evil age (Gal. 1:4). Biblically, love is not an emotional response but a decision of the will. Thus, to love the appearing of Jesus Christ is to invest one's time and energy with a view to future realities like Paul did, not live for this present age alone.

For Paul, to love his appearing also meant contending in the good contest, finishing the race, keeping the believing: this would include faithfully executing and completing the call and office of his apostleship, which was given to him by Jesus Christ. It doesn't mean he lived a

---

[89] In the Greek New Testament, the word translated as "world" in verse 10 is *aiōn*, which means age or ages.

perfect, faultless life but that he was faithful to do all that God, in Christ, had called him to do. He did not quit. He contended according to the rules. Paul *finished* the race. That is to say, it isn't enough to start the race. One must finish in order to receive the crown.

In 2 Timothy 4, Paul encouraged Timothy to remain faithful to carry out his own ministry. And he reminded Timothy of Demas, who did not remain faithful to his ministry because he loved this present age instead. Sandwiched in between is Paul's own example of someone faithfully carrying out and completing his ministry.

All believers in Christ can love the lord's appearing throughout their lifetime by choosing to set their priorities on things above, not on things on the earth.[90] All are to run the race set before them and finish it. For ministers, that means faithfully executing the office and function of their ministry as Paul did.

Imperishable Crown

1 Corinthians 9:24-25
[24]Do you not know that in a race all the runners run, but only one receives the prize? So run that you may obtain it.
[25]Every athlete exercises self-control in all things. They do it to receive a perishable **wreath** [crown], but we an imperishable.

Earlier in this chapter, we saw that the prize in verse 24 is the imperishable wreath in verse 25. It refers to the crown given to a winning athlete at the public Games. This wreath was made from perishable material like pine, celery, or oak leaves. Many sculptures, urns, and coins from antiquity depict people wearing leafy wreaths on their heads. Because it was made from leaves, a crown would wilt and perish, as all cut vegetation does. That is what "perishable" means in verse 25—it will corrupt and perish.

---

[90] See Col. 3:1-4.

While athletes in the Games strive to obtain a perishable crown, sons of God are to seek to obtain an *imperishable* one. The end of verse 25 contains a figure of speech, ellipsis, where the word "crown" is omitted but readily supplied by the reader: "but we an imperishable [*crown*]." Omitting the word "crown" emphasizes its imperishability. In order to receive this imperishable crown, the believer is to exercise self-control in all things. Paul encouraged all Christians to run so they may obtain it.

The Crown of Life

James 1:1-12

¹James, a servant of God and of the Lord Jesus Christ,
To the twelve tribes in the Dispersion: Greetings.
²Count it all joy, my brothers, when you meet **trials** (*peirasmos*) of various kinds,
³for you know that the testing of your faith produces steadfastness.
⁴And let steadfastness have its full effect, that you may be perfect and complete, lacking in nothing.
⁵If any of you lacks wisdom, let him ask God, who gives generously to all without reproach, and it will be given him.
⁶But let him ask in faith, with no doubting, for the one who doubts is like a wave of the sea that is driven and tossed by the wind.
⁷For that person must not suppose that he will receive anything from the Lord;
⁸he is a double-minded man, unstable in all his ways.
⁹Let the lowly brother boast in his exaltation,
¹⁰and the rich in his humiliation, because like a flower of the grass he will pass away.

¹¹For the sun rises with its scorching heat and withers the grass; its flower falls, and its beauty perishes. So also will the rich man fade away in the midst of his pursuits. ¹²Blessed is the man who remains steadfast under **trial** (*peirasmos*), for when he has stood the test he will receive **the crown of life**, which God has promised to those who love him.

The crown of life is given to those who remain steadfast under trial. In the Greek New Testament, the word translated as "trial" in verse 12 is *peirasmos*, meaning "proof, test, trial... a putting to the proof as metals, etc., by fire." [91] Biblically speaking, a temptation to do evil does *not* originate from the One True God (James 1:13) but originates either from one's carnal old man nature (James 1:4-14) or from the devil and his hosts (Matt. 4:3, 1 Thess. 3:5). Tests, however, may originate from God to strengthen and to prove an individual, to prove their believing, or to test their obedience. God may test a person by giving him His Word to see if that person carries it out. For example, note what God said to Israel regarding the manna that He had provided for them in the wilderness:

> **Exodus 16:4**
> Then the LORD said to Moses, "Behold, I am about to rain bread from heaven for you, and the people shall go out and gather a day's portion every day, that I may **test** (*peirasmos*) them, whether they will walk in my law or not.[92]

God gave specific instructions to the Israelites regarding the gathering of the manna to *test their obedience to His Word.* He could have miraculously provided all the bread they would need for a lifetime, but God designed the manna to be collected according to His express commands. He did this so that He could test them to see whether they

---

91   Bullinger, *A Critical Lexicon and Concordance*, s.v. "trial."
92   In the LXX, the word "test" is a translation of the Greek word *peirasmos*.

would walk in His law or not. This was not a temptation to do evil but a test to see whether they would obey God's specific directions. That's not to say that all tests come from God. Life itself presents enough challenges and obstacles to test our believing. But the Scriptures are clear that God can test someone.[93] One way of doing this is by giving them His Word and seeing whether that person will obey or not.

Today, we may not clearly understand what the Bible means by a trial. Perhaps we think about a courtroom where someone is on trial for a crime, or we may think of how trying it is to work side-by-side with an obnoxious colleague. However, the biblical meaning of the word "trial" has the connotation of being tested or proven.[94]

James 1:3 further tells us that the "testing of your faith" produces steadfastness. It isn't one's intelligence or virtue being tested but one's faith or believing. Consider this example. Say you do not have enough money in the bank to cover the repairs on your car. Do you worry about this situation, or do you remember that God promises to meet all your needs according to His riches in glory in Christ Jesus (Phil. 4:19)? This type of stressful situation tests our believing: will we rely on God and believe His Word, or will we rely on something else?

In his first epistle, the apostle Peter also wrote about trials.

1 Peter 1:6-7
[6]In this you rejoice, though now for a little while, if necessary, you have been grieved by various **trials** (*peirasmos*),
[7]so that the tested genuineness of your faith—more precious than gold that perishes though it is tested by fire—may be found to result in praise and glory and honor at the revelation of Jesus Christ.

---

[93] See also Genesis 22.

[94] See also John 6:5-7 where Jesus Christ tested Philip to see how he would respond, and 2 Cor. 2:9 where Paul wrote to the Corinthians to test them if they were obedient in all things.

1 Peter 4:12-13

[12]Beloved, do not be surprised at the fiery **trial** (*peirasmos*) when it comes upon you to test you, as though something strange were happening to you.
[13]But rejoice insofar as you share Christ's sufferings, that you may also rejoice and be glad when his glory is revealed.

Once again, we see that trials test an individual's faith or believing. Peter admonished his readers to rejoice during such trials because this testing would refine their faith, resulting in praise, glory, and honor at the appearance of Jesus Christ. The saints were not to rejoice in the trial itself but to rejoice because of what it might produce: refined believing, which would result in future recognition at the return of Christ.

Further, in his explanation of the Parable of the Seed and Sower, Jesus Christ had something vital to say about the nature of trials.

Luke 8:11-15

[11]Now the parable is this: The seed is the word of God.
[12]The ones along the path are those who have heard; then the devil comes and takes away the word from their hearts, so that they may not believe and be saved.
[13]And the ones on the rock are those who, when they hear the word, receive it with joy. But these have no root; they believe for a while, and in time of **testing** (*peirasmos*) fall away.
[14]And as for what fell among the thorns, they are those who hear, but as they go on their way they are choked by the cares and riches and pleasures of life, and their fruit does not mature.
[15]As for that in the good soil, they are those who, hearing the word, hold it fast in an honest and good heart, and bear fruit with patience.

This parable reveals that some people who hear the Word of God and receive it with joy will believe for a while, but some will fall away when tested *because they are not rooted in the Word of God*. Note how it does not give a psychological or a socioeconomic reason for falling away. Instead, the reason for failing the test and falling away is that the individual is not rooted in God's Word. Note again what is being tested: the person's believing in God's Word.

So, to remain steadfast under trials means to withstand testing by continuing to believe God. Let's next move on to consider what the word "steadfast" in James 1:12 means. In the Greek New Testament, the word translated as "steadfast" is *hupomonē*, which means to endure, wait behind, remain, and persevere.[95] Note its use in the following passage:

2 Corinthians 1:3-7
³Blessed be the God and Father of our Lord Jesus Christ, the Father of mercies and God of all comfort,
⁴who comforts us in all our affliction, so that we may be able to comfort those who are in any affliction, with the comfort with which we ourselves are comforted by God.
⁵For as we share abundantly in Christ's sufferings, so through Christ we share abundantly in comfort too.
⁶If we are afflicted, it is for your comfort and salvation; and if we are comforted, it is for your comfort, which you experience when you **patiently endure** (*hupomonē*), the same sufferings that we suffer.
⁷Our hope for you is unshaken, for we know that as you share in our sufferings, you will also share in our comfort.

Paul and other ministers experienced great comfort from God as they patiently endured affliction and suffering on behalf of the saints. In like manner, the Corinthians would experience the same comfort if they were to endure as Paul and others had.

---

95 Strong, *The New Strong's Expanded* s.v. "*hupomonē*."

Later in the same epistle, Paul again wrote about endurance:

2 Corinthians 6:1-5
[1]Working together with him, then, we appeal to you not
to receive the grace of God in vain.
[2]For he says, "In a favorable time I listened to you, and
in a day of salvation I have helped you." Behold, now is
the favorable time; behold, now is the day of salvation.
[3]We put no obstacle in anyone's way, so that no fault
may be found with our ministry,
[4]but as servants of God we commend ourselves in every
way: by great **endurance** (*hupomonē*), in afflictions,
hardships, calamities,
[5]beatings, imprisonments, riots, labors, sleepless nights,
hunger;

Paul and others endured despite afflictions, hardships, calamities,
beatings, imprisonments, riots, labors, sleepless nights, and hunger.

2 Thessalonians 1:4
Therefore we ourselves boast about you in the churches
of God for your **steadfastness** (*hupomonē*) and faith in
all your persecutions and in the afflictions that you are
enduring.

We can begin to appreciate that steadfastness, biblically speaking,
means to bear up under all kinds of adverse conditions.
In his second epistle to Timothy, Paul wrote:

2 Timothy 3:10-11
[10]You, however, have followed my teaching, my conduct,
my aim in life, my faith, my patience, my love, my
steadfastness (*hupomonē*),

¹¹my persecutions and sufferings that happened to me at Antioch, at Iconium, and at Lystra—which persecutions I endured; yet from them all the Lord rescued me.

Paul remained steadfast in the face of persecution and suffering.

In the Epistle of James, Job is given as an example of steadfastness.

James 5:11

Behold, we consider those blessed who remained **steadfast** (*hupomonē*). You have heard of the **steadfastness** (*hupomonē*) of Job, and you have seen the purpose of the Lord, how the Lord is compassionate and merciful.

If you read the book of Job, you will see that Job sometimes expressed anger, sarcasm, and even bitterness. He didn't endure heartache and affliction without any show of emotion. At times, he responded in frustration at his miserable comforters, and yet he is given as an example of steadfastness. Why? Because despite all the miserable circumstances he faced and all the temptations that originated from Satan, Job did not stop believing the Word of God concerning the coming Christ. He never cursed God. Despite all the pressures and temptations from Satan—losing all his children, wealth, and health—Job was steadfast in believing. It may be easy to remain steadfast when everything is rosy, but it is much more challenging when life seems to pull the rug out from under you. No wonder Job is given as an example of steadfastness. We also should note that God was compassionate and merciful to Job during his afflictions. Indeed, God blessed Job at the end of his life more than at the beginning (Job 42:12).

As we have seen, to be steadfast under trial means to remain firm in believing despite persecutions and afflictions. *Steadfast believers remain faithful in believing, no matter the circumstances.* Paul and his companions were faithful to God during the many trials and perils they encountered, as did Job. They stand as examples to us all.

Nineteenth-century clergyman George Mueller, who by faith and prayer alone trusted God to provide for tens of thousands of orphans in his lifetime, wrote the following about the testing of one's faith:

We should not shrink from opportunities where our faith may be tried. The more I am in a position to be tried by faith, the more I will have the opportunity of seeing God's help and deliverance. Every fresh instance in which He helps and delivers me will increase my faith.

The believer should not shrink from situations, positions, or circumstances in which his faith may be tried, but he should cheerfully embrace them as opportunities to see the hand of God stretched out in help and deliverance. Thus his faith will be strengthened.[96]

Mueller understood that if sons of God remain steadfast when tried, they will grow in believing. They will learn that God is faithful to help and to deliver.

The Unfading Crown of Glory

1 Peter 5:1-4

[1]So I exhort the elders among you, as a fellow elder and a witness of the sufferings of Christ, as well as a partaker in the glory that is going to be revealed:
[2]shepherd the flock of God that is among you, exercising oversight, not under compulsion, but willingly, as God would have you; not for shameful gain, but eagerly;
[3]not domineering over those in your charge, but being examples to the flock.
[4]And when the chief Shepherd appears, you will receive the unfading **crown** (*stephanos*) **of glory**.

This passage is addressed explicitly to elders in the Church. Here we read that the unfading crown of glory will be given by the chief

---

[96] Mueller, *A Narrative of the Lord's Dealings*, 469.

Shepherd, meaning Jesus Christ, to elders in the Church if they fulfill the responsibilities of an elder as outlined in the Scriptures. Verses 2 and 3 describe some of these responsibilities.

First, elders are to "feed the flock of God." The word "feed" means more than providing nourishment but includes exercising "the whole office of a shepherd, which involves not merely the feeding on grass ... but the entire leading, guiding, guarding, and folding of the flock."[97] Second, elders are to take the oversight of God's people not out of compulsion, nor out of a greedy desire for financial gain, but out of a ready mind. In other words, elders should not have ulterior or selfish motives. Third, the elders are not to domineer over God's people but instead to be examples to them.

This passage has a repeated "not...but" construction:

Not	But
not under compulsion	but willingly
not for shameful gain	but eagerly
not domineering over those in your charge	but being examples to the flock

This repetition draws attention to the characteristics and attitudes an elder should and should not exhibit when overseeing God's people.

At this point, let's read other passages that speak about an elder's responsibilities in the Church. (The reader is asked to remember that this is not a comprehensive treatment of the subject.) For instance, in the first chapter of Paul's epistle to Titus, we read some of the qualifications of elders:

Titus 1:5-9
⁵This is why I left you in Crete, so that you might put what remained into order, and appoint elders in every town as I directed you—

---

97   Bullinger, *A Critical Lexicon and Concordance*, s.v. "feed."

⁶if anyone is above reproach, the husband of one wife, and his children are believers and not open to the charge of debauchery or insubordination.

⁷For an **overseer**, as God's steward, must be above reproach. He must not be arrogant or quick-tempered or a drunkard or violent or greedy for gain,

⁸but hospitable, a lover of good, self-controlled, upright, holy, and disciplined.

⁹He must hold firm to the trustworthy word as taught, so that he may be able to give instruction in sound doctrine and also to rebuke those who contradict it.⁹⁸

Here we learn that an elder is to be beyond accusation, a husband of one wife, with faithful children who are not accused of living a debauched or insubordinate lifestyle. An overseer is not to be arrogant or quick-tempered, not a drunkard or a quarrelsome bully, and not someone greedy for material gain. Rather, he is to be hospitable, a lover of good, self-controlled, upright, holy, and disciplined. He must hold firm to the faithful Word so that he can teach sound doctrine and rebuke those who contradict the sound doctrine.

Paul's first epistle to Timothy has more to say about the overseer's qualifications.

1 Timothy 3:1-7
¹The saying is trustworthy: If anyone aspires to the office of overseer, he desires a noble task.

²Therefore an overseer must be above reproach, the husband of one wife, sober-minded, self-controlled, respectable, hospitable, able to teach,

³not a drunkard, not violent but gentle, not quarrelsome, not a lover of money.

---

⁹⁸ In the Greek New Testament, the word translated "elder" in verse 5 and "overseer" in verse 7 are different words. Some suggest that they are synonyms while others argue that an overseer is an elder who oversees other elders. Either way, it seems that an overseer is an elder, though not all elders are necessarily overseers.

⁴He must manage his own household well, with all dignity keeping his children submissive,

⁵for if someone does not know how to manage his own household, how will he care for God's church?

⁶He must not be a recent convert, or he may become puffed up with conceit and fall into the condemnation of the devil.

⁷Moreover, he must be well thought of by outsiders, so that he may not fall into disgrace, into a snare of the devil.

According to this passage from 1 Timothy 3, we see that the overseer must:

- Be above accusation and not a recent convert
- Be the husband of one wife with his household well managed
- Be sober-minded, not a drunkard
- Be self-controlled, not a lover of money
- Be respectable and hospitable
- Be able to teach
- Be gentle, not argumentative
- Be well thought of by those outside the Church

Note how the word "must" is repeated in verses 2, 4, 6, and 7. The responsibilities and conduct of elders in the Church, as specified in the Scriptures, are not optional for an overseer of God's people.

We may learn even more about the function of elders in the Church from the record in Acts 20, where Paul addressed the elders at Ephesus. In verses 18-21, Paul first presented himself as an example for the elders to emulate. He spoke of serving the Lord with all humility, keeping nothing back that was profitable, teaching and testifying to both Jews and Greeks the Gospel of Jesus Christ. Then, Paul charged the overseers:

Acts 20:28-36

²⁸Pay careful attention to yourselves and to all the flock, in which the Holy Spirit has made you overseers, to

care for the church of God, which he obtained with his own blood.

²⁹I know that after my departure fierce wolves will come in among you, not sparing the flock;

³⁰and from among your own selves will arise men speaking twisted things, to draw away the disciples after them.

³¹Therefore be alert, remembering that for three years I did not cease night or day to admonish every one with tears.

³²And now I commend you to God and to the word of his grace, which is able to build you up and to give you the inheritance among all those who are sanctified.

³³I coveted no one's silver or gold or apparel.

³⁴You yourselves know that these hands ministered to my necessities and to those who were with me.

³⁵In all things I have shown you that by working hard in this way we must help the weak and remember the words of the Lord Jesus, how he himself said, 'It is more blessed to give than to receive.' "

³⁶And when he had said these things, he knelt down and prayed with them all.

In verse 28, we see that it is God who makes a person an overseer. The same verse also uses the shepherd metaphor to magnify the relationship between an elder and those he oversees: he is to feed and shepherd God's people like a shepherd provides for and protects his flock. The shepherding imagery continues, as those who cause division in the Church are called "fierce wolves" (v. 29) who do not spare the flock. The fierce wolves spoken of would come from outside the Church and from within the elders in the Church ("from among you"). Because of these fierce wolves, elders were to be on alert.

While a comprehensive study of the topic of elders and overseers in the Church is outside the scope of this chapter, these passages give the reader insight into the unique responsibilities of elders and overseers in the Church. The reader is encouraged to study these records in more detail and to study the life of Jesus Christ as *the* Overseer of God's people: "For you were straying like sheep but have now returned to the Shepherd and Overseer of your souls" (1 Pet. 2:25).

How Many Crowns?

In the previous section, we learned about the crown of righteousness, the imperishable crown, the crown of life, and the crown of unfading glory. We saw that the crown refers to a specific reward available to all Christian believers if they fulfill the requirements outlined in the Scriptures.

The question naturally presents itself—are there four different crowns? And if so, can a believer receive more than one crown? Are there two crowns, one for elders and one for those who are not elders in the Church? We believe that the Scriptures teach there is only one crown for the following reasons:

1. Various descriptors

Our home has a fireplace, and on the mantle sits a decorative candlestick. In describing this candlestick, we may refer to it as *tall*, for it is about 14 inches. We may refer to it as *shiny* because the metal material has a bright sheen to it. And we may refer to it as *silver*, for that is its color. While we may choose to talk about the candlestick in light of its particular characteristics—tall, shiny, silver—we are still talking about the same candlestick. It is common to refer to one thing as having different characteristics.

We see this throughout the Bible. For example, a son of God may be referred to as a sanctified one, a saint, a believer, a Christian, a joint heir with Christ, and so forth. Are these descriptors speaking about different people, or are they different descriptors used to speak about the same thing? Along the same lines, God may be described as "Almighty God," "the Lord of Hosts," "the Ancient of Days," "Heavenly Father," and so forth. Each name highlights a different aspect of God's nature, but each description still speaks about the One True God. So, although there are various descriptors of the crown, they all refer to the same crown. It is one crown with different descriptors: imperishable, righteous, living, and unfading.[99]

2. Genitive case

We must take a quick detour into Greek grammar to consider how the genitive case functions.

In English, we ordinarily use an adjective to describe a noun. We speak of a "white cat" and "humorous books," but the Greek language uses the genitive case. So, the literal English translation would be "the cat of white" and "books of humor." In the Bible, we read about "sons of God," meaning God's sons, or "children of Abraham," meaning Abraham's children. In English, "of" is usually the sign of the genitive case.

The accusative case is used in reference to the imperishable crown, so, it is already translated as a descriptor: "imperishable crown." However, the genitive construction is used in the other three references to the crown:

- Crown of righteousness
- Crown of life
- Unfading Crown of glory

What does this genitive construction signify? Bullinger lists nine distinct classes of the genitive case, each with its own function and emphasis.[100] (For examples, see the table in Appendix B: Four Apparent Contradictions about the Inheritance)

When it comes to the crown, we see the genitive of relation being used. In English, we could translate this genitive of relation as "pertaining to." So, it would be the crown pertaining to righteousness, the crown pertaining to life, the unfading crown pertaining to glory.

Perhaps to our mind, the "of ____" construction somehow makes

---

[99] The words "unfading" and "imperishable" might be considered synonyms, words used to describe something that lasts.

[100] See also Bullinger, *The Companion Bible*, Appendix 17.

these seem like three distinctive crowns. But recognizing how the genitive case functions in Greek helps us to see that it is *one* crown associated with righteousness, life, and glory. (It is also an imperishable and unfading crown, although those are not genitive constructions in Greek.)

3. Singular in number

In the Greek New Testament, *stephanos* is always singular, with the exception of three occurrences in the book of Revelation.[101]

Further, we know that the prize and the crown are the same. The prize is only spoken of in the singular. Why don't we read about prizes and crowns if multiple crowns are available? The Scriptures only speak of the prize (singular) and the crown (singular) except for the three instances mentioned in Revelation.

Finally, why would Paul write that only the crown of righteousness awaited him? Why didn't he say that three crowns awaited him? Indeed, Paul would have qualified for the crown of life and the crown of glory. Why, then, would he have received only one crown, not the others? Because there is one crown, spoken of as having different characteristics.

4. Definite article

In the Scriptures, the crown is set apart by the definite article.[102]

---

[101] Rev. 4:4, 4:10, and 9:7 mention crowns, plural. However, the people and things wearing the crowns are plural in number, so naturally, the crown would agree in number. That is, there are 24 elders wearing crowns in Rev. 4:4, 10, and there are locusts with what looked like gold crowns on their heads in Rev. 9:7. In all three instances from the book of Revelation, the persons or objects wearing the crowns are plural in number, so the crowns are plural in number. There is no textual evidence to suggest that these people or objects were each wearing multiple crowns.

[102] The definite article occurs in all Greek texts consulted: Stevens, Nestle, Westcott-Hort, Tischendorf, Textus Receptus, and SBL Greek New Testament.

2 Timothy 4:8
Henceforth there is laid up for me **the** crown of
righteousness, which the Lord, the righteous judge, will
award to me on that day, and not only to me but also to
all who have loved his appearing.

According to the Greek New Testament, it should literally read "*the*
crown of *the* righteousness."

James 1:12
Blessed is the man who remains steadfast under trial, for
when he has stood the test he will receive **the crown of
life**, which God has promised to those who love him.

According to the Greek New Testament, it should literally read "*the*
crown of *the* life."

1 Peter 5:4
And when the chief Shepherd appears, you will receive
the unfading crown of glory.

According to the Greek New Testament, it should literally read "*the*
unfading crown of *the* glory." The definite article in these verses
marks out the crown as *the* crown, distinct from all other crowns. The
singularity of the crown is made emphatic. It is *the* crown, meaning
one, singular crown.[103]

For these reasons, we believe that the Scriptures speak of one crown
that is available to the Christian believer.

---

[103] Material culture supports the idea that an athlete was crowned with one crown.
For instance, if we look at historic artifacts that depict the ancient public Games,
we see the victor being crowned with one *stephanos*. Artifacts such as sculptures,
inscriptions, and coins from the Roman and Greek time periods show athletes
wearing a singular crown. To a reader in the first century who was familiar with the
public Games, the thought of an athlete having multiple crowns piled on his head
would seem ridiculous. Though this evidence does not have the same authority as
the Scriptures, it in no way contradicts the argument that there is one crown.

Two Crowns for Elders?

Some argue that the faithful elder will receive two crowns. After all, the Scriptures speak of elders being worthy of "double honor" in this life (1 Tim. 5:17). Wouldn't that translate into eternal life, too?

We conclude that there is one crown available to the Christian believer, whether he is an elder or not, and we offer the following reasons.

1. As we have already discussed, if elders do not faithfully fulfill the criteria outlined in the Scriptures, they will receive no crown. On the other hand, if they faithfully meet these criteria, they will receive the unfading crown of glory. Surely, if elders fulfill the criteria for the crown of glory, they will also have fulfilled the criteria for the crown of life and crown of righteousness *if* they were different crowns. The elder's added responsibility is a sober reminder to the elders in the Church to faithfully execute the office and function God has given them. To do otherwise could mean forfeiting the crown. This is in keeping with what the lord taught, that "to whom much is given, much is required" (Luke 12:48). Elders have been given more responsibility in the Church, so more is expected of them.

2. The Scriptures say that one who receives a prophet in the name of a prophet will receive a prophet's reward (Matt. 10:41). In other words, the person receiving the words of the prophet will be rewarded the same as the one delivering the message. A function is no guarantee of more reward. Scriptures warn believers not to value one function over another in the Body of Christ and to have the same care for one another. A function is no measure of reward. Faithfulness is.

3. The parable of the workers in the vineyard indicates that God is a righteous judge who will reward justly (Matt. 20). In this parable, all the workers received the same reward, even though some of them did more work than others.

4. Joshua and Caleb both "wholly followed the Lord" (Num. 32:12) and thus received the reward of entering the promised land. Yet only Joshua was appointed the leader of Israel. That is to say, Joshua had been given more responsibility than Caleb, yet both received the same reward. Most of Israel received their inheritance by lot. Only Joshua and Caleb got to choose what land they wanted for their inheritance.

5. Paul only spoke of receiving the crown of righteousness. Yet we saw from the record in Acts 20:17-36 that he spoke of himself as a model for all elders. Why doesn't he say he will receive the crown of glory and life? Further, in 1 Corinthians 9:24 he tells the saints to run to obtain a crown (singular), and he pursued the same thing, not different crowns.

God is faithful and just to reward according to His generosity and kindness. But God set the conditions to receive the crown, so we must accept His terms.

Disqualified

Let's close the chapter by briefly considering what it means to be disqualified from receiving the prize (crown). This topic is expanded and explained in much more detail in Appendix F, and the reader may want to read that material before proceeding. But, for the sake of brevity, we offer the following shortened explanation of what it means to be disqualified from receiving the prize (crown).

1 Corinthians 9:24-27
[24]Do you not know that in a race all the runners run, but only one receives the **prize**? So run that you may obtain it.
[25]Every athlete exercises self-control in all things. They do it to receive a perishable **wreath** [crown], but we an imperishable.

²⁶So I do not run aimlessly; I do not box as one beating the air.

²⁷But I discipline my body and keep it under control, lest after preaching to others I myself should be **disqualified**.

The crown (prize) is not automatically given to all Christians but is dependent upon how one runs the race, meaning how one conducts their life. A Christian can be disqualified from receiving the crown. What does this mean? If we ignore the chapter break and keep reading, we will see that the context answers this question.

1 Corinthians 10:1-14

¹For I do not want you to be unaware, brothers, that our fathers were all under the cloud, and all passed through the sea,

²and all were baptized into Moses in the cloud and in the sea,

³and all ate the same spiritual food,

⁴and all drank the same spiritual drink. For they drank from the spiritual Rock that followed them, and the Rock was Christ.

⁵Nevertheless, with most of them God was not pleased, for they were overthrown in the wilderness.

⁶Now these things took place as examples for us, that we might not desire evil as they did.

⁷Do not be idolaters as some of them were; as it is written, "The people sat down to eat and drink and rose up to play."

⁸We must not indulge in sexual immorality as some of them did, and twenty-three thousand fell in a single day.

⁹We must not put Christ to the test, as some of them did and were destroyed by serpents,

¹⁰nor grumble, as some of them did and were destroyed by the Destroyer.

¹¹Now these things happened to them as an example, but they were written down for our instruction, on whom the end of the ages has come.

¹²Therefore let anyone who thinks that he stands take heed lest he fall.

¹³No temptation has overtaken you that is not common to man. God is faithful, and he will not let you be tempted beyond your ability, but with the temptation he will also provide the way of escape, that you may be able to endure it.

¹⁴Therefore, my beloved, flee from idolatry.

This passage contains numerous references and allusions to records from the Old Testament. While we won't take the time to consider the significance of each allusion (we do this in the Appendix), in a word, Paul said, don't be like the Israelites in the wilderness. Don't desire evil as they did. Don't be idolaters like they were. Don't commit fornication (often used in the Scriptures to refer to worshipping other gods) as they did.[104] Don't put the Lord to the test as they did. And don't grumble as they did.

Israel's actions in the wilderness were an example to the Corinthians—an example to avoid. The provocation against God was not one single act but a series of actions. Numbers 14:22 tells us that Israel provoked God and disobeyed Him *ten times*. These records from the Old Testament exemplify how Israel disobeyed God, tested Him, sinned against Him, and turned from Him to serve idols.

After alluding to or quoting from Old Testament passages that speak of Israel's sin and idolatry, Paul issued two warnings: "Therefore let anyone who thinks that he stands take heed lest he fall" (v. 12) and "therefore, my beloved, flee from idolatry" (v. 14). These warnings are with a view to the future realities concerning the Hope. While *all* saints are saved and have eternal life, not all will automatically receive the prize. While *all* run the race, not all will be crowned. Just

---

104   Cummins, *A Journey Through the Acts*, Vol. 1, 297.

as most Israelites failed to enter the promised land, Christian believers today might fail to receive the crown. How? By imitating Israel in the wilderness when they craved evil and were idolaters. This is what it means to be disqualified from the prize (crown).

Between the two warnings comes this marvelous promise: "No temptation has overtaken you that is not common to man. God is faithful, and he will not let you be tempted beyond your ability, but with the temptation, he will also provide the way of escape, that you may be able to endure it" (v. 13). Contextually, the temptation is to imitate Israel's sin and idolatry. This is what disqualifies a son of God from receiving the crown.

Remember, Paul wrote in 1 Corinthians 9:27 that he disciplined his body and kept it under control so he would not be disqualified. Was Paul referring to diet and exercise? Was he referring to denying the flesh and its needs? Religious tradition may put a self-denial spin on this, where discipline means punishing the flesh and self-control means avoiding excess. However, the Scriptures we have considered in this section indicate that discipline also involves *not worshipping idols,* and self-control also involves not *lusting after other gods.* Therefore, it's essential to strip away religious connotations of these concepts and look, with clear thinking, at the sober warnings given to the Church in 1 Corinthians 9 and 10.

Recall that in Colossians 2:18, the saints were warned to not allow themselves to be disqualified from the prize (the crown) through worshipping of angels or other such practices.

Christians are to be self-controlled in all things, and this is not limited to bodily restraint. It includes not turning away from God to idols. If one turns from God to idols, he forfeits the crown. Why would Paul need to give such stark warnings to the Corinthians? Because so much was at stake.

Summary and Conclusion

As we have discovered, the prize and crown are both athletic terms derived from the world of sports, specifically, the ancient Games. Both the prize and the crown are metaphors, figures of comparison that underscore the singularity and value of this specific reward. From our study of the Scriptures, we understand that the prize and the crown refer to the same thing. The prize is a general term, and the crown is specific. Although the Bible seems to speak of different crowns—the imperishable crown, the crown of righteousness, the crown of life, the unfading crown of glory—we have come to understand that this refers to the same crown with different characteristics.

One then naturally wonders, what is the crown? We know the crown is not a wreath of eternally green oak leaves but a metaphor representing something. What does it represent? Just as the athlete's crown in the ancient Games represented something, so does the Christian's crown. Because it is compared to the victor's crown in the ancient Games, the crown represents *singular* honor, glory, and praise in the ages to come. It is a special reward for the highest commitment to God and the Lord Jesus Christ. While we don't know all the crown entails, we do know that the crown is a special reward carrying singular, eternal honor in heaven.

Chapter 7

The Nature of the Reward

Today, when we think about the compensation one receives as a reward, we may think of money, goods, or other material items. But what about the nature of the reward in heaven? Will there be mansions or piles of money waiting for us? Is the compensation going to be material in nature or something else entirely? When it comes to questions like this, we look to only one place for answers—the Scriptures. In this chapter, we seek to learn what the Scriptures say about the nature of the Christian's reward.

Jesus Christ's Teachings

Let's start with a record we handled in Chapter 4.

> **Matthew 19:27-29**
> ²⁷Then Peter said in reply, "See, we have left everything and followed you. What then will we have?"
> ²⁸Jesus said to them, "Truly, I say to you, in the new world, when the Son of Man will sit on his glorious throne, you who have followed me will also sit on twelve thrones, judging (*krinō*) the twelve tribes of Israel.
> ²⁹And everyone who has left houses or brothers or sisters or father or mother or children or lands, for my name's sake, will receive a hundredfold and will inherit eternal life.

In answer to Peter's question about what they would have for forsaking all and following him, Jesus Christ said the apostles would "sit on twelve thrones, judging the twelve tribes of Israel." This would occur in the future when the Son of Man sits on his glorious throne. In verse 28, the word translated as "judging" is *krinō,* which ordinarily means to give an opinion between right or wrong. But according to Thayer, in this particular occurrence, *krinō* is a Hebraism connoting "to rule, govern, to preside over with the power of giving judicial decision."[105] In other words, the promise given here to the twelve apostles for their sacrifice and faithful service was not only to judge between right and wrong but also to preside over the twelve tribes of Israel. They would reign over them. In this passage, we see that the promised compensation was *positions of authority and responsibility.*

Sometime after this, James and John's mother asked Jesus Christ for a favor for her sons.

Matthew 20:20-23

²⁰Then the mother of the sons of Zebedee came up to him with her sons, and kneeling before him she asked him for something.
²¹And he said to her, "What do you want?" She said to him, "Say that these two sons of mine are to sit, one at your right hand and one at your left, in your kingdom."
²²Jesus answered, "You do not know what you are asking. Are you able to drink the cup that I am to drink?" They said to him, "We are able."
²³He said to them, "You will drink my cup, but to sit at my right hand and at my left is not mine to grant, but it is for those for whom it has been prepared by my Father."

Now let's read the parallel record in Mark.

Mark 10:35-40

³⁵And James and John, the sons of Zebedee, came up to him and said to him, "Teacher, we want you to do for us whatever we ask of you."

---

[105] Thayer, *A Greek-English Lexicon,* s.v. "*krinō.*"

³⁶And he said to them, "What do you want me to do for you?"

³⁷And they said to him, "Grant us to sit, one at your right hand and one at your left, in your glory."

³⁸Jesus said to them, "You do not know what you are asking. Are you able to drink the cup that I drink, or to be baptized with the baptism with which I am baptized?"

³⁹And they said to him, "We are able." And Jesus said to them, "The cup that I drink you will drink, and with the baptism with which I am baptized, you will be baptized, ⁴⁰but to sit at my right hand or at my left is not mine to grant, but it is for those for whom it has been prepared."

James and John, accompanied by their mother, asked Jesus Christ for the honor of sitting in his kingdom on his right and left hand. In the Greek New Testament, the word translated as "sit" in verse 37 is *kathizō*. This word means more than just sitting down to rest but implies exercising authority. (See "Appendix G: A Study of *Kathizō* (Seated)"). They were not asking for a comfortable place to sit; they were asking for positions of distinction in Christ's kingdom.

Recall that the apostles had already been promised they would sit on twelve thrones, judging the twelve tribes of Israel. James and John wanted more. In response, Jesus Christ first asked the brothers if they were able to share his responsibility and commitment.[106] Then he told them that these positions were not his to give but were up to God to decide. Notice how he did not say, "No such positions exist." Nor did he rebuke James and John or their mother for requesting these exalted stations. When so many denied him as the Christ, here were some who recognized and acknowledged his future kingdom of power and glory. They did not doubt that Christ would have a kingdom but wanted to share in the corresponding glory. This passage indicates that there are positions of authority in Christ's kingdom.

---

[106] According to numerous sources, the phrase "drink the cup" is an idiom meaning to participate or share in the responsibility.

Rank within the Kingdom

What was the reaction of the other apostles to the brothers' request?

> **Matthew 20:24-28**
> [24] And when the ten heard it, they were indignant at the two brothers.
> [25] But Jesus called them to him and said, "You know that the rulers of the Gentiles lord it over them, and their great ones exercise authority over them.
> [26] It shall not be so among you. But whoever would be great among you must be your servant,
> [27] and whoever would be first among you must be your slave,
> [28] even as the Son of Man came not to be served but to serve, and to give his life as a ransom for many."

James and John's request did not go over well with the other apostles. But let's note that Jesus Christ wasn't upset by their request. Instead, he gave them a plain answer and then taught them that the path to exaltation in his kingdom was one of service. Whoever desired to be great among them should be their *servant*, and whoever wanted to be first among them should be their *slave*.

In the Greek New Testament, the word translated "servant" in verse 26 is *diakonos*, a general term for someone who performs the commands of a master or superior, whether they serve a king at court or serve people food and drink at table.[107] However, the word translated "slave" in verse 27 is *doulos*, meaning "someone who belongs to another; a bond-slave, without any ownership rights of their own...metaphorically, one who gives himself up wholly to another's will."[108] "Servant" and "slave" are not synonyms but are words indicating differing degrees of service.

Note there are degrees of service and degrees of corresponding honor in Christ's kingdom. Being a servant resulted in great recognition;

---

107   Thayer, *A Greek-English Lexicon*, s.v. "*diakonos*."
108   Thayer, *A Greek-English Lexicon*, s.v. "*doulos*."

being a bondslave resulted in being first, the highest recognition. If one wanted to be exalted in the kingdom of God, he was to serve. However, if one wanted to be of the *first rank* in the kingdom of God, he was to be a bondslave. This passage suggests that there are degrees of authority in Christ's kingdom and corresponding degrees of exaltation, based on service.

Jesus Christ taught that the greater the service in this age, the greater the recognition in the kingdom of God in the future age. Christ himself exemplified this kind of service. Though he was God's Only Begotten Son, he came to serve, not to be served. The supreme act of this service was demonstrated when he gave his life as a ransom for many. And as a result of his obedience and sacrifice, Jesus Christ was elevated to the highest position available in the heavenly places—at God's right hand (Eph. 1:20-22; Phil. 2:8-11). Christ did not deny the existence of positions of authority in his kingdom, nor did he scold his apostles when they asked questions about these positions. Instead, he taught his apostles *how* to be great or first in the kingdom of God—by serving. His own life exemplified this kind of service to the fullest degree.

This was not the only time Jesus Christ had to address the matter of preeminence in the kingdom of God with his disciples:

> **Mark 9:33-37**
> [33]And they came to Capernaum. And when he was in the house he asked them, "What were you discussing on the way?"
> [34]But they kept silent, for on the way they had argued with one another about who was the greatest.
> [35]And he sat down and called the twelve. And he said to them, "If anyone would be first, he must be last of all and servant of all."
> [36]And he took a child and put him in the midst of them, and taking him in his arms, he said to them,
> [37]"Whoever receives one such child in my name receives me, and whoever receives me, receives not me but him who sent me."

On their way to Capernaum, the twelve apostles argued about who was the greatest. When they were together in a house, Jesus Christ asked them what they had been discussing. The apostles did not reply. So, Jesus called the Twelve together and taught them how one would be first: be servant of all. Note that Jesus did not say, "everyone is equal," or "everyone has the same position." Instead, he taught them that if one wanted to be first in rank or position, he was to be the greatest servant. By way of illustration, he brought a child and put him in their midst.

Let's read the parallel record in Luke.

Luke 9:46-48

[46]An argument arose among them as to which of them was the greatest.

[47]But Jesus, knowing the reasoning of their hearts, took a child and put him by his side

[48]and said to them, "Whoever receives this child in my name receives me, and whoever receives me receives him who sent me. For he who is least among you all is the one who is great."

In biblical culture, a child would have virtually no rank in society. He was the epitome of humility and lowliness. At another time, Jesus had used the example of a child to teach his disciples about humility.

Matthew 18:2-4

[2]And calling to him a child, he put him in the midst of them

[3]and said, "Truly, I say to you, unless you turn and become like children, you will never enter the kingdom of heaven.

[4]Whoever humbles himself like this child is the greatest in the kingdom of heaven.

In using this powerful illustration of the child, Jesus Christ underscored that the way to be great in his kingdom was to be humble. In addition to being servants, they were to be humble like children.

One may think the apostles finally got the message. But let's read a record from Luke, which describes some of the events that occurred during what is commonly called "the Last Supper."

> **Luke 22:24-30**
> [24]A dispute also arose among them, as to which of them was to be regarded as the greatest.
> [25]And he said to them, "The kings of the Gentiles exercise lordship over them, and those in authority over them are called benefactors.
> [26]But not so with you. Rather, let the greatest among you become as the youngest, and the leader as one who serves.
> [27]For who is the greater, one who reclines at table or one who serves? Is it not the one who reclines at table? But I am among you as the one who serves.
> [28]"You are those who have stayed with me in my trials,
> [29]and I assign to you, as my Father assigned to me, a kingdom,
> [30]that you may eat and drink at my table in my kingdom and sit on thrones judging the twelve tribes of Israel.

The apostles were again arguing about who would be the greatest among them. This took place during a very trying time for Jesus Christ, as he was preparing to give up his life. Despite the heaviness of the situation, he patiently explained to them, once again, that the way to become the greatest in the kingdom of God was not by domineering over others as worldly leaders do but by serving. Jesus Christ pointed to his own life as an example. For a second time, he talked about the apostles sitting on thrones, judging the twelve tribes of Israel. But this time, he qualified it by adding "those who stayed with me in my trials." In other words, the promise of sitting on thrones could not apply to Judas Iscariot, who would betray the lord.[109]

---

[109] By the time Jesus Christ said this, it is possible Judas had left to betray him. The exact timing may not be possible to establish. However, since Judas did not continue with Jesus Christ, and since he forfeited his office, it is not possible that the promise of sitting on thrones would apply to Judas. The apostles are still called the Twelve in Acts 6:2, with Matthias having replaced Judas.

While there are many other lessons one might glean from this passage, for our purposes, let's note that Jesus Christ spoke of "greater" and "greatest" in his kingdom. He did not say there would be no rank in his kingdom.

In the following passage, Jesus Christ also speaks of great and least in the kingdom.

> ### Matthew 5:17-19
>
> [17]"Do not think that I have come to abolish the Law or the Prophets; I have not come to abolish them but to fulfill them.
>
> [18]For truly, I say to you, until heaven and earth pass away, not an iota, not a dot, will pass from the Law until all is accomplished.
>
> [19]Therefore whoever relaxes one of the least of these commandments and teaches others to do the same will be called **least in the kingdom of heaven**, but whoever does them and teaches them will be called **great in the kingdom of heaven.**

In verse 19, the word "least" can mean the least or the smallest in size, amount, dignity, or least in rank.[110] The term "great" can mean large, important, powerful, or great in rank.[111] When Jesus Christ spoke of least and great in this passage, what degree is he talking about—least or great in size, or least or great in importance, position, or rank?

Jesus Christ taught that anyone who would break the least of the commandments and teach others to do the same would be called "least" in the kingdom of heaven. Notice that this person would still be *in the kingdom*, but he would be called "least." In contrast, someone who kept the commandments and taught others would be called "great." Both would be *in* the kingdom, but one would be least in rank and one great in rank. They would not necessarily have the same position, authority, or responsibility. Contextually, he was speaking about least and great in importance, position, or rank within the kingdom of heaven. Let's

---

110   Strong, *The New Strong's Expanded*, s.v. *"elachistos."*

111   Thayer, *A Greek-English Lexicon*, s.v *"megas."*

also remember that he was answering their question about who would be least and great in the kingdom.

A kingdom implies dominion, rule, authority, and order. A kingdom also means having an authority structure with the king at the top and others under him who serve in various positions and levels. Jesus Christ said there were positions to his left and right hand in his kingdom but that it was up to God to grant those positions. Further, he promised his apostles who continued with him in his trials that they would sit on thrones judging the twelve tribes of Israel. Rather than denying that such seats of authority and responsibility exist, Jesus Christ made promises concerning some of these positions. He taught his disciples that the way to become great in his kingdom was by humility and service. From all the passages we have considered in this section, we may conclude that the nature of future reward includes having positions of authority and responsibility within Christ's kingdom.

Having looked at passages in the Gospels where Jesus Christ taught about the least and greatest in the kingdom of God, let's now read two parables about the kingdom. While there are many lessons to be learned from these parables, for our purposes we will focus on what they teach us about the nature of future reward.

Parable of the Minas

The first parable is sometimes called the "parable of the minas."[112] A mina is a Greek monetary unit.

> **Luke 19:11-27**
> [11]As they heard these things, he proceeded to tell a parable, because he was near to Jerusalem, and because they supposed that the kingdom of God was to appear immediately.

---

[112] This is referred to as the "parable of the pounds" in the KJV and other Bible versions.

[12]He said therefore, "A nobleman went into a far country to receive for himself a kingdom and then return. [13]Calling ten of his servants, he gave them ten minas, and said to them, 'Engage in business until I come.' [14]But his citizens hated him and sent a delegation after him, saying, 'We do not want this man to reign over us.' [15]When he returned, having received the kingdom, he ordered these servants to whom he had given the money to be called to him, that he might know what they had gained by doing business. [16]The first came before him, saying, 'Lord, your mina has made ten minas more.' [17]And he said to him, 'Well done, good servant! Because you have been faithful in a very little, you shall have authority over ten cities.' [18]And the second came, saying, 'Lord, your mina has made five minas.' [19]And he said to him, 'And you are to be over five cities.' [20]Then another came, saying, 'Lord, here is your mina, which I kept laid away in a handkerchief; [21]for I was afraid of you, because you are a severe man. You take what you did not deposit, and reap what you did not sow.' [22]He said to him, 'I will condemn you with your own words, you wicked servant! You knew that I was a severe man, taking what I did not deposit and reaping what I did not sow? [23]Why then did you not put my money in the bank, and at my coming I might have collected it with interest?' [24]And he said to those who stood by, 'Take the mina from him, and give it to the one who has the ten minas.' [25]And they said to him, 'Lord, he has ten minas!' [26]'I tell you that to everyone who has, more will be given, but from the one who has not, even what he has will be taken away.

²⁷But as for these enemies of mine, who did not want me to reign over them, bring them here and slaughter them before me.'"

In the parable, a nobleman went into a far country to receive a kingdom for himself and then returned. Before going away, he gave his servants some money to conduct business. Each servant received the same amount, one mina. They were all given the same money and the same responsibility. After some time, the nobleman returned and called his servants to see how they had fared.

The first servant had gained ten minas and was commended with, "Well done, good servant." Because he had been faithful and gotten ten fold in return, he was given *authority* over much—ten cities. The second servant had gained five minas. He received no commendation from the nobleman, but he was given *authority* over five cities. The third servant had gained nothing from his one mina, for he had hidden it out of fear. The nobleman called this servant "wicked" because he did nothing with what was entrusted to him. Even though he knew that his lord would return and expect something back, he hid the money out of fear. And so, the nobleman gave this man's mina to the first servant. This wicked servant was not given anything.

Jesus Christ explained, "I tell you that to everyone who has, more will be given, but from the one who has not, even what he has will be taken away" (v. 26). There is an ellipsis in this verse, with the words "been faithful" missing but readily supplied by the context. It would therefore read, "I tell you that to everyone who has [been faithful], more will be given, but from the one who has not [been faithful], even what he has will be taken away."[113] In other words, everyone who had been *faithful* to gain more according to what he had been given would receive more in return. In this case, what was received was more responsibility.

---

[113] Based on the Greek word for "has," which means "to own or possess," this technically would be translated, "I tell you that to everyone who has (possesses) *faithfulness*, more will be given, but from the one who has (possesses) not *faithfulness*, even what he has will be taken away." But we opted for a rendering that is clearer in English.

In contrast, everyone who had not been faithful to gain more according to what he had been given would not receive anything in return. He would not be given added responsibility. Jesus Christ was talking about future reward based on the degree of faithfulness. (This parable also shows that Jesus Christ's kingdom was future and that those who did not accept him—his enemies in verse 27—would perish.)

Parable of the Talents

Let's consider another parable about the kingdom of God, sometimes called the "parable of the talents." In this passage, a talent is a monetary unit, not an innate ability.

> ### Matthew 25:14-18
> [14]"For it [the kingdom of God] will be like a man going on a journey, who called his servants and entrusted to them his property.[114]
> [15]To one he gave five talents, to another two, to another one, to **each according to his ability.** Then he went away.
> [16]He who had received the five talents went at once and traded with them, and he made five talents more.
> [17]So also he who had the two talents made two talents more.
> [18]But he who had received the one talent went and dug in the ground and hid his master's money.

In the parable, a man entrusted his property to his servants while he went on a journey. He gave one servant five talents, he gave another two talents, and to the third, he gave one talent. Unlike the servants in the parable of the minas, the servants in this parable are *not* given the same amount when the man leaves on his journey. Instead, each is given an amount according to his own ability (v. 15). Let's see what the servants did with their talents.

---

[114] Matt. 25:1 tells us that Jesus Christ was teaching parables about the kingdom of heaven. In verse 14, he is still speaking about the kingdom of heaven.

Matthew 25:19-30

[19]Now after a long time the master of those servants came and settled accounts with them.

[20]And he who had received the five talents came forward, bringing five talents more, saying, 'Master, you delivered to me five talents; here, I have made five talents more.'

[21]His master said to him, 'Well done, good and faithful servant. You have been faithful over a little; I will **set you over** much. Enter into the joy of your master.'

[22]And he also who had the two talents came forward, saying, 'Master, you delivered to me two talents; here, I have made two talents more.'

[23]His master said to him, 'Well done, good and faithful servant. You have been faithful over a little; I will **set you over** much. Enter into the joy of your master.'

[24]He also who had received the one talent came forward, saying, 'Master, I knew you to be a hard man, reaping where you did not sow, and gathering where you scattered no seed,

[25]so I was afraid, and I went and hid your talent in the ground. Here, you have what is yours.'

[26]But his master answered him, 'You wicked and slothful servant! You knew that I reap where I have not sown and gather where I scattered no seed?

[27]Then you ought to have invested my money with the bankers, and at my coming I should have received what was my own with interest.

[28]So take the talent from him and give it to him who has the ten talents.

[29]For to everyone who has will more be given, and he will have an abundance. But from the one who has not, even what he has will be taken away.

^{30}And cast the worthless servant into the outer darkness. In that place there will be weeping and gnashing of teeth.'

When the master returned, he received the report. The first servant who had been given five talents made five more; likewise, the second servant who had been given two talents made two more. Even though these two servants had been given different amounts, they both made the most of their talents according to their ability. Both got a 100% return, so to speak, even though they started with different amounts. *Both* got the *same* commendation: "Well done, good and faithful servant. You have been faithful over a little; I will set you over much. Enter into the joy of your master." What was the reward for their faithfulness? Both would be "set over" (*kathistēmi*) much, meaning they would be appointed, or set over others.[115]

The third servant, however, hid his one talent because he was afraid. The master called him a "wicked and slothful servant," took his one talent, and gave it to the first servant. The "worthless" servant was cast out into outer darkness, signifying no reward. Then Jesus Christ concluded: "For to everyone who has will more be given, and he will have an abundance. But from the one who has not, even what he has will be taken away" (v. 29). This verse may seem unclear without recognizing that there is a figure of speech, ellipsis, with the words "been faithful" being omitted. The context indicates that the subject matter is faithfulness. Verse 29 might therefore be clearer if rendered as follows: "For to everyone who has [been faithful] will more be given, and he will have an abundance. But from the one who has not [been faithful], even what he has will be taken away."[116]

In the parable of the talents, each servant was accountable for the amount he was given, which was commensurate with his ability.

---

[115] Thayer, *A Greek-English Lexicon*, s.v. "*kathistēmi*."

[116] Based on the Greek word "has," this technically would be translated, "For to everyone who has (possesses) *faithfulness* will more be given, and he will have an abundance. But from the one who has (possesses) not *faithfulness*, even what he has will be taken away." But we opted for the clearer English rendering.

Each was rewarded according to how faithful he was in carrying out that responsibility. Those who were faithful with their allotted portion were *set over* much, while the servant who made nothing of his talent was given nothing in return. In fact, that servant had to relinquish his responsibility altogether.

The parable of the minas and the parable of the talents shed light on the nature of future reward. In both parables, faithful ones receive more authority, while unfaithful ones receive less or none. In both parables, the faithful servants were commended and rewarded, and each servant was held accountable for what he did with his own mina or talent. In both parables, the context reveals that the man going on a journey represents the Lord Jesus Christ, who would go away to receive the kingdom. The servants were those who waited for his return and were given responsibilities while waiting. They were rewarded according to their faithfulness when the lord returned. The nature of the reward they received was *authority and responsibility* within the kingdom, commensurate with their service.

God has Highly Exalted Him

No one exemplifies service and humility like the Lord Jesus Christ. And the Scriptures tell us because he humbled himself and was obedient, God highly exalted him.

> ### Philippians 2:3-11
> ³Do nothing from selfish ambition or conceit, but in humility count others more significant than yourselves.
> ⁴Let each of you look not only to his own interests, but also to the interests of others.
> ⁵Have this mind among yourselves, which is yours in Christ Jesus,
> ⁶who, though he was in the form of God, did not count equality with God a thing to be grasped,

⁷but emptied himself, by taking the form of a servant, being born in the likeness of men.

⁸And being found in human form, he humbled himself by becoming obedient to the point of death, even death on a cross.

⁹**Therefore** God has highly exalted him and bestowed on him the name that is above every name,

¹⁰so that at the name of Jesus every knee should bow, in heaven and on earth and under the earth,

¹¹and every tongue confess that Jesus Christ is Lord, to the glory of God the Father.

The word "therefore" in verse 9 indicates a reason. God highly exalted Jesus Christ and gave him a singular name *because* he humbled himself and became obedient, even to the point of an ignominious death on the cross. These were deliberate decisions by Jesus Christ. While preparing for what was to come, Jesus Christ prayed in the Garden of Gethsemane for another way to accomplish God's purpose. Three times he asked God if there was another way to fulfill His will, and yet three times he said, "not my will, but yours be done" (Luke 22:42). Though it was not easy, Jesus Christ obeyed God and gave up his life.

Jesus Christ certainly exemplified his own teaching concerning humility and service. As God's only begotten Son, he had certain rights and privileges, but instead of using those rights for personal gain, he emptied himself and obeyed God. And how did God reward him? By giving him an elevated position at His right hand and a name above all names in heaven and on earth. That is a highly exalted position indeed! Jesus Christ *obtained* his highly exalted position by his humble, obedient service to God.

During his temptations by the devil, Jesus Christ was offered an exalted position:

Luke 4:5-8

⁵And the devil took him up and showed him all the kingdoms of the world in a moment of time,

⁶and said to him, "To you I will give all this authority and their glory, for it has been delivered to me, and I give it to whom I will.

⁷If you, then, will worship me, it will all be yours."

⁸And Jesus answered him, "It is written, " 'You shall worship the Lord your God, and him only shall you serve.' "

The devil offered Jesus Christ all the authority and glory of the world's kingdoms if he (Jesus) would bow down and worship him (the devil). Had he accepted this offer, Jesus Christ would have had all the authority and glory of the world's kingdoms. And, perhaps most of all, he wouldn't have had to go through the suffering and pain of crucifixion.

However, Jesus Christ refused the devil's offer and instead chose the path of humility and obedience. As a result, Jesus Christ was given authority not only over the earth *but also in heaven!* As for glory, Jesus Christ alone occupies a singular seat of authority at God's right hand, and his future is filled with even more glorification. Jesus Christ is the ultimate example of one who was rewarded with a position of authority and responsibility within God's kingdom. This position is unparalleled in this age and in the age to come.

Reign with Christ

We have seen that the apostles were promised thrones in Christ's kingdom, meaning that they would reign with him. But the Scriptures also speak of the availability for Christians to reign with Christ.

2 Timothy 2:10-12

¹⁰Therefore I endure everything for the sake of the elect, that they also may obtain the salvation that is in Christ Jesus with eternal glory.

¹¹The saying is trustworthy, for: **If** we have died with him, we will also live with him;

¹²**if** we endure, we will also **reign** with him; **if** we deny
him, he also will deny us;

To reign essentially means to rule. For example, Archelaus reigned
over Jerusalem after his father, Herod (Matt. 2:22), and the angel
Gabriel prophesied that Jesus would reign over the house of Jacob
forever (Luke 1:32-33). In these and other occurrences, the word "reign"
means to rule. Here in 2 Timothy 2:12, we read of reigning *with* Christ
in the future. We also see that reigning *with* Christ is conditional: *if*
we endure.

This reigning with Christ is not to be confused with reigning in life
through Christ, which we read about in the book of Romans.

Romans 5:17, 21

For if, because of one man's trespass, death **reigned**
through that one man, much more will those who receive
the abundance of grace and the free gift of righteousness
reign in life through the one man Jesus Christ.

Verse 21

so that, as sin **reigned** in death, grace also might **reign**
through righteousness leading to eternal life through
Jesus Christ our Lord.

In verse 17, we see that because of Adam's transgression, death—the loss
of spirit life—ruled man. But because of God's grace and His gift of holy
spirit, the saints are freed from that reign of death. Now, all born again
ones reign in life through the one man, Jesus Christ. This reigning in life
is an accomplished reality for every saint. This truth operates on several
levels. In the here and now, we reign in life through Christ because we
are more than conquerors through him. But we also reign in life because
we have received the gift of eternal life, and the consequences of Adam's
disobedience no longer rule over us! Put simply, to reign in life through
Christ means that we no longer are under the dominion of death, for we

have passed from death unto eternal life. It is an accomplished reality for each Christian, thanks to God's grace and mercy.

However, reigning *with* Christ is a future possibility, based on the conditions set forth in 2 Timothy 2:10-12. Let's reread the passage:

2 Timothy 2:10-12
[10]Therefore I endure everything for the sake of the elect, that they also may obtain the salvation that is in Christ Jesus with eternal glory.
[11]The saying is trustworthy, for: **If** we have died with him, we will also live with him;
[12]**if** we endure, we will also **reign** with him; **if** we deny him, he also will deny us;

Notice the three "if" clauses in verses 11 and 12: "*if* we have died with him," "*if* we endure," and "*if* we deny him." The first condition, stated in verse 11, speaks to our identification with Christ. We have already died with him, and so we will also live with him, signifying eternal life. However, the conditions stated in verse 12 are another matter altogether.

> Reign in life through Christ— accomplished reality
> Reign with Christ— possible future reality

Verse 12 tells us that if one endures, one will reign with Christ in the coming age. Reigning with Christ is conditional. Because not all saints will satisfy this condition, not all saints will reign. While all saints reign *in* life now *through* Jesus Christ, not all saints will automatically reign *with* Christ in the future because reigning with Christ is dependent upon enduring. To reign means to rule, and so to reign with Christ means to rule with him in his kingdom.

What does it mean to endure? The context gives us the answer. Part of enduring is not denying Christ. "If we deny him, he will deny us" can only mean that if we do not endure, we will lose out on reward. What will be denied us is reigning with Christ. It cannot mean that Christ will deny us eternal life or our inheritance, for those are guaranteed to each Christian believer. However, to reign with Christ in the future is conditional upon one's walk, and that includes not denying Christ, and not being ashamed of the Gospel.

In Matthew 10:33, Jesus Christ said, "but whoever denies me before men, I also will deny before my Father who is in heaven." In Luke 9:28a, he said, "for whoever is ashamed of me and my words, of him will the Son of Man be ashamed when he comes in his glory...." In both cases, he was addressing his disciples, and he was speaking about future realities, including future reward. To deny Christ, then, is to become ashamed of Christ and the Gospel. The result would be loss of reward.

When 2 Timothy was written, the state of the Church was dire. Paul was in prison, and all who had once believed the Gospel in Asia had turned away from him and his teachings. Some leaders were teaching the wrong doctrine, and many were ashamed of the apostle Paul. Three times in the opening chapter of the epistle, we read about not being ashamed of the Gospel.

2 Timothy 1:8, 12, 16
Therefore do not be **ashamed** of the testimony about our Lord, nor of me his prisoner, but share in suffering for the gospel by the power of God,

Verse 12
which is why I suffer as I do. But I am not **ashamed**, for I know whom I have believed, and I am convinced that he is able to guard until that day what has been entrusted to me.

Verse 16
May the Lord grant mercy to the household of Onesiphorus, for he often refreshed me and was not **ashamed** of my chains,

For Paul to encourage Timothy not to be ashamed of him or the Gospel indicates that he may have been tempted to do so. He also reminded

Timothy that there were still some, like Onesiphorus, who had helped Paul and were not ashamed of his imprisonment. With so many having turned away from Paul and the right doctrine, it was understandably a dark time for the Church.

In the next chapter, Paul continues to teach Timothy about the need for endurance.

2 Timothy 2:1-13

[1]You then, my child, be strengthened by the grace that is in Christ Jesus,

[2]and what you have heard from me in the presence of many witnesses entrust to faithful men, who will be able to teach others also.

[3]Share in suffering as a good **soldier** of Christ Jesus.

[4]No **soldier** gets entangled in civilian pursuits, since his aim is to please the one who enlisted him.

[5]An **athlete** is not crowned unless he competes according to the rules.

[6]It is the hard-working **farmer** who ought to have the first share of the crops.

[7]Think over what I say, for the Lord will give you understanding in everything.

[8]Remember Jesus Christ, risen from the dead, the offspring of David, as preached in my gospel,

[9]for which I am suffering, bound with chains as a criminal. But the word of God is not bound!

[10]Therefore I **endure** everything for the sake of the elect, that they also may obtain the salvation that is in Christ Jesus with eternal glory.

[11]The saying is trustworthy, for: If we have died with him, we will also live with him;

[12]if we **endure**, we will also reign with him; if we deny him, he also will deny us;

[13]if we are faithless, he remains faithful—for he cannot deny himself.

Notice how in verse 3, Paul again admonishes Timothy to "share in suffering" as he had earlier in 2 Timothy 1:8. He then provides three illustrations of the soldier, athlete, and farmer. These illustrations underscore aspects of endurance. Timothy was to endure hardship, like a soldier, and not be entangled with the affairs of this world, so as to please his master. He was to contend according to the rules like an athlete, which would include teaching the right doctrine, rightly interpreting the Word of Truth, and not being ashamed of the Gospel, among other matters. And he was to work hard in his ministry like a farmer. Accordingly, he would be rewarded in the same way the hardworking farmer partakes of his harvest.

It is in *this* context that we read about reigning with Christ. In light of the condition of the Church at the time, it would take courage and fortitude for Timothy to endure and remain faithful.

We know that not all who worked with Paul were willing to endure the hardships that arose for the Gospel's sake.[117] If they did not endure, then they would not reign with Christ. And so, when we read about reigning with Christ in 2 Timothy 2:12, we understand that this promise pertains to those in the Church who endure and remain faithful. Reigning with Christ is not given to those who deny the Lord Jesus Christ, who are ashamed of his testimony, and who forsake the Gospel when suffering and persecution arise. While their salvation and eternal inheritance are assured, they will not reign with Christ in the coming age.[118]

---

[117] For instance, Hymenaeus and Alexander. See 1 Tim.1:19-20.

[118] According to Rev. 3:20-21, the possibility of sitting with Christ on his throne is offered to the "one who conquers." In the context of the book of Revelation, this means staying faithful during the Great Tribulation, which makes up part of the Day of the Lord. Although the people addressed in the book of Revelation are not part of the Church of the One Body, we still see that some would be granted the privilege of reigning with Christ on the earth, *if* they were faithful during the Great Tribulation time period.

Summary and Conclusion

In this chapter, we have seen that Jesus Christ promised the apostles that they would judge the twelve tribes of Israel as a reward for their sacrifice and faithful service. This judging includes ruling or presiding over others. We saw that according to Christ's teachings, there is rank within the Kingdom of God. We learned that the nature of the reward includes having positions of authority and responsibility in that kingdom. From the parables of the minas and the talents, we learned that faithful ones receive more authority while unfaithful ones receive less or none.

All kingdoms have order and hierarchies, and this is true of the kingdom of God. On several occasions, the disciples asked Jesus Christ who would be the greatest in the kingdom of God. Not once did Jesus Christ say, "There are no positions within the kingdom." Not once did he say, "Everyone is equal in the kingdom." Not once did he say, "No one is least or greatest in the kingdom." He also did not reprove his disciples for *desiring* positions or recognition but merely instructed them *how* to become the greatest in the kingdom. Jesus Christ taught that the greater the service one rendered, the greater the recognition would be in the age to come. His own example illustrates that the nature of the reward includes having authority, for he was rewarded for his obedience with a singular, highly exalted position at God's right hand.

Finally, we saw that reigning in life by Christ now is not the same as reigning with Christ in a future age. Reigning in life by Christ means that all born again ones are rescued from the power of darkness and delivered from death and given the assurance of eternal life. But reigning with Christ is dependent upon enduring. We are given to understand that reigning with Christ is a very esteemed position of authority and responsibility in the age to come. Therefore, Christian believers can commit to enduring to the end, knowing about God's glorious promises regarding future reward.

Chapter 8

The New Authority Structure in Christ

As we learned in Chapter 1, the whole creation is waiting for the revealing of the sons of God.

Romans 8:19-22

[19]For the creation waits with eager longing for the revealing of the sons of God.

[20]For the creation was subjected to futility, not willingly, but because of him who subjected it, in hope

[21]that the creation itself will be set free from its bondage to corruption and obtain the freedom of the glory of the children of God.

[22]For we know that the whole creation has been groaning together in the pains of childbirth until now.

The whole creation, which includes angels, was subject to futility and the bondage of corruption. What caused all creation to be put into such bondage? How is God going to bring about deliverance from this bondage?

Most Christians are familiar with the fall of man recorded in Genesis 3. When Adam sinned in the Garden, his action caused devastation to the order God set up for man on the earth. Man was to have dominion over everything, replenish the earth and bring everything into subjection. But by disobeying God's command, Adam disrupted the relationship between God and man and brought about calamity upon the earth.

While many understand the effects of the fall of man, there is another fall that has had even more cataclysmic effects.

Isaiah 14:12-15

[12]"How you are fallen from heaven, O Day Star, son of Dawn! How you are cut down to the ground, you who laid the nations low!

[13]You said in your heart, 'I will ascend to heaven; above the stars of God I will set my throne on high; I will sit on the mount of assembly in the far reaches of the north;

[14]I will ascend above the heights of the clouds; I will make myself like the Most High.'

[15]But you are brought down to Sheol, to the far reaches of the pit.

The "Day Star" in verse 12 is rendered "Lucifer" in the King James Version. [119] This same entity is also called "Satan" and the "devil" in God's Word. He attempted to usurp God's position but instead is said to have "fallen from heaven."

This same being is spoken of in a record in the book of Ezekiel:

Ezekiel 28:12-17

[12]"Son of man, raise a lamentation over the king of Tyre, and say to him, Thus says the Lord God: "You were the signet of perfection, full of wisdom and perfect in beauty.

[13]You were in Eden, the garden of God; every precious stone was your covering, sardius, topaz, and diamond, beryl, onyx, and jasper, sapphire, emerald, and carbuncle; and crafted in gold were your settings and your engravings. On the day that you were created they were prepared.

---

[119] A more thorough study of the fall of Lucifer, along with a biblical survey of his kingdom, are beyond the scope of this book. Most biblical scholars concur that the record in Isaiah 14 and the following record in Ezekiel 28 both indirectly refer to the one who is called the serpent, Satan, and the devil. For the purposes of our study, we are only noting his fall from heaven. For more understanding of the devil and his kingdom, the reader is referred to other sources such as Appendix 19, "The Serpent of Genesis 3," in *The Companion Bible*.

¹⁴You were an anointed guardian cherub. I placed you; you were on the holy mountain of God; in the midst of the stones of fire you walked.

¹⁵You were blameless in your ways from the day you were created, till unrighteousness was found in you.

¹⁶In the abundance of your trade you were filled with violence in your midst, and you sinned; so I cast you as a profane thing from the mountain of God, and I destroyed you, O guardian cherub, from the midst of the stones of fire.

¹⁷Your heart was proud because of your beauty; you corrupted your wisdom for the sake of your splendor. I cast you to the ground; I exposed you before kings, to feast their eyes on you.

This record from Ezekiel starts by addressing the king of Tyre, but it is also referring to the power behind the king's throne. It speaks of a supernatural spiritual being awesome in his power, "the anointed guardian cherub" (v. 14). This anointed cherub was in God's holy mountain, meaning heaven, and he was blameless until unrighteousness was found in him. Then, he sinned (v. 16) and was cast out of the mountain of God. This anointed cherub who sinned is God's arch enemy, the devil. Carefully note that this sin took place in *heaven*.

In 2 Peter 2:4 we read, that "God did not spare angels when they sinned but cast them into hell and committed them to chains of gloomy darkness to be kept until the judgment." Some of these angels also sinned along with Lucifer in heaven, resulting in their imprisonment. This sin of both Lucifer and some of the angels caused defilement in heaven.

What was God's plan to cleanse this defilement? To answer this, we turn to the book of Hebrews.

Hebrews 9:22-24

²²Indeed, under the law almost everything is purified with blood, and without the shedding of blood there is no forgiveness of sins.

[23]Thus it was necessary for the copies of the heavenly things to be purified with these rites, but the heavenly things themselves with better sacrifices than these. [24]For Christ has entered, not into holy places [the most holy place] made with hands, which are copies of the true things, but into heaven itself, now to appear in the presence of God on our behalf.

When the high priest entered the most holy place, he sprinkled the mercy seat and other things therein with blood to purify them. While the earthly things were purified with the blood of animals, the heavenly things required a better sacrifice. The "better sacrifices" (v. 23) is a figurative way of speaking of the one great sacrifice of Jesus Christ himself. This infinitely better sacrifice was necessary to purify the things in heaven.

The devil's sin and fall preceded Adam's sin and fall.[120] While Adam's sin took place on earth, Lucifer's sin occurred in heaven. Lucifer's rebellion in heaven and Adam's disobedience on earth brought about cataclysmic changes to God's creation. Their rebellions brought about disorder in both realms. How would God deal with the state of rebellion that existed in heaven and earth? CHRIST!

Headed up in Christ

When Jesus Christ was carrying out his earthly ministry, he declared that all he had to do was appeal to the Father, and God would send more than twelve legions of angels to assist him (Matt. 26:53). But after his resurrection, Jesus Christ said that all authority in heaven and earth had been given to him (Matt. 28:18). After the ascension, Christ went into heaven and is at God's right hand, with angels, authorities, and powers having been subjected to him (1 Pet. 3:22). In Ephesians, we read more about Christ's singular position as head over all.

---

[120] We know this because by the time the devil is addressed in Genesis 3, he is called "the serpent." Rev. 12:9 and 20:2 tell us that this serpent is the devil also called Satan. Before his fall, he was called the "Day Star" (Is. 14:12).

Ephesians 1:7-10

[7]In him [Christ] we have redemption through his blood, the forgiveness of our trespasses, according to the riches of his grace,

[8]which he lavished upon us, in all wisdom and insight [9]making known to us the mystery of his will, according to his purpose, which he set forth in Christ

[10]as a plan for the fullness of time, to unite all things in him, things in heaven and things on earth.

Note how other versions render verses 9 and 10:

Ephesians 1:9-10 (NASB95)

[9]He made known to us the mystery of His will, according to His kind intention which He purposed in Him

[10]with a view to an **administration** suitable to the fullness of the times, that is, the summing up of all things in Christ, things in the heavens and things on the earth.

Ephesians 1:9-10 (WT)

[9] He has made known to us the mystery of His will in accordance with His good pleasure, which He Himself purposed in him [*Christ*],

[10] so that in the **administration** of the fullness of the times He might bring all things together under one head in the Christ, *that is*, the things in heaven and the things upon the earth in him [*the Christ*].

The word "administration" in verse 10 means "the management of household affairs, stewardship."[121] God has a purpose in Christ for the "fullness of time," meaning the future. God's will is to have Christ as "head manager," so to speak, of both the heavens and the earth. All things on earth and in heaven are to be headed up in Christ.

---

[121] Strong, *The New Strong's Expanded*, s.v. "*oikonomia*."

In the Garden, Adam had dominion over the earth; but after his fall, that dominion was transferred to Satan, the devil.[122] But in the ages to come, Christ will have headship over all things in heaven and earth. Though we read earlier that Jesus Christ has already been given all authority in heaven and earth, the process is ongoing. It will not be completed until the "fullness of times" when God's purpose is fully and finally realized.

Let's return to Ephesians chapter 1.

Ephesians 1:16-23

[16]I do not cease to give thanks for you, remembering you in my prayers,

[17]that the God of our Lord Jesus Christ, the Father of glory, may give you the Spirit of wisdom and of revelation in the knowledge of him,

[18]having the eyes of your hearts enlightened, that you may know what is the hope to which he has called you, what are the riches of his glorious inheritance in the saints,

[19]and what is the immeasurable greatness of his power toward us who believe, according to the working of his great might

[20]that he worked in Christ when he raised him from the dead and seated him at his right hand in the heavenly places,

[21]far above all rule and authority and power and dominion, and above every name that is named, not only in this age but also in the one to come.

[22]And he put all things under his feet and gave him as head over all things to the church,

[23]which is his body, the fullness of him who fills all in all.

---

[122] When Jesus Christ was tempted by the devil, the devil offered him all the kingdoms of the world and their glory. In making this offer, the devil said, "to you I will give all this authority and their glory, for it has been delivered to me, and I give it to whom I will" (Luke 4:6).

Christ's position at God's right hand in the heavenlies is far above all "rule and authority and power and dominion and above every name that is named, not only in this age but also in the one to come" (v. 21). To go from the grave to God's right hand is quite an exaltation! Christ's highly elevated position is far above all exercised or conferred power, all celestial and earthly lordship, and above every name that is named. Except for God, Jesus Christ occupies the highest position possible. What's more, there are other positions of authority under Christ (rule, authority, power, dominion). Whatever these positions of authority might be, Jesus Christ is *far* above them all. In order to administer the heavens and earth with Christ as the head, a new authority structure was required.

A New Authority Structure in Christ

Colossians 1:13-18 describes the new arrangement with Christ as the head. To appreciate the significance of this new arrangement, we need to study this passage carefully. First, the pronouns "he" and "him" could refer to God or Jesus Christ. Based on the context and other passages, we have supplied the antecedent for each masculine pronoun to avoid confusion.

Colossians 1:13-20

¹³He [God] has delivered us from the domain of darkness and transferred us to the kingdom of his beloved Son,
¹⁴in whom [Christ] we have redemption, the forgiveness of sins.
¹⁵He [Christ] is the image of the invisible God, the firstborn of all **creation** (*ktsis*).
¹⁶For by him [Christ] all things were **created** (*ktizō*), in heaven and on earth, visible and invisible, whether thrones or dominions or rulers or authorities—all things were **created** (*ktizō*) through him [Christ] and for him [Christ].

[17]And he [Christ] is before all things, and in him [Christ] all things hold together.

[18]And he [Christ] is the head of the body, the church. He [Christ] is the beginning, the firstborn from the dead, that in everything he [Christ] might be preeminent.

[19]For in him [Christ] all the fullness of God was pleased to dwell,

[20]and through him [Christ] to reconcile to himself all things, whether on earth or in heaven, making peace by the blood of his [Christ's] cross.

In verse 13, we read that born again ones have been delivered out of the domain or authority of darkness and have been transferred to Christ's kingdom. The saints have been transferred from one authority structure to another.[123] Jesus Christ is referred to as "the firstborn of all creation" and "the beginning, the firstborn from the dead." In these verses, "firstborn" refers to Christ's resurrection from the dead, not his physical birth. Jesus Christ is the only man to have died and been raised to immortality, and it is in this regard that he is the "firstborn."

In verses 15 and 16, we see the words "creation" and "created." This does not refer to the creation record in Genesis 1 but to something new that has been created in Christ. Furthermore, the phrase "by him" in verse 16 should read "in him."[124] Note how the NIV renders this verse:

Colossians 1:16 (NIV)
For **in him** [Christ] all things were created: things in heaven and on earth, visible and invisible, whether thrones or powers or rulers or authorities; all things have been created through him and for him.

---

[123] While we have gone from the authority of darkness to the authority of Christ's kingdom, the physical transfer is still future. See 2 Pet. 1:11 for example.

[124] According to the Greek, the word "*en*" occurs in verse 16, which is normally translated "in."

In him, that is, in Christ, all things were "created." From the immediate context, we see that the phrase "all things" refers to thrones, powers, rulers, and authorities, words that signify exercised or conferred power. These are the new positions of authority created in Christ.

In the Greek New Testament, the word translated as "creation" (v. 15) is *ktisis*, and "created" (v. 16) is *ktizō*. Both are from the same root word, which means "to people a country, build houses and cities in it, hence, to found, set up, establish, produce, bring into being."[125] Note how *ktisis* is translated in the following verse:

1 Peter 2:13-14
[13]Be subject for the Lord's sake to every human **institution** (*ktisis*), whether it be to the emperor as supreme,
[14]or to governors as sent by him to punish those who do evil and to praise those who do good.

Most English Bibles translate *ktisis* (v. 13) as "institution." Peter encouraged the believers to submit themselves to every human institution, whether a supreme leader, like an emperor, or a lesser ranking official, like a governor. We see, then, that *ktisis* can mean an authority structure.

And so, when we read that in Christ, all things were created (*ktizō*) in heaven and earth, it refers to a newly created authority structure. One author explains it thus:

> The creation spoken of in Colossians chapter 1 is the creation of authority through God's only begotten Son.... It does not say that Christ created the heaven and the earth, but that all things in heaven and on earth were created in him.[126]

That is to say, the "all things created in him" refers to thrones, powers, rulers, authorities—a new authority structure. These newly created

---

125 Bullinger, *A Critical Lexicon*. s.v. "create."
126 Carden, *One God*, 155.

things are in heaven and on earth, with some visible and some invisible. For instance, one of the newly created authority structures in Christ on earth is the Church of the One Body, where Christ is the head. Christ has the right to delegate authority within the Church.

In Colossians 1:17, Christ is said to be "before all things." The word "before" can mean before in place, time, or superiority.[127] All of these apply to the headship of Jesus Christ. He is first in *place* because he is in a preeminent position at God's right hand. He is first in *time* because he is the firstborn from the dead. Jesus Christ is first in *superiority* because everything is subject to him. Is it any wonder that in verse 18, he is described as being "preeminent"?

> Jesus Christ is the first in *place*.
> Jesus Christ is the first in *time*.
> Jesus Christ is the first in *superiority*.

Note how other versions render verse 18:

Colossians 1:18 (NASB95)
He is also head of the body, the church; and He is the beginning, the firstborn from the dead, so that He Himself **will come to have first place** in everything.

Colossians 1:18 (Darby)
And he is the head of the body, the assembly; who is [the] beginning, firstborn from among the dead, that he might have the **first place** in all things:

Whatever this newly created authority structure in heaven and on earth involves, Christ will occupy first place, under God. From God's perspective, Christ has already been granted the highest position. However, because there are still things in heaven and earth that need to be brought into subjection to Christ, his premier position is described

---

[127] Bullinger, *A Critical Lexicon and Concordance*, s.v. "before."

as in the process of being fully realized. Perhaps David's example of being anointed as king serves as a parallel. He was anointed by Samuel when he was just a youth but didn't come into power until he was thirty years old. In other words, he had been given the position of the king but didn't execute his function until he was on the throne. In a similar manner, Christ has been given the preeminent position, but he is still waiting for his enemies to be made his footstool.[128]

Colossians 1:20 says, "and through him [Christ] to reconcile to himself all things, whether on earth or in heaven, making peace by the blood of his [Christ's] cross." This reconciliation of all things is in heaven and on earth. Recall that Satan and Adam's rebellions brought disorder to heaven and earth. Jesus Christ's obedience will bring about the reconciliation of things in both realms!

In sum, rather than referring to the Genesis 1 creation, the creation spoken of in Colossians 1:13-20 refers to the risen Christ and new authority structure that has been created *in him*.

Becoming Preeminent

We have seen that the saints have been transferred from the kingdom of darkness into Christ's kingdom and that there is a new authority structure in heaven and on earth in Christ. From God's perspective, Christ has already been granted the highest position. However, the process is ongoing, for not everything has been subjected to Christ, as we will see in this section. Let's begin with 1 Corinthians 15. In this passage, the pronouns "he" and "him" could refer either to God or Jesus Christ. Based on the context and other passages, we have supplied the antecedent for each masculine pronoun to avoid confusion.

1 Corinthians 15:24-28
[24]Then comes the end, when he [Christ] delivers the kingdom to God the Father after destroying every rule and every authority and power.

---

[128]   See for example Acts 2:34-35; Heb. 1:13, 10:12-13.

25For he [Christ] must reign until he [God] has put all his [Christ's] enemies under his [Christ's] feet.
26The last enemy to be destroyed is death.
27For "God has put all things in **subjection** under his [Christ's] feet." But when it says, "all things are put in **subjection**," it is plain that he [God] is excepted who put all things in **subjection** under him [Christ].
28When all things are **subjected** to him [Christ], then the Son himself will also be **subjected** to him [God] who put all things in **subjection** under him [Christ], that God may be all in all.

Note how the same root word "subject" is repeated six times in the space of two verses. This constitutes the figure *polyptoton* or the repetition of the same word in different inflections.[129] This figure emphasizes that all things are to be *subject* to Jesus Christ, with the sole exception of God Himself. God has given Jesus Christ this highly exalted position. He has been given all authority on earth and in heaven in this age *and* the age to come. The repetition of "subject" and "subjection" makes this truth most emphatic.

Verse 24 speaks about the destruction of every rule, every authority, and every power. From the context, we can understand that this does not mean the authorities that are already in subjection to Christ, nor to the new authority structure, but to his enemies on earth and in the heavenly places. Christ's enemies will be destroyed.

Moreover, the "end" referred to in verse 24 is still in the future. According to Revelation 11:15, 12:10, and other records, Jesus Christ's complete and total dominion will be fully realized in the future. Some things have already been put under subjection to him, but there are some things that God has yet to subdue under Christ.

In sum, we have seen that:

- Jesus Christ's reconciling work extends to both heaven and earth.
- In Christ, a new authority structure has been created.

---

129   Hans, *Go Figure!* 61.

- Jesus Christ has first place in this new authority structure.
- Jesus Christ's highly exalted position extends to things in heaven and on earth.
- Jesus Christ is *far* above all rule and authority.
- Jesus Christ is in the process of becoming preeminent in all things.
- All of Christ's enemies will be destroyed.
- Christ will deliver the kingdom to God so that God may be all in all.

Seated in the Heavenly Places

Let's next consider what the new authority structure created in Christ might mean for the Church. If you recall, Ephesians 1:20 stated that Christ is seated at God's right hand in the heavenly places. In biblical culture, to sit at someone's right hand signified a position of honor and authority, likely because the right hand was associated with a blessing.

What's more, in raising Christ from the dead and seating him at His own right hand, God exercised tremendous power described as the "immeasurable greatness of His power" (Eph. 1:19). This power is "toward us who believe." If we continue reading from Ephesians chapter 1 into chapter 2, we begin to see, at least in part, the far-reaching implications of this exercised power.

> **Ephesians 2:5-7**
> ⁵even when we were dead in our trespasses, made us alive together with Christ—by grace you have been saved—
> ⁶and raised us up with him and **seated us with** (*sunkathizō*) **him in the heavenly places** in Christ Jesus,
> ⁷so that in the coming ages he might show the immeasurable riches of his grace in kindness toward us in Christ Jesus.

Saved ones, who were once dead in trespasses and sins, are now *seated with Christ* in the heavenly places. How can the Church be seated in the heavenly places with Christ and yet still be on the earth? This seating together with Christ is a spiritual reality now but will be fully realized when Christ returns. Note some of the parallels between God's exercised power in Christ and toward the Church.

Christ	The Church, His Body
God's power worked in Christ.	God's power towards us who believe.
Raised from the dead.	Once dead in trespasses and sins but now raised with Christ.
Seated at God's right hand in the heavenly places, far above all.	Seated with Christ in the heavenly places.

In the Greek New Testament, the word translated as "seated with" (Eph. 2:6) is *sunkathizō*, a compound word from *sun*, meaning together, and *kathizō*, meaning to sit. While *kathizō* can mean to sit someplace physically, like sitting on the ground or on a chair, it often means to sit so as to carry out authority, judgment, or rulership. It indicates a purpose other than just resting. Here are a few examples: [130]

- Jesus Christ sat down (*kathizō*) to teach. (John 8:2)
- Pilate sat (*kathizō*) on his judgment seat to judge. (Matt. 27:19)
- James and John asked to be seated (*kathizō*) at the lord's left and right hand in his glory to rule. (Matt. 20:20-23)
- The scribes and the Pharisees sat (*kathizō*) on Moses' seat to exercise rule over the people. (Matt. 23:2)

While not every occurrence of *kathizō* in the Bible has this connotation, most do. So, when we read that the Church is "seated together" in the heavenly places in Christ, this implies that the Church is sitting in a place of honor, power, and authority.

---

[130] For a fuller explanation, see Appendix G: "A Study of *Kathizō* (Seated)."

What might this mean for the Church? Perhaps 1 Corinthians 6 gives us a glimpse:

1 Corinthians 6:2-3

²Or do you not know that the saints will judge the world? And if the world is to be judged by you, are you incompetent to try trivial cases?

³Do you not know that we are to judge angels? How much more, then, matters pertaining to this life!

The thought of the Church judging the world and angels is stunning. How is this possible? Because the saints are seated in the heavenly places with Christ. This spiritual blessing now will become an actuality in the age to come. Because Jesus Christ occupies the highest position of authority in the cosmos next to God and we are seated *with him*, the saints too will exercise authority, under Christ, in the coming age.

Does this mean that all saints will exercise the *same* authority or rulership? No, for we have seen that there are different ranks in the kingdom of God. Recall that there are "thrones, powers, rulers, and authorities," (Col. 1:16), which are words with different shades of meaning, suggesting varying degrees of rule. We also know that not everyone will receive the same reward and that not everyone will reign with Christ.

We see a similar arrangement in our American judicial system, where there is a Supreme Court, a Lower Court, and a District Court. All judges carry out judgment, but not all have the same degree of authority. As another example, Moses judged Israel, but he also delegated authority by appointing capable men over the Twelve Tribes by thousands, hundreds, fifties, and tens (Exod. 18:25-26). These men judged the affairs of Israel.[131] They all judged, but their conferred power differed in degree. This is true of all kingdoms, whether earthly or spiritual, and it is true of the new authority structure created in Christ.

---

[131] In the Hebrew culture, judging implied ruling also, not just merely judging between right and wrong. Consider the Judges of Israel, for instance, who not only judged matters within the Twelve Tribes but ruled as well.

Summary and Conclusion

In this chapter, we saw that the rebellions of Lucifer and Adam had consequences in heaven and earth. Their rebellions brought about serious upheaval to God's order, leaving all creation groaning and travailing in pain. God's work in Christ not only brought reconciliation to man on earth but also to things in heaven. God's will for the administration of the fullness of times is to put all things, in heaven and on earth, in subjection to Christ. The full and complete realization of this arrangement is still future.

We also learned that when the Scriptures describe Jesus Christ as "seated in the heavenly places," it refers to his singular honor, power, and authority, under God. Finally, we have seen that because the Church is seated together with Christ, the Church will share in Christ's authority, in a subject position. While we may not comprehend the full extent of the Church's role with Christ, just a glimpse is enough to give the saint a reason to stay faithful.

This new authority structure, created by God, realized in Christ, will bring restoration to God's creation on earth and in heaven. All enemies will be brought into subjection, causing rebellion to cease.

In Ephesians we read:

> **Ephesians 2:6-7**
> ⁶and raised us up with him and seated us with him in the heavenly places in Christ Jesus,
> ⁷**so that** in the coming ages he might show the immeasurable riches of his grace in kindness toward us in Christ Jesus.

God has exercised tremendous power towards Christ and the Church. And in the coming ages, He will reveal the immeasurable riches of His grace and kindness to us in Christ. By His grace, our heavenly Father has already richly blessed us in Christ, but there is so *much more* to come!

Chapter 9

Running the Race to the Finish

In his second epistle to the Thessalonians, Paul wrote:

2 Thessalonians 1:3-4
³We ought always to give thanks to God for you, brothers, as is right, because your faith is growing abundantly, and the love of every one of you for one another is increasing.
⁴Therefore we ourselves boast about you in the churches of God for your steadfastness and faith in all your persecutions and in the afflictions that you are enduring.

Paul boasted about the Thessalonians for their steadfastness, or patient endurance, and for their believing amidst severe trouble. The Thessalonians were exemplary in that they faced great adversity with steadfast believing. Rather than allow the circumstances to discourage them, they *grew* in their believing and love. To remain steadfast in believing may be easy when all is going well, when loving, supportive people surround us, and when circumstances are rosy. But what happens when we aren't supported or when circumstances are dire? What about in times of heartbreak or disillusionment? During such times, we may be tempted to quit "running the race," one of the metaphors used in the Scriptures to describe the Christian's life.

Running the Race

It is self-evident that if anyone runs in a race, they cannot hope to obtain any kind of prize without finishing. Quitting near the beginning, the middle, or even close to the end, means automatic disqualification. In several places in the Bible, the Christian's walk is compared to a race. Note this metaphor in the following verses:

1 Corinthians 9:24-27

[24]Do you not know that in a **race all the runners run**, but only one receives the prize? So **run** that you may obtain it.

[25]Every athlete exercises self-control in all things. They do it to receive a perishable wreath, but we an imperishable.

[26]So I do not **run** aimlessly; I do not box as one beating the air.

[27]But I discipline my body and keep it under control, lest after preaching to others I myself should be disqualified.

Paul is not speaking about running a literal race. He is using a metaphor to compare the Christian's life to running in a race.

In the book of Hebrews, we again see this metaphor.

Hebrews 12:1

Therefore, since we are surrounded by so great a cloud of witnesses, let us also lay aside every weight, and sin which clings so closely, and let us **run with endurance the race that is set before us**,

Runners in ancient times would ordinarily run naked so as not to be encumbered by any weight or entangled by any loose garments. Imagine running a race while wearing a heavy suit of armor or layers of flowing garments that could easily slip down around your ankles. One could hardly run a race with such impediments. Here, the saints are encouraged to lay aside anything that weighs down or entangles them (such as sin) so that they can run the race set before them with endurance.

The apostle Paul used the metaphor of running a race to describe his own life and ministry.

Acts 20:24

But I do not account my life of any value nor as precious to myself, if only I may finish my **course** (*dromos*) and the ministry that I received from the Lord Jesus, to testify to the Gospel of the grace of God.

In the Greek New Testament, the word translated as "course" is *dromos*, meaning a "running, course, career, or race."[132] This word is used two other times in the Greek New Testament.

2 Timothy 4:7

I have fought the good fight, I have finished the **race** (*dromos*), I have kept the faith.

Acts 13:25

And as John was finishing his **course** (*dromos*), he said, 'What do you suppose that I am? I am not he. No, but behold, after me one is coming, the sandals of whose feet I am not worthy to untie.'

In all three occurrences, *dromos* is used figuratively to signify one's course or course of life: specifically, John the Baptist's and Paul's office and ministries. When Paul spoke about finishing his course, he was addressing the Ephesian elders before taking his journey to Jerusalem, where he was eventually taken prisoner.[133] By this point in his ministry, all Asia had heard the Word of the Lord to the end that it prevailed (Acts 19:10, 20). This was not at the beginning of Paul's ministry but many years after he had received his commission from Jesus Christ.[134] Paul could have chosen to sit back and rest on his laurels. Instead, he wanted to *finish* his course and fulfill his commission. At the time of his

---

[132] Strong, *The New Strong's Expanded*, s.v. "*dromos.*"

[133] Even though the context of the record indicates that Paul was going to Jerusalem contrary to God's will, he was intent on fulfilling his ministry and finishing the race. See Acts 20:16-21:14.

[134] For more on this commission, see Acts 9:3-19.

speaking in Acts 20:24, Paul had run a successful race, but he wanted to keep running it to the finish.

Then, in Philippians, Paul again uses this metaphor to describe his life and ministry:

> **Philippians 3:12-14**
> [12]Not that I have already obtained this or am already perfect, but I **press on** (*diōkō*) to make it my own, because Christ Jesus has made me his own.
> [13]Brothers, I do not consider that I have made it my own. But one thing I do: forgetting what lies behind and straining forward to what lies ahead,
> [14]I **press on** (*diōkō*) toward the goal for the prize of the upward call of God in Christ Jesus.

In the Greek New Testament, the word translated as "press on" in verses 12 and 14 is *diōkō*, meaning "to run swiftly to catch some person or thing, to run after."[135] When Paul wrote the epistle to the Philippians, he was still actively running the race, still pursuing the prize. He did not say the prize was his yet. Paul wrote these verses while he was in prison after he had spoken to the Ephesian elders and after he had gone to Jerusalem. Yet, he was still pressing on and straining towards the end goal; he was still running the race.

Paul is near the end of his life when he wrote:

> **2 Timothy 4:6-8**
> [6]For I am already being poured out as a drink offering, and the time of my departure has come.
> [7]I have fought the good fight, I have **finished the race**, I have kept the faith.
> [8]Henceforth there is laid up for me the **crown** of righteousness, which the Lord, the righteous judge, will award to me on that day, and not only to me but also to all who have loved his appearing.

---

[135]   Thayer, *A Greek-English Lexicon*, s.v. "*diōkō*."

By this time in his life, Paul had finished the race; subsequently, the crown awaited him. Paul did not say that the crown was promised to him the moment he was born again. Instead, he wrote, by revelation, that the crown awaited him because he had finished his race. He had kept the faith.

Early in his life, Paul wrote that he was running the race and desired to finish the course. Later, he wrote that he was still running the race and was pressing on toward the prize. He had not yet obtained it. At the end of his life, he had finished the race set before him, and the crown awaited him.

> In Acts 20:24, Paul is running the race
> and desires to finish his course.
> In Philippians 3:14, Paul is running the race,
> pursuing the prize.
> In 2 Timothy 4:7, Paul has finished his race,
> and the crown awaits him.

The appeal to press on towards the prize, to finish the race, is given to all Christians. Let's return to Philippians 3:

Philippians 3:13-21

[13]Brothers, I do not consider that I have made it my own. But one thing I do: forgetting what lies behind and straining forward to what lies ahead,

[14]I press on toward the goal for the prize of the upward call of God in Christ Jesus.

[15]Let those of us who are mature think this way, and if in anything you think otherwise, God will reveal that also to you.

[16]Only let us hold true to what we have attained.

[17]Brothers, join in imitating me, and keep your eyes on those who walk according to the example you have in us.

[18]For many, of whom I have often told you and now tell you even with tears, walk as enemies of the cross of Christ.

[19]Their end is destruction, their god is their belly, and they glory in their shame, with minds set on earthly things.

[20]But our citizenship is in heaven, and from it we await a Savior, the Lord Jesus Christ,

[21]who will transform our lowly body to be like his glorious body, by the power that enables him even to subject all things to himself.

Here, Paul encouraged all who were mature to think as he did with regard to pressing on toward the prize. Paul urged the Philippians not to be like the "enemies of the cross of Christ" (v. 18) but to imitate him and to keep watching those who, like Paul, were examples of believing and faithfulness. The enemies fulfilled their own desires and focused on "earthly things" (v. 19). He reminded the Philippians that their citizenship was in heaven, not on earth and that they were waiting for Christ to return and give them new, glorious bodies. We see, then, that to "think this way" (v. 15) is to focus on eternal rather than temporal or earthly things. All Christians are exhorted to run the race set before them with a view to obtaining the prize, which is the crown.

Paul's endurance, his finishing the race, his completing the course and ministry given to him by Jesus Christ speaks volumes. Because of his faithful service, Paul was assured of receiving the crown. The Scriptures are clear that the crown is available to all sons of God, but like Paul, they must run the race *to the finish*. All Christians are not called to fulfill the ministry that Paul himself carried out, but all can serve. All are called to present their bodies as living sacrifices. All are urged to labor in the lord, and all have functions to fulfill.[136] All can be faithful. All can run the race to the finish to obtain the crown.

---

[136] See for example Rom. 12:1-8; 1 Cor. 4:1, 15:58.

Future Glory in View

As we know, Paul faced dangers, crises, pain, suffering, hardships, and other troubles as he preached the Gospel.[137] Frequent beatings, being shipwrecked three times, being in constant danger, facing much hardship—these are just some of the afflictions Paul faced as a servant of Christ. Note how he described one pressure situation:

2 Corinthians 1:8-10

[8]For we do not want you to be unaware, brothers, of the affliction we experienced in Asia. For we were so utterly burdened beyond our strength that we despaired of life itself.

[9]Indeed, we felt that we had received the sentence of death. But that was to make us rely not on ourselves but on God who raises the dead.

[10]He delivered us from such a deadly peril, and he will deliver us. On him we have set our hope that he will deliver us again.

The affliction he and his companions faced was utterly beyond their strength. It was so bad, they thought they might die. This was not some minor inconvenience or a bad day at the office. This affliction was life-threatening and seemingly impossible to bear. How did Paul endure despite these kinds of pressures? The following passage provides an answer.

2 Corinthians 4:8-18

[8]We are afflicted in every way, but not crushed; perplexed, but not driven to despair;

[9]persecuted, but not forsaken; struck down, but not destroyed;

[10]always carrying in the body the death of Jesus, so that the life of Jesus may also be manifested in our bodies.

---

[137] See for instance 2 Cor.11:23-28.

[11]For we who live are always being given over to death for Jesus' sake, so that the life of Jesus also may be manifested in our mortal flesh.

[12]So death is at work in us, but life in you.

[13]Since we have the same spirit of faith according to what has been written, "I believed, and so I spoke," we also believe, and so we also speak,

[14]knowing that he who raised the Lord Jesus will raise us also with Jesus and bring us with you into his presence.

[15]For it is all for your sake, so that as grace extends to more and more people it may increase thanksgiving, to the glory of God.

[16]So we do not lose heart. Though our outer self is wasting away, our inner self is being renewed day by day.

[17]For this light momentary affliction is preparing for us an eternal weight of glory beyond all comparison,

[18]as we look not to the things that are seen but to the things that are unseen. For the things that are seen are transient, but the things that are unseen are eternal.

They did not lose heart in the face of such distress because they knew Christ would return and they would be gathered together. Paul had his eyes set on future glory. He concluded that the future glory was so great, his affliction was light and momentary in comparison. To drive home this point, verses 17 and 18 contain a series of opposites:

Present Affliction	Future Glory
light	heavy beyond comparison
momentary	eternal
seen	unseen

The afflictions we experience in our lifetime, from disappointments to tragedy to heartbreaks, are real enough, but they are *light* compared to the weight of the glory that awaits us. They are also *momentary*, whereas our future glory as sons of God is eternal! For Paul and others, the coming glory was so extraordinary it was beyond any comparison to their current adversities. What was described earlier as something utterly beyond their strength—life threatening—was now relegated to the category of momentary and light, in view of future glory.

Let's consider some passages that will help us to begin to understand what this glory entails.

Romans 8:17-18

[17]and if children, then heirs—heirs of God and fellow heirs with Christ, provided we suffer with him in order that we may also be **glorified with him**.

[18]For I consider that the sufferings of this present time are not worth comparing with the **glory** that is to be revealed to us.

The Scriptures do not deny Christians' sufferings, nor how painful they might be. But the Scriptures make it plain that the sufferings of this present time are *not worth comparing* to future glory. "Glory" is a word that has many shades of meaning, encompassing such things as power, recognition, authority, and radiance. The basic definition of glory is light, brightness, splendor, and radiance from light. It can even refer to manifested power (John 2:11; Rom. 6:4). Glory can signify honor, praise, and acclaim.

Recall how when the devil tempted Jesus Christ in the wilderness, he offered him all the kingdoms of the world and their *glory* if Jesus would bow down and worship him (Matt. 4:8-9). Can you imagine what this would mean? Think of the adulation that takes place at a rock concert or the kind of prestige and power enjoyed by heads of state. Or think of the honor and praise given to Nobel prize winners, the tributes showered upon sports celebrities, or the thunderous applause given to stars of stage and screen. Then maybe add all that glory together, multiply it many times, and you might have an approximation of the recognition that was offered to Jesus Christ that day. The offer of all the world's glory was *not* trivial.

Yet Jesus Christ refused to bow down and worship Satan and rejected his offer of all the world's glory. Jesus Christ was only interested in the glory that comes from God.

John 5:41-44

[41]I do not receive **glory** from people.

[42]But I know that you do not have the love of God within you.

[43]I have come in my Father's name, and you do not receive me. If another comes in his own name, you will receive him.

[44]How can you believe, when you receive **glory** from one another and do not seek the **glory** that comes from the only God?

Jesus Christ categorically stated that he did not receive glory from people but God alone.

Further, 1 Peter 1:24 describes the fleeting nature of man's glory:

1 Peter 1:24

for "All flesh is like grass and all its glory like the flower of grass. The grass withers, and the flower falls,

Man's glory is like the flower of grass, which dries up and falls off the plant. It is short-lived. How often do we see a person reach the peak of earthly glory, only to fall into oblivion? They may even try to reclaim some of their former glory but fail miserably. There is a vast difference between man's glory and God's glory. The glory that comes from God is not momentary or fading but is eternal.

The Christian's hope is an expectation of future *glory*, but this is not the glory that comes from man. In one of his prayers, Jesus Christ said, "The glory that you have given me I have given to them, that they may be one even as we are one" (John 17:22). Whatever glory God gave to Jesus Christ, he wanted to share it with us, his followers. No wonder our hope is a hope of *glory*!

In Colossians, Paul writes again about this future glory:

Colossians 3:3-4
³For you have died, and your life is hidden with Christ in God.
⁴When Christ who is your life appears, then you also will appear with him in **glory**.

When we appear with Christ at his return, we won't appear with him in some dimly lit backwater; we will appear with him in *glory*.

George Mueller wrote, "The longer I live, the more I am enabled to realize that I have but one life to live on earth, and that this one life is but a brief life, for sowing, in comparison with eternity, for reaping."[138] Mueller's point is that in relation to eternity, this present life on earth is fleeting. If what we do in this lifetime determines, at least in part, what we enjoy for eternity in the ages to come, then it stands to reason that we should assess how we spend our limited time on this earth. We have written this book, *Christ Jesus our Hope*, to encourage the saints to live in light of this glorious Hope.

In the book of Hebrews, we read:

Hebrews 12:1-4
¹Therefore, since we are surrounded by so great a cloud of witnesses, let us also lay aside every weight, and sin which clings so closely, and let us run with endurance the race that is set before us,
²looking to Jesus, the founder and perfecter of our faith, who for the joy that was set before him endured the cross, despising the shame, and is seated at the right hand of the throne of God.

---

[138] Mueller, "George Mueller Quotes."

³Consider him who endured from sinners such hostility against himself, so that you may not grow weary or fainthearted.

⁴In your struggle against sin you have not yet resisted to the point of shedding your blood.

In running the race, we are to look to Jesus as the supreme example of enduring until the end. Indeed, he finished the course set before him (John 4:24; 17:4). Jesus Christ is set forth here as the example of someone who believed God all the way to the end—he is the "perfecter of faith." The word "looking" in verse 2 means "to turn the eyes away from other things and fix them on something."¹³⁹ We are not to focus on the circumstances (every weight and sin), but on him who endured.

Verse 2 tells us how he endured, despite the agony and shame of the cross and the hatred of sinners: it was because of the "joy that was set before him." In other words, Jesus Christ looked to future reward, future glory. Verse 3 tells us to "consider" him who endured. Considering requires more than a passing thought. If you carefully study the records of Jesus Christ after his betrayal and arrest leading to his crucifixion, you will see that he said very little, so much so that "Pilate was amazed."¹⁴⁰ Thus it is all the more enlightening to note what he *did* say when he spoke. He repeatedly foretold of his future glory. For example, when the high priest questioned him during his arrest, Jesus Christ said, "From now on you will see the Son of Man seated at the right hand of Power and coming on the clouds of heaven" (Matt. 26:64). The next day at his mock trial before the elders, chief priests and scribes he said, "From now on the Son of Man shall be seated at the right hand of the power of God" (Luke 22:69). Before Pilate, he declared "My kingdom is not of this world" (John 18:36). Jesus Christ had the joy of future glory set before his eyes.

While he was being unjustly tried and beaten, the promise of being seated at God's right hand was still future. While he was dying on the

---

¹³⁹ Thayer, *A Greek-English Lexicon*. s.v. "*aphoraō*"

¹⁴⁰ Various Scriptures note how little he spoke during his questioning by the chief priests and Pilate. See for example Matt. 26:62-63, 27:12-14; Mark 15:5; Luke 23:9.

tree, future glory was something intangible. How tempting it would have been to quit under such severe pressure. But Jesus Christ endured the pain, suffering, and shame by looking forward to the joy of his future glorification, which included being seated at the right hand of God! We are to look at and consider his example, so we do not grow weary and fainthearted. Our glory is still a future reality today, but it is as certain as the promises of God. With Christ as our example, we too can finish our race by looking forward to our future glory, which will be fully revealed when Christ returns.

The Scriptures encourage all saints to believe God's Word, to live fruitful Christian lives, and to serve and love God. This is what it means to run the race to the finish. In the ancient Games, no matter how skilled, an athlete would not receive the crown unless he *finished the race*. It wasn't enough to compete hard and then quit. He had to *finish* the race in order to win the prize.

Summary and Conclusion

In the opening chapter of this book, we saw that Jesus Christ has always been the hope for humanity. Old Testament believers like Moses and Abraham made life-altering decisions because of the knowledge of Christ's first coming. Having recognized the impact of Christ's first coming, we next studied the return of Christ for the Church. We saw how the Gathering Together is the triggering event that sets into motion all the events of the future ages. Following that, we learned that our inheritance is sure, imperishable, undefiled, and unfading and that God is the One Who made us adequate to receive this inheritance. This inheritance brings us into the very presence of God. With this essential background, we then studied what the Scriptures say about the Christian's reward. We learned that each person will receive his own reward according to his own work or labor, and labor in the lord is not in vain. To address the concern some may have, we delved into how the truth of future reward does not repudiate God's grace but magnifies it. Next, we learned about the prize, which is the crown. We saw that the crown is a specific type of reward available to all Christian believers who fulfill the criteria outlined in the Scriptures. Moving on, we considered some truths regarding the nature of future reward, which includes having positions of authority and responsibility in Christ's kingdom. We learned that the path to exaltation is humility and service, with Christ being the supreme example. We also considered Christ's exaltation, where he is to be head over all things in heaven and on earth. This led to an examination of the new authority structure that has been created in Christ and the Church's heavenly seating in Christ. We then discussed what it meant to run the race to the finish. We learned that the glory that awaits the Church is so spectacular, the afflictions and pains of this life, no matter how severe, can't be compared to it.

All sons of God have been raised with Christ to a new life and all are encouraged to set their thinking heavenward:

Colossians 3:1-4
[1]If then you have been raised with Christ, seek the things that are above, where Christ is, seated at the right hand of God.
[2]Set your minds on things that are above, not on things that are on earth.
[3]For you have died, and your life is hidden with Christ in God.
[4]When Christ who is your life appears, then you also will appear with him in glory.

Christ Jesus is our life and our hope. One day, we will appear with him in glory. There may be heartaches, there may be disappointments, and there may be trials along the way, but one glimpse of him in glory will the toils of life repay. With our eyes on Christ, we can run the race with patience, keeping our hearts and minds on things above. Like Paul, we can choose to fight the good fight of believing, finish the course, and love his appearing. May it be soon!

Appendix A

The Day of the Lord

In chapter 2, we briefly considered the Day of the Lord in relation to the coming of Christ for the Church. From the records in 1 and 2 Thessalonians, we learned that the Day of the Lord could not come until the Church had first departed. Therefore, the gathering together of the Church *precedes* the Day of the Lord.

Despite the clarity of the Scriptures, there remains much confusion about Christ's coming *for* the Church and Christ's coming later during the Day of the Lord. In order to clear up some of this confusion and better understand some aspects of the Day of the Lord, we have written this appendix. This topic could fill a book, so please note that our examination here is only introductory. There are many more passages that we do not cover. In this appendix, we will first discuss some of the characteristics of the Day of the Lord, and then we move on to a study of the wrath of God, which is associated with the Day of the Lord. We conclude with a brief examination of Matthew 24 and 25.

Some may ask, "If the Day of the Lord occurs after the Gathering Together, why should we bother to study it at all?" Understanding basic truths regarding the Day of the Lord helps avoid confusion and the potential misinterpretation of the Scriptures. In Paul's time, the Day of the Lord was used to shake up and alarm the Thessalonian saints, even as it is used to confuse and frighten people today. Thus, a good Scriptural understanding of the Day of the Lord is important so that we are not deceived by false teachers. Even today, many believe that the saints will have to go through the Great Tribulation, and some insist that we are going through it now. Part of this confusion has been caused by mixing up Jesus Christ's coming for the Church with his coming during the Day of the Lord.

Characteristics of the Day of the Lord

1 Thessalonians 5:2-3

²For you yourselves are fully aware that the day of the Lord will come like a thief in the night.

³While people are saying, "There is peace and security," then sudden destruction will come upon them as labor pains come upon a pregnant woman, and they will not escape.

Verse 2 compares the coming of the Day of the Lord to the coming of a thief in the night. As we know, a thief does not announce his intentions before coming to steal. Instead, he comes suddenly under cover of darkness without being expected. This is a key characteristic of the Day of the Lord—it comes without warning.

Perhaps you have heard people say that the signs of our times indicate that the Day of the Lord is near. Some have suggested that they can tell from world events that the Day of the Lord is close at hand. From the confidence with which these theories are propounded, one would think the Day of the Lord is not coming as a thief in the night but as a marching band in a parade. However, the Scriptures are unambiguous that the Day of the Lord will come like a thief in the night. It will be sudden, without warning.

This truth is reiterated in Peter's second epistle:

2 Peter 3:10

But the day of the Lord will come like a thief, and then the heavens will pass away with a roar, and the heavenly bodies will be burned up and dissolved, and the earth and the works that are done on it will be exposed.

The Day of the Lord will come like a thief (unannounced and sudden), and cataclysmic events will take place. The Day of the Lord is *not a single day* but covers a period of time. Many things occur during this period that affect both the heavens and earth. This will become evident as we consider more records about the Day of the Lord.

The Scriptures reveal one of the central purposes of the Day of the Lord:

Isaiah 2:11-22

[11]The **haughty** looks of man shall be brought low, and the **lofty pride** of men shall be humbled, and the LORD alone will be exalted in that day.

[12]For the LORD of hosts has a day against all that is **proud** and **lofty**, against all that is **lifted up**—and it shall be brought low;

[13]against all the cedars of Lebanon, **lofty and lifted up**; and against all the oaks of Bashan;

[14]against all the **lofty** mountains, and against all the **uplifted** hills;

[15]against every **high** tower, and against every fortified wall;

[16]against all the ships of Tarshish, and against all the beautiful craft.

[17]And the **haughtiness** of man shall be humbled, and **the lofty pride** of men shall be brought low, and the LORD alone will be exalted in that day.

[18]And the idols shall utterly pass away.

[19]And people shall enter the caves of the rocks and the holes of the ground, from before the terror of the LORD, and from the splendor of his majesty, when he rises to terrify the earth.

[20]In that day mankind will cast away their idols of silver and their idols of gold, which they made for themselves to worship, to the moles and to the bats,

[21]to enter the caverns of the rocks and the clefts of the cliffs, from before the terror of the LORD, and from the splendor of his majesty, when he rises to terrify the earth.

229

²²Stop regarding man in whose nostrils is breath, for of what account is he?

Verses 11 to 17 have an astonishing amount of repetition, where synonyms for pride occur: "haughty," "high," "lifted up," "haughtiness," "lofty," and so forth. Further, verses 11 and 17 are nearly identical in wording:

- Verse 11: "The haughty looks of man shall be brought low, and the lofty pride of men shall be humbled, and the LORD alone will be exalted in that day."
- Verse 17: "And the haughtiness of man shall be humbled, and the lofty pride of men shall be brought low, and the LORD alone will be exalted in that day."

This repetition is like a refrain in a song, where a key line is repeated for emphasis. This passage's unusual amount of repetition dramatically underscores the truth that the Day of the Lord is a time when man's pride and all that is lofty will be humbled. Man's haughty ways will be utterly shattered, and the Lord alone will be exalted.

Then in verses 19 to 21, we learn that the Day of the Lord is on the earth and that it involves God's rising to "terrify the earth." The book of Isaiah speaks of the vision Isaiah saw concerning Judah and Jerusalem (see Isa. 1:1, 2:1), but Judah and Jerusalem will not be the only ones affected by the Day of the Lord. The Day of the Lord will impact *the whole earth*. What's more, idols will be utterly abolished (vv. 18-20). It is a time when people will cast their idols aside and try to hide for fear of the Lord and the splendor of His majesty. The Day of the Lord is a fearsome time that will destroy all that is prideful and haughty.

So far, we have seen the following characteristics of the Day of the Lord:

- It will come suddenly, without warning.
- The pride of man will be made low.
- It will affect the whole earth.

- Idols shall utterly pass away.
- Man will hide for fear.
- God alone will be exalted.

Let's read another record about the Day of the Lord.

Isaiah 13:6-20

⁶Wail, for the day of the LORD is near; as destruction from the Almighty it will come!

⁷Therefore all hands will be feeble, and every human heart will melt.

⁸They will be dismayed: pangs and agony will seize them; they will be in anguish like a woman in labor. They will look aghast at one another; their faces will be aflame.

⁹Behold, the day of the LORD comes, cruel, with wrath and fierce anger, to make the land a desolation and to destroy its sinners from it.

¹⁰For the stars of the heavens and their constellations will not give their light; the sun will be dark at its rising, and the moon will not shed its light.

¹¹I will punish the world for its evil, and the wicked for their iniquity; I will put an end to the pomp of the arrogant, and lay low the pompous pride of the ruthless.

¹²I will make people more rare than fine gold, and mankind than the gold of Ophir.

¹³Therefore I will make the heavens tremble, and the earth will be shaken out of its place, at the wrath of the LORD of hosts in the day of his fierce anger.

¹⁴And like a hunted gazelle, or like sheep with none to gather them, each will turn to his own people, and each will flee to his own land.

¹⁵Whoever is found will be thrust through, and whoever is caught will fall by the sword.

¹⁶Their infants will be dashed in pieces before their eyes; their houses will be plundered and their wives ravished. ¹⁷Behold, I am stirring up the Medes against them, who have no regard for silver and do not delight in gold. ¹⁸Their bows will slaughter the young men; they will have no mercy on the fruit of the womb; their eyes will not pity children. ¹⁹And Babylon, the glory of kingdoms, the splendor and pomp of the Chaldeans, will be like Sodom and Gomorrah when God overthrew them. ²⁰It will never be inhabited or lived in for all generations; no Arab will pitch his tent there; no shepherds will make their flocks lie down there.

Even though this was written long before Christ's first coming, the Day of the Lord was spoken of as being near (v. 6).[141] We know that the Day of the Lord has not come because the Church has not departed, so how is it "near"? This is an idiom used to give a sense of time from God's perspective to whom a thousand years is as one day and one day as a thousand years (2 Pet. 3:8). Though it may not be literally near in terms of years and centuries, it is near from God's perspective.[142]

This record reveals once more that the Day of the Lord is not a desirable time for those caught by it. It comes as "destruction from the Almighty." There are references to people's hands being feeble, hearts melting, and people being dismayed and in pain. People will have agony

---

[141] There are several references in the Old Testament that indicate the Day of the Lord is at hand, meaning near: Isa. 13:6; Joel 1:15, 2:1; Zeph. 1:7, 14.

[142] When God speaks of a definite period of time, we can be assured that He is exact. For example, when He spoke of Jesus Christ being in the heart of the earth for three days and three nights, we can be assured that it was three days and three nights. However, when God speaks of time in a relative manner; that is, being "near" or "a little while," we dare not take our own definitions and apply them to God's Word. The Day of the Lord was future at the time of the writing of the book of Isaiah, it was future at the time of Christ, it was future when the epistles to the Thessalonians were written, and it is future today. What God calls "near" from His perspective may span thousands of years from man's perspective.

like a woman going into labor. The Day of the Lord comes "cruel with wrath and fierce anger, to make the land a desolation." God, by Isaiah, makes the purpose of the Day of the Lord clear: "I will punish the world for its evil, and the wicked for their iniquity; I will put an end to the pomp of the arrogant, and lay low the pompous pride of the ruthless."

What's more, there are references to cataclysmic events such as the stars and the constellations not giving light, the sun being dark, the moon not shining, the heavens being shaken, and the earth being moved out of its place. During this time, there will be so much destruction man will be "more rare than fine gold." Gold is precious or costly because of its rarity, so the implication is that few people will survive.

Significantly, we read about the "wrath of the LORD of hosts" and the "day of his fierce anger." A key characteristic of the Day of the Lord is that it is associated with the wrath of God, directed towards all that is prideful, evil, and wicked.

From this passage, we see the following characteristics of the Day of the Lord:

- It comes with destruction from the Almighty.
- It brings fear, anguish, pain, and agony to those present.
- It comes with God's wrath and fierce anger against all who are prideful, arrogant, evil, wicked, and ruthless.
- It is accompanied by cataclysmic celestial events, such as the stars and moon not giving light.
- Few people will survive.

Isaiah was not the only prophet to write about the Day of the Lord. The prophet Joel also spoke quite vividly about this day.

Joel 2:1-11
¹Blow a trumpet in Zion; sound an alarm on my holy mountain! Let all the inhabitants of the land tremble, for the day of the LORD is coming; it is near,
²a day of darkness and gloom, a day of clouds and thick darkness! Like blackness there is spread upon the

mountains a great and powerful people; their like has never been before, nor will be again after them through the years of all generations.

[3]Fire devours before them, and behind them a flame burns. The land is like the garden of Eden before them, but behind them a desolate wilderness, and nothing escapes them.

[4]Their appearance is like the appearance of horses, and like war horses they run.

[5]As with the rumbling of chariots, they leap on the tops of the mountains, like the crackling of a flame of fire devouring the stubble, like a powerful army drawn up for battle.

[6]Before them peoples are in anguish; all faces grow pale.

[7]Like warriors they charge; like soldiers they scale the wall. They march each on his way; they do not swerve from their paths.

[8]They do not jostle one another; each marches in his path; they burst through the weapons and are not halted.

[9]They leap upon the city, they run upon the walls, they climb up into the houses, they enter through the windows like a thief.

[10]The earth quakes before them; the heavens tremble. The sun and the moon are darkened, and the stars withdraw their shining.

[11]The LORD utters his voice before his army, for his camp is exceedingly great; he who executes his word is powerful. For the day of the LORD is great and very awesome; who can endure it?

In this passage, the Lord's army is described as a fearsome, consuming force during the Day of the Lord. They spread so thickly on the mountains that the mountains look black. What a picture! Before them is a lush land like the Garden of Eden, and behind them is scorched earth. Before them and behind them is a consuming fire. The Lord's army is compared to a powerful force that is drawn for battle: they charge forward and scale up the walls without ever breaking rank.[143] In their presence, the earth quakes, the heavens tremble, the sun and moon are darkened, and the stars no longer shine. The Day of the Lord is described in such shocking and frightful terms.

Later in Joel, we read more references to the Day of the Lord.

Joel 3:13-16

[13]Put in the sickle, for the harvest is ripe. Go in, tread, for the winepress is full. The vats overflow, for their evil is great.

[14]Multitudes, multitudes, in the valley of decision! For the day of the LORD is near in the valley of decision.

[15]The sun and the moon are darkened, and the stars withdraw their shining.

[16]The LORD roars from Zion, and utters his voice from Jerusalem, and the heavens and the earth quake. But the LORD is a refuge to his people, a stronghold to the people of Israel.

The darkening of the sun, moon, and stars is described in many records that speak of the Day of the Lord.[144] However, verse 16 mentions a different aspect: "But the LORD is a refuge to his people, a stronghold to the people of Israel." Many records in the Old Testament, the Gospels, and the New Testament attest to God's particular dealings with Israel during the Day of the Lord. Some of these records speak of the gathering of the children of Israel back to the land of Israel, the city of Jerusalem becoming the focal point of all the earth, and the reign of the Messiah, Jesus Christ, on the earth. We won't look at this aspect of

---

[143] Several English Bibles, like the NKJV, translate verse 7, "They run like mighty men, they climb the wall like men of war; Everyone marches in formation, And they do not break ranks."

[144] See for example, Isaiah 13:6-13; Jer. 4:23-28; Joel 2:1-3, 10-11, 30-32, 3:14-16; Amos 5:18-20, 8:9; Matt. 24:29; Mark 13:24; Luke 21:25; Acts 2:16-21; Rev. 6:12-17.

the Day of the Lord in detail, but for now, let's note that the Lord is a refuge to His people during the Day of the Lord.

The prophet Amos also spoke of the Day of the Lord:

Amos 5:18-20

¹⁸Woe to you who desire the day of the LORD! Why would you have the day of the LORD? It is darkness, and not light,

¹⁹as if a man fled from a lion, and a bear met him, or went into the house and leaned his hand against the wall, and a serpent bit him.

²⁰Is not the day of the LORD darkness, and not light, and gloom with no brightness in it?

The illustration in verse 19 speaks of how inescapable the Day of the Lord will be. A person may escape from a lion only to be met by a bear. Or he goes into his house to lean on the wall and is bitten by a serpent! This is a dramatic description of the inescapability of that time.

Zephaniah also prophesied about the Day of the Lord:

Zephaniah 1:14-18

¹⁴The great day of the LORD is near, near and hastening fast; the sound of the day of the LORD is bitter; the mighty man cries aloud there.

¹⁵A day of wrath is that day, a day of distress and anguish, a day of ruin and devastation, a day of darkness and gloom, a day of clouds and thick darkness,

¹⁶a day of trumpet blast and battle cry against the fortified cities and against the lofty battlements.

¹⁷I will bring distress on mankind, so that they shall walk like the blind, because they have sinned against the LORD; their blood shall be poured out like dust, and their flesh like dung.

¹⁸Neither their silver nor their gold shall be able to deliver them on the day of the wrath of the LORD. In the

fire of his jealousy, all the earth shall be consumed; for a full and sudden end he will make of all the inhabitants of the earth.

Zephaniah describes some aspects of the Day of the Lord that we have seen in other records: there is distress and anguish, ruin and devastation, darkness and gloom, clouds and thick darkness, trumpet blasts and battle cries, and the wrath of God. Notice how the Day of the Lord affects the whole earth.

The emphasis on God's wrath or anger during the Day of the Lord is repeated in chapter 2 of Zephaniah.

Zephaniah 2:1-3
¹Gather together, yes, gather, O shameless nation,
²before the decree takes effect —before the day passes away like chaff— before there comes upon you the burning anger of the LORD, before there comes upon you the day of the anger of the LORD.
³Seek the LORD, all you humble of the land, who do his just commands; seek righteousness; seek humility; perhaps you may be hidden on the day of the anger of the LORD.

The Day of the Lord is also called "the day of the anger of the Lord." Is there any doubt that the Lord's anger comes during the Day of the Lord?

Many other records in the Old Testament speak of the Day of the Lord, and the reader is encouraged to search the Scriptures on this topic. The passages covered in this section are given to provide the reader with an introduction to the topic and some key characteristics of the Day of the Lord.

Having read some Old Testament records that speak of the Day of the Lord, let's return to a passage in 1 Thessalonians 5 that we looked at earlier.

1 Thessalonians 5:1-5
¹Now concerning the times and the seasons, brothers, you have no need to have anything written to you.

> [2]For you yourselves are fully aware that the day of the Lord will come like a thief in the night.
> [3]While people are saying, "There is peace and security," then sudden destruction will come upon them as labor pains come upon a pregnant woman, and they will not escape.
> [4]But you are not in darkness, brothers, for that day to surprise you like a thief.
> [5]For you are all children of light, children of the day. We are not of the night or of the darkness.

Recall that the Day of the Lord comes as a thief in the night, meaning suddenly and by surprise. People will think everything is just fine, but then there will be sudden destruction. From the Old Testament records we read, we know how severe and inescapable this destruction will be. However, remember that the gathering together of the Church occurs before the Day of the Lord and that Christian believers will not be subjected to the death and destruction that accompanies that Day. We can now better appreciate why the Thessalonian saints did not need to be told about the times and seasons. They had been instructed that they would not be part of that Day. They were saved from the wrath which accompanies the Day of the Lord:

1 Thessalonians 5:9-11
[9]For God has not destined us for wrath, but to obtain salvation through our Lord Jesus Christ,
[10]who died for us so that whether we are awake or asleep we might live with him.
[11]Therefore encourage one another and build one another up, just as you are doing.

Instead of fearing that that day would come upon them, they could take comfort in and encouragement from knowing they were saved from this wrath and that they would be gathered together before the events of the Day of the Lord started to unfold.

The Day of the Lord is also spoken of in 2 Thessalonians 2:

2 Thessalonians 2:1-3

[1]Now concerning the coming of our Lord Jesus Christ and our being gathered together to him, we ask you, brothers, [2]not to be quickly shaken in mind or alarmed, either by a spirit or a spoken word, or a letter seeming to be from us, to the effect that the day of the Lord has come. [3]Let no one deceive you in any way. For that day will not come, unless the rebellion comes first, and the man of lawlessness is revealed, the son of destruction,

In chapter 2, we discussed this record in detail, so we won't take the time to reiterate our findings now. But having studied the frightful events that accompany the Day of the Lord, we can appreciate why the Thessalonian believers could have easily been "shaken in mind or alarmed." Someone had falsely taught them that the Day of the Lord had come. Knowing all they did about the fearsome Day of the Lord, no wonder the Thessalonians were shaken up!

To close this section, let's return to Peter's second epistle.

2 Peter 3:7-10

[7]But by the same word the heavens and earth that now exist are stored up for fire, being kept until the day of judgment and destruction of the ungodly. [8]But do not overlook this one fact, beloved, that with the Lord one day is as a thousand years, and a thousand years as one day. [9]The Lord is not slow to fulfill his promise as some count slowness, but is patient toward you, not wishing that any should perish, but that all should reach repentance. [10]But the day of the Lord will come like a thief, and then the heavens will pass away with a roar, and the heavenly bodies will be burned up and dissolved, and the earth and the works that are done on it will be exposed.

The Day of the Lord has been "near" and "at hand" for thousands of years, and we have already discussed God's reckoning of time and how it differs from man's. It's important to remember, therefore, that "The Lord is not slow to fulfill his promise" (v. 9). Just because it has not come to pass does not mean God is failing to uphold His promise. On the contrary, He has patiently waited because He is "not wishing that any should perish, but that all should reach repentance." No matter how long it takes for the Day of the Lord to come—one more day or one more century—we know that the Day of the Lord *will* come. God's anger and wrath will be against the prideful, the wicked, the evil, and the sinful. There will be cataclysmic events in the heavens so no one can miss their occurrence. The heavens will pass away with a roar, and the heavenly bodies will be burned up and dissolved. The earth and its works will be exposed. However, Christian believers can consider these events without fear because they have been delivered from the wrath to come, which is part of the Day of the Lord.

Summary:

- The Day of the Lord comes after the gathering together of the Church.
- Born-again ones are saved from the wrath to come, which takes place during the Day of the Lord.
- The Day of the Lord comes as a thief in the night, taking everyone by surprise. There are no signs to announce its coming.
- The Day of the Lord is against the pride and sin of man. It is a time when man's pride will be humbled, and the Lord alone will be exalted.
- The Day of the Lord is accompanied by many catastrophic events, destruction, and death.
- It is a Day when God will judge idolatry and destroy all idols.
- The Day of the Lord is not to be desired by anyone. It is inescapable for those overtaken by it.

- The Day of the Lord has been "at hand" or "near" for seemingly a long time. However, God's view of time is not the same as man's.
- The Day of the Lord is associated with the wrath of God.

The Wrath of God

In the previous section, we read that the wrath of God is associated with the Day of the Lord. In this section, we will present passages that speak about the wrath of God and its purposes, but the reader is asked to keep in mind that this is not a comprehensive study. Before delving into the Scriptures on this topic, it's essential to recall that Christians are saved from the wrath to come (Rom 5:9; 1 Thess. 1:10). The wrath of God during the Day of the Lord is not directed towards any Christian, for all Christians are saved from this future wrath.

God's Wrath

Before examining the topic of God's wrath during the Day of the Lord, we should first acknowledge God's tremendous loving and merciful nature. Indeed, the Bible is filled with declarations of how merciful, gracious, longsuffering, and slow to anger God is.

Exodus 34:6-7
⁶The LORD passed before him and proclaimed, "The LORD, the LORD, a God merciful and gracious, slow to anger, and abounding in steadfast love and faithfulness, ⁷keeping steadfast love for thousands, forgiving iniquity and transgression and sin, but who will by no means clear the guilty, visiting the iniquity of the fathers on the children and the children's children, to the third and the fourth generation."

Psalm 145:8
The LORD is gracious and merciful, slow to anger and abounding in steadfast love.

Psalm 30:5
For his anger is but for a moment, and his favor is for a lifetime. Weeping may tarry for the night, but joy comes with the morning.

God is not quick-tempered but very slow to become angry, and His anger lasts only for a moment, while His favor lasts for a lifetime. Therefore, to depict God as a vengeful, angry God without remembering His steadfast love, grace, and mercy is to distort the truth of the Scriptures concerning the nature of God. At the same time, to depict God as a loving, forgiving, compassionate God without acknowledging that He is justifiably angry at times or that there is a period in the future where God's wrath will be on full display is also to distort the truth of the Scriptures concerning the nature of God.

A record in Exodus provides important insight into the nature of God's wrath. In this passage, Moses had gone up to the mountain of God and was there for forty days. During that time, the children of Israel incited Aaron to make a golden calf to worship. Let's note what God said to Moses about this:

Exodus 32:7-10
7And the LORD said to Moses, "Go down, for your people, whom you brought up out of the land of Egypt, have corrupted themselves.
8They have turned aside quickly out of the way that I commanded them. They have made for themselves a golden calf and have worshiped it and sacrificed to it and said, 'These are your gods, O Israel, who brought you up out of the land of Egypt!' "
9And the LORD said to Moses, "I have seen this people, and behold, it is a stiff-necked people.

¹⁰Now therefore let me alone, that my wrath may burn hot against them and I may consume them, in order that I may make a great nation of you."

God called Israel a "stiff-necked people" and said He was ready to "consume them." God said to Moses that He wanted to be left alone so "that my wrath may burn hot against them." In other words, God wanted to let his wrath develop into a full burning rage against these idolatrous people. God's anger was directed not toward Moses but at the people who had made and worshipped the golden calf. Thus, we see God's wrath was justifiable, for it was in response to Israel's idolatry, a profound act of disobedience. We also see God's wrath was deliberate and under His command, not an emotional outburst like man's might be. God's wrath is under His control, and He could choose to let His anger "burn hot against them," or He could relent.

Let's continue with the record.

Exodus 32:11-14
¹¹But Moses implored the LORD his God and said, "O LORD, why does your wrath burn hot against your people, whom you have brought out of the land of Egypt with great power and with a mighty hand?
¹²Why should the Egyptians say, 'With evil intent did he bring them out, to kill them in the mountains and to consume them from the face of the earth'? Turn from your burning anger and relent from this disaster against your people.
¹³Remember Abraham, Isaac, and Israel, your servants, to whom you swore by your own self, and said to them, 'I will multiply your offspring as the stars of heaven, and all this land that I have promised I will give to your offspring, and they shall inherit it forever.' "
¹⁴And the LORD relented from the disaster that he had spoken of bringing on his people.

Moses interceded for the people, and God decided not to bring His wrath upon them. In this instance, Moses had to mediate for the people to stay God's wrath. Moses' intercession for Israel saved them from the utter destruction that would have indeed come to pass if God's anger had been given full sway. While this record does not speak of the wrath of God that takes place during the Day of the Lord, we can nonetheless appreciate that God's wrath is deliberate (He could let it burn hot or relent) and that it is in response to something, in this case, idolatry. When God's wrath is exercised, it is justified.

Let's reread a passage from Zephaniah that speaks of God's wrath during the Day of the Lord.

> **Zephaniah 1:14-18**
> [14]The great day of the LORD is near, near and hastening fast; the sound of the day of the LORD is bitter; the mighty man cries aloud there.
> [15]A day of wrath is that day, a day of distress and anguish, a day of ruin and devastation, a day of darkness and gloom, a day of clouds and thick darkness,
> [16]a day of trumpet blast and battle cry against the fortified cities and against the lofty battlements.
> [17]I will bring distress on mankind, so that they shall walk like the blind, because they have sinned against the LORD; their blood shall be poured out like dust, and their flesh like dung.
> [18]Neither their silver nor their gold shall be able to deliver them on the day of the wrath of the LORD. In the fire of his jealousy, all the earth shall be consumed; for a full and sudden end he will make of all the inhabitants of the earth.

Verse 15 tells us that the Day of the Lord is a day of wrath, meaning that this is a period characterized by God's wrath. During this time period, God's wrath will have its full sway. No wonder it is a day of ruin, darkness, and devastation. God's wrath is again compared to fire, a fire that is so powerful it will consume all the earth. Note also at whom this anger is directed: at the "mighty man," "the lofty battlements," and those who have "sinned against the Lord." Like many of the passages from Isaiah that speak about the Day of the Lord and the wrath of God, this passage also indicates that God's wrath is leveled at those who sin against Him and against those who are prideful and lofty.

Other records in the Scriptures speak of fire and judgment being part of God's wrath during the Day of the Lord. (In the Bible, fire is often associated with judgment.)[145]

Isaiah 66:13-16

[13]As one whom his mother comforts, so I will comfort you; you shall be comforted in Jerusalem.

[14]You shall see, and your heart shall rejoice; your bones shall flourish like the grass; and the hand of the LORD shall be known to his servants, and he shall show his indignation against his enemies.

[15]"For behold, the LORD will come in fire, and his chariots like the whirlwind, to render his anger in fury, and his rebuke with flames of fire.

[16]For by fire will the LORD enter into judgment, and by his sword, with all flesh; and those slain by the LORD shall be many.

This record, in part, deals with events that are still in the future and are part of the Day of the Lord. Note that once again, God's anger is directed toward His enemies. God's fury will come in flaming fire. This fire signifies God's judgment upon His enemies, as stated in verse 16.

While God is slow to anger, there is a time coming when God's wrath will be exhibited. God's anger is not an emotional outburst as it often is with a man but is in just response to things such as idolatry, sin, and wickedness. We have also seen that the Day of the Lord is a day of God's wrath and that His wrath is compared to an all-consuming fire.

---

[145] For example, see Isa. 4:4, 29:6, 66:16; Ezek. 28:18; Zech. 12:6; 1 Cor. 3:13, 15; Heb. 10:27.

The fire of God's wrath comes in judgment against the wicked, the prideful, and the sinful. God's wrath is just.

The Wrath of God in the Book of Romans

Having looked at key passages from the Old Testament about the Day of the Lord, we now turn to the book of Romans.

Romans 1:16-18

[16]For I am not ashamed of the gospel, for it is the power of God for salvation to everyone who believes, to the Jew first and also to the Greek.

[17]For in it the righteousness of God is revealed from faith for faith, as it is written, "The righteous shall live by faith."

[18]For the **wrath** of God is revealed from heaven against all ungodliness and unrighteousness of men, who by their unrighteousness suppress the truth.

Verse 18 speaks of the wrath of God that is revealed from heaven. Although this is expressed in the present tense ("is revealed"), this does not mean that God's wrath has yet been unleashed. This is a figurative way of saying that God's wrath will assuredly be revealed from heaven. Further, note at whom this expressed wrath is directed: all ungodliness and unrighteousness of men, and those who suppress the truth. Those who reject God, the Gospel of Jesus Christ, and suppress the truth will face God's righteous wrath. God has been patient throughout the ages, but His wrath will be manifested.

Is there any doubt that God's wrath is justifiable?

Romans 1:19-20

[19]For what can be known about God is plain to them, because God has shown it to them.

²⁰For his invisible attributes, namely, his eternal power and divine nature, have been clearly perceived, ever since the creation of the world, in the things that have been made. So they are without excuse.

God has not kept Himself hidden. He has made Himself known in His Word, His creation, and by His Son Jesus Christ. Man is without excuse. All men have the option to know God and to accept His plan of salvation, but not all men will choose God's ways and God's plan. Those who willfully reject God and the Gospel of Jesus Christ will face the expressed wrath of God. These are the people described in Romans 1:18-32. They are without excuse because God has not hidden Himself or the Gospel.

The passage continues:

Romans 1:21-25
²¹For although they knew God, they did not honor him as God or give thanks to him, but they became futile in their thinking, and their foolish hearts were darkened.
²²Claiming to be wise, they became fools,
²³and exchanged the glory of the immortal God for images resembling mortal man and birds and animals and creeping things.
²⁴Therefore God gave them up in the lusts of their hearts to impurity, to the dishonoring of their bodies among themselves,
²⁵because they exchanged the truth about God for a lie and worshiped and served the creature rather than the Creator, who is blessed forever! Amen.

Those who suppress the truth disregard God by not giving Him honor or thanks. Instead, they worship the creation—man, animals, angels, planets, stars—rather than the Creator, and they do this with full knowledge. They know God but chose to disregard God and worship something else instead.

Those who willfully disregard God and worship the creation rather than the Creator are described in the following verses:

Romans 1:26-32

[26]For this reason God gave them up to dishonorable passions. For their women exchanged natural relations for those that are contrary to nature;

[27]and the men likewise gave up natural relations with women and were consumed with passion for one another, men committing shameless acts with men and receiving in themselves the due penalty for their error.

[28]And since they did not see fit to acknowledge God, God gave them up to a debased mind to do what ought not to be done.

[29]They were filled with all manner of unrighteousness, evil, covetousness, malice. They are full of envy, murder, strife, deceit, maliciousness. They are gossips,

[30]slanderers, haters of God, insolent, haughty, boastful, inventors of evil, disobedient to parents,

[31]foolish, faithless, heartless, ruthless.

[32]Though they know God's righteous decree that those who practice such things deserve to die, they not only do them but give approval to those who practice them.

These people are *filled* with all manner of unrighteousness. They are evil, covetous, and malicious. They are *full* of envy, murder, deceit, and so forth. They hate God. They are foolish, faithless, heartless, and ruthless. And even though they *know* that according to God's righteous standard, they deserve to die, they not only continue in their unrighteousness but also applaud those who are just like them. Is it any wonder God's wrath is directed towards people like these? From this, we learn a self-evident truth: God's wrath is not arbitrary. It is just. And God's wrath is directed against "all ungodliness and unrighteousness of men, who by their unrighteousness suppress the truth."

Romans 2 states a conclusion to the matter:

Romans 2:1-3

¹Therefore you have no excuse, O man, every one of you who judges. For in passing judgment on another you condemn yourself, because you, the judge, practice the very same things.

²We know that the judgment of God rightly falls on those who practice such things.

³Do you suppose, O man—you who judge those who practice such things and yet do them yourself—that you will escape the judgment of God?

The truth that the ungodly and unrighteous are without excuse frames this passage (1:20, 2:1). God's judgment "rightly falls" on those who practice such things. Today, people may ignore God and scoff at His Word, but His righteous judgment *will* occur. In the Old Testament, the inescapability of the Day of the Lord is expressed in vivid detail (Amos 5:18-20). In Romans 2:3, that truth is made emphatic through a rhetorical question: "Do you suppose you will escape the judgment of God?"

The following passage makes known more about God's wrath and at whom it is directed.

Romans 2:5-10

⁵But because of your hard and impenitent heart you are storing up **wrath** for yourself on the day of **wrath** when God's righteous judgment will be revealed.

⁶He will render to each one according to his works:

⁷to those who by patience in well-doing seek for glory and honor and immortality, he will give eternal life;

⁸but for those who are self-seeking and do not obey the truth, but obey unrighteousness, there will be **wrath and fury.**

> ⁹There will be tribulation and distress for every human being who does evil, the Jew first and also the Greek, ¹⁰but glory and honor and peace for everyone who does good, the Jew first and also the Greek.

God has exercised forbearance and longsuffering, and in His goodness, He gives people the opportunity to repent and accept Jesus Christ as their lord and savior. However, if some continue to be hard-hearted and unrepentant, they will face God's wrath during the Day of the Lord. Verse 5 says God's righteous judgment will be revealed during the day of wrath. When God exercises His anger, it will be per His righteous judgment. Verse 7 speaks of those who are "self-seeking and do not obey the truth but obey unrighteousness." Upon these, God will render wrath and fury. Once again, we should be attentive to the truth that God will *not* arbitrarily inflict wrath. Man has been given ample opportunity to know God and the truth.

Chapter 3 of Romans continues to speak about God's wrath.

Romans 3:3-6

> ³What if some were unfaithful? Does their faithlessness nullify the faithfulness of God?
> ⁴By no means! Let God be true though every one were a liar, as it is written, "That you may be justified in your words, and prevail when you are judged."
> ⁵But if our unrighteousness serves to show the righteousness of God, what shall we say? That God is unrighteous to inflict **wrath** on us? (I speak in a human way.)
> ⁶By no means! For then how could God judge the world?

God is not unrighteous in inflicting His wrath. He will judge the world, and His judgment will be just, but wrath is part of God's judgment. When men respond angrily, they often act unfairly or in the heat of passion. When man metes out punishment, it is often unjust. Not so with God. God's justice is according to truth, and He will impose His expressed wrath with perfect justice.

In His great love and mercy, God has given people the opportunity to avoid His wrath.

Romans 10:9-10

[9]because, if you confess with your mouth that Jesus is Lord and believe in your heart that God raised him from the dead, you will be saved.

[10]For with the heart one believes and is justified, and with the mouth one confesses and is saved.

This salvation is made available by God's grace because of the "redemption that is in Christ Jesus." Therefore, believing concerning Christ has been made available to all. Because this grace has been extended to all, all have the option to believe or not. This sets the basis for God's righteous judgment and the imposition of wrath against those who choose not to believe.

It should be obvious but worth repeating that since the wrath is against those who are filled with unrighteousness, a Christian believer who is made righteous in Christ will _not_ face God's wrath.

Romans 5:8-10

[8]but God shows his love for us in that while we were still sinners, Christ died for us.

[9]Since, therefore, we have now been justified by his blood, much more shall we be saved by him from the **wrath** of God.

[10]For if while we were enemies we were reconciled to God by the death of his Son, much more, now that we are reconciled, shall we be saved by his life.

Those who have believed in Christ are saved from God's expressed wrath. What a tremendous comfort that is.

In Romans chapter 9, we read more about God's wrath.

Romans 9:19-24

¹⁹You will say to me then, "Why does he still find fault? For who can resist his will?"

²⁰But who are you, O man, to answer back to God? Will what is molded say to its molder, "Why have you made me like this?"

²¹Has the potter no right over the clay, to make out of the same lump one vessel for honorable use and another for dishonorable use?

²²What if God, desiring to show his **wrath** and to make known his power, has endured with much patience vessels of **wrath** prepared for destruction,

²³in order to make known the riches of his glory for vessels of mercy, which he has prepared beforehand for glory—

²⁴even us whom he has called, not from the Jews only but also from the Gentiles?

Here we read about vessels of wrath and vessels of mercy. What does this mean? In this context, "vessel" is used to signify a person.[146] One group are "vessels of wrath," meaning people who will face God's wrath. They are prepared for destruction. A second group are "vessels of mercy," meaning those who have believed the Gospel of God concerning His Son Jesus Christ. They have received God's mercy and are prepared for glory.

At first blush, the word "prepared" in verses 22 and 23 seems to imply that God preordained some to wrath and some to glory. This cannot be, for God has given man free will to choose. But verse 22 speaks hypothetically ("what IF God") and does not imply that God predetermined who would face His wrath and receive His mercy. What if God had chosen to exercise His wrath during the golden calf incident or before Jesus Christ came or before the Day of Pentecost? God has

---

[146] This is either a metonymy or a metaphor where the word "vessel" is put for a person. See also Jer. 22:28, 25:34, 51:34; Hos. 8:8; 2 Tim. 2:21; 1 Pet. 3:7 where "vessel" is put for a person or for a group of people.

been slow to anger. Many have deserved His wrath throughout the generations, but God has been slow to anger so that those who would believe could receive His mercy. This passage from Romans 9 indicates that those who do not believe in Jesus Christ will face wrath and destruction. Those who choose to believe will receive mercy and glory.

We have considered the wrath of God and God's purpose in imposing wrath. We have also seen that God's wrath will be accompanied by righteous judgment. However, there is another aspect of God's wrath worth considering:

Romans 12:19

Beloved, never avenge yourselves, but leave it to the **wrath** of God, for it is written, "Vengeance is mine, I will repay, says the Lord."

Christians are exhorted not to avenge themselves but to leave it to the wrath of God, which will come in the future. God will take vengeance during the day of His anger; therefore, Christians are not to avenge themselves or try to bring about justice by their own methods. When Christians are treated unjustly, they can take great comfort in knowing that true justice will one day be exercised.

In this section on the wrath of God in the book of Romans, we have learned the following:

- The righteousness of God is revealed to those who believe the Gospel concerning His Son, Jesus Christ, our lord.
- The wrath of God is revealed against the ungodliness and unrighteousness of men and against those who, by their unrighteousness, suppress the truth.
- All men are without excuse.
- God will be justified when He exercises His wrath.
- God has exercised tremendous forbearance and longsuffering, and His goodness gives all men a chance to repent. But, on the other hand, if they refuse God's goodness, they will face His wrath during the Day of the Lord.

- God is not unrighteous in inflicting wrath.
- Christian believers are saved from the coming wrath by being justified freely by Christ's blood.
- Christians are exhorted not to avenge themselves but to give place to the wrath of God because He will execute justice.

2 Thessalonians

Let's next look at two passages in 2 Thessalonians that speak about the wrath of God during the Day of the Lord.

2 Thessalonians 1:3-10

[3]We ought always to give thanks to God for you, brothers, as is right, because your faith is growing abundantly, and the love of every one of you for one another is increasing.

[4]Therefore we ourselves boast about you in the churches of God for your steadfastness and faith in all your persecutions and in the afflictions that you are enduring.

[5]This is evidence of the righteous judgment of God, that you may be considered worthy of the kingdom of God, for which you are also suffering—

[6]since indeed God considers it just to repay with affliction those who afflict you,

[7]and to grant relief to you who are afflicted as well as to us, when the Lord Jesus is revealed from heaven with his mighty angels

[8]in flaming fire, inflicting **vengeance** on those who do not know God and on those who do not obey the gospel of our Lord Jesus.

[9]They will suffer the punishment of eternal destruction, away from the presence of the Lord and from the glory of his might,

^{10}when he comes on that day to be glorified in his saints, and to be marveled at among all who have believed, because our testimony to you was believed.

While the word "wrath" is not used in this passage, the vengeance described in verses 8 to 10 refers to the vengeance that takes place during the Day of the Lord, when the righteous judgment of God will be executed. This will occur when Jesus Christ is revealed from heaven during the Day of the Lord after he has gathered together the Church. Again, note that the wrath of God is directed toward those who do not know God and those who do not obey the Gospel of our Lord Jesus Christ.

These people upon whom God will take vengeance during the Day of the Lord are again referred to in 2 Thessalonians:

2 Thessalonians 2:8-12
^{8}And then the lawless one will be revealed, whom the Lord Jesus will kill with the breath of his mouth and bring to nothing by the appearance of his coming.
^{9}The coming of the lawless one is by the activity of Satan with all power and false signs and wonders,
^{10}and with all wicked deception for those who are perishing, because they refused to love the truth and so be saved.
^{11}Therefore God sends them a strong delusion, so that they may believe what is false,
^{12}in order that all may be condemned who did not believe the truth but had pleasure in unrighteousness.

In verses 8 and 9, we read that the lawless one to be revealed comes by the "activity of Satan" and is accompanied by "all power and false signs and wonders," which will deceive those who refuse to believe the truth and be saved. In other words, they had a choice to accept the truth, but they chose to believe "what is false" instead, which had been offered to them by Satan.

255

In these passages from 2 Thessalonians, we again see that the wrath of God during the Day of the Lord is not arbitrarily imposed upon all mankind but is against those who don't believe the truth and have pleasure in unrighteousness.

The Wrath of God during the Lord's Day in the Book of Revelation

No study of the Day of the Lord would be complete without discussing the book of Revelation, for it contains much information about that Day.

> **Revelation 1:9-10**
> [9]I, John, your brother and partner in the tribulation and the kingdom and the patient endurance that are in Jesus, was on the island called Patmos on account of the word of God and the testimony of Jesus.
> [10]I was in the Spirit on the Lord's day, and I heard behind me a loud voice like a trumpet

Verse 10 indicates that what John saw was "on the Lord's Day," which is the same as the day of the Lord.[147] We know that the Day of the Lord occurs after the gathering together of the Church, so what is being revealed to John will occur *after* the Church has departed. This truth must be kept in mind when considering the events recorded in the book of Revelation.

In Revelation 6, we read:

> **Revelation 6:12-17**
> [12]When he [Jesus Christ] opened the sixth seal, I looked, and behold, there was a great earthquake, and the sun became black as sackcloth, the full moon became like blood,

---

[147] The Lord's Day and the Day of the Lord mean the same thing. "The Day of the Lord" is simply a genitive construction.

¹³and the stars of the sky fell to the earth as the fig tree sheds its winter fruit when shaken by a gale.

¹⁴The sky vanished like a scroll that is being rolled up, and every mountain and island was removed from its place.

¹⁵Then the kings of the earth and the great ones and the generals and the rich and the powerful, and everyone, slave and free, hid themselves in the caves and among the rocks of the mountains,

¹⁶calling to the mountains and rocks, "Fall on us and hide us from the face of him who is seated on the throne, and from the **wrath** of the Lamb,

¹⁷for the great day of their **wrath** has come, and who can stand?"

The "he" of verse 12 refers to Jesus Christ. Note that Jesus Christ is involved in executing the wrath of God and that the Day of the Lord is referred to as "the great day of *their* wrath." Note how these events recall many details from Old Testament passages describing the Day of the Lord.

In Revelation 11, we read:

Revelation 11:15-18

¹⁵Then the seventh angel blew his trumpet, and there were loud voices in heaven, saying, "The kingdom of the world has become the kingdom of our Lord and of his Christ, and he shall reign forever and ever."

¹⁶And the twenty-four elders who sit on their thrones before God fell on their faces and worshiped God,

¹⁷saying, "We give thanks to you, Lord God Almighty, who is and who was, for you have taken your great power and begun to reign.

¹⁸The nations raged, but your **wrath** came, and the time for the dead to be judged, and for rewarding your servants, the prophets and saints, and those who fear your name, both small and great, and for destroying the destroyers of the earth."

Along with God's wrath is the "time of the dead that they should be judged." God's wrath and His judgment are associated.

Then, in chapter 19, we read more about Jesus Christ's role during the Day of the Lord.

> **Revelation 19:13-15**
> [13]He [Jesus Christ] is clothed in a robe dipped in blood, and the name by which he is called is The Word of God.
> [14]And the armies of heaven, arrayed in fine linen, white and pure, were following him on white horses.
> [15]From his mouth comes a sharp sword with which to strike down the nations, and he will rule them with a rod of iron. He [Jesus Christ] will tread the winepress of the **fury** of the **wrath** of God the Almighty.

The "he" in verses 13 and 15 refers to Jesus Christ. When verse 15 reads, "He will tread the winepress of the fury of the wrath of God the Almighty," we understand that it is Jesus Christ who is involved in carrying out the wrath of God. This same truth was expressed in Revelation 6:17. In other words, Jesus Christ is the agent for exercising the wrath of God.

In sum, concerning the wrath of God during the Day of the Lord in the book of Revelation, we have seen the following:

- The descriptions of God's wrath during the Day of the Lord echo numerous Old Testament descriptions.
- Judgment is associated with wrath.
- Jesus Christ is the agent of God's wrath.

A Brief Study of Matthew 24 and 25

From the records in the Church epistles, we learned about the Gathering Together, which is Christ's coming for the Church (2 Thess. 2:1). Other records tell us about some of the events that occur when Christ returns during the Day of the Lord. It's important to keep these two comings of Christ separate and distinct: one is to gather the Church, and the other takes place during the Day of the Lord. We cover Matthew 24 and 25 because these chapters are often misconstrued as describing the Gathering Together when they actually describe Christ's coming *during the Day of the Lord*. While we focus our attention on Matthew's Gospel, the reader is encouraged to consider the parallel records in Mark 13 and Luke 21. Please note that we don't discuss every detail and how they relate to the end times but only address the often-confused passages.

Matthew 24

In Matthew 24, the disciples asked Jesus Christ about the sign of his coming.

Matthew 24:1-3

¹Jesus left the temple and was going away, when his disciples came to point out to him the buildings of the temple.

²But he answered them, "You see all these, do you not? Truly, I say to you, there will not be left here one stone upon another that will not be thrown down."

³As he sat on the Mount of Olives, the disciples came to him privately, saying, "Tell us, when will these things be, and what will be the **sign of your coming** and of the end of the age?"

Does verse 3 refer to Christ's coming for the Church or his coming during the Day of the Lord? We should already realize that this cannot refer to his coming to gather the Church because, as we read in 1 Corinthians 15, this was a secret revealed to the apostle Paul sometime later.

Let's continue with the record.

Matthew 24:4-22

[4]And Jesus answered them, "See that no one leads you astray.

[5]For many will come in my name, saying, 'I am the Christ,' and they will lead many astray.

[6]And you will hear of wars and rumors of wars. See that you are not alarmed, for this must take place, but the end is not yet.

[7]For nation will rise against nation, and kingdom against kingdom, and there will be famines and earthquakes in various places.

[8]All these are but the beginning of the birth pains.

[9]"Then they will deliver you up to tribulation and put you to death, and you will be hated by all nations for my name's sake.

[10]And then many will fall away and betray one another and hate one another.

[11]And many false prophets will arise and lead many astray.

[12]And because lawlessness will be increased, the love of many will grow cold.

[13]But the one who endures to the end will be saved.

[14]And this gospel of the kingdom will be proclaimed throughout the whole world as a testimony to all nations, and then the end will come.

[15]"So when you see the abomination of desolation spoken of by the prophet Daniel, standing in the holy place (let the reader understand),

[16]then let those who are in Judea flee to the mountains.

[17]Let the one who is on the housetop not go down to take what is in his house,

[18]and let the one who is in the field not turn back to take his cloak.

[19]And alas for women who are pregnant and for those who are nursing infants in those days!

²⁰Pray that your flight may not be in winter or on a Sabbath.

²¹For then there will be **great tribulation**, such as has not been from the beginning of the world until now, no, and never will be.

²²And if those days had not been cut short, no human being would be saved. But for the sake of the elect those days will be cut short.

After alluding to the deception that would cause people to go astray, Jesus Christ spoke about wars, rumors of wars, nations rising against nations, famines, earthquakes, and other tribulations. These events are referred to as "the beginning of the birth pains" (v. 8). Jesus Christ then goes on to speak of false prophets that would arise to deceive many, and he then speaks of the "great tribulation." The period he is describing is a time of great lawlessness, which takes place during the Day of the Lord.¹⁴⁸ The parallel record in Luke 21:22-23 describes this period as a time of vengeance, distress, and wrath.

In Matthew 24:13, Christ made a statement that should alert us that he *cannot* be addressing Christians: "The one who endures to the end will be saved." We know that today, salvation unto eternal life is not dependent on "enduring until the end" but upon confessing Jesus as lord and believing in the heart that God has raised him from the dead (Rom. 10:9-10). And so, when Christ refers to people being saved in verse 13, he refers to those alive during the Great Tribulation who endure in believing.¹⁴⁹ Therefore, the "elect" in verse 22 refers to those who remain steadfast during the Great Tribulation; it does not refer to the elect of God who are born again. The "sign of his coming" (v. 3) takes place during the period leading up to the Day of the Lord. It does not refer to his return for the Church.

---

¹⁴⁸ We noted earlier from 2 Thess. 2:8 about the coming of the lawless one *after* the departure of the Church. This period of lawlessness is associated with the appearance of the lawless one.

¹⁴⁹ People surviving the Great Tribulation are also mentioned in the book of Revelation (see Rev. 7:14).

Let's continue with the record in Matthew 24:

Matthew 24:23-28

²³Then if anyone says to you, 'Look, here is the Christ!' or 'There he is!' do not believe it.

²⁴For false christs and false prophets will arise and perform great signs and wonders, so as to lead astray, if possible, even the elect.

²⁵See, I have told you beforehand.

²⁶So, if they say to you, 'Look, he is in the wilderness,' do not go out. If they say, 'Look, he is in the inner rooms,' do not believe it.

²⁷For as the lightning comes from the east and shines as far as the west, so will be the coming of the Son of Man.

²⁸Wherever the corpse is, there the vultures will gather.

During this Great Tribulation, false christs and prophets will show great signs to deceive "even the elect." Jesus Christ compared his coming during the Day of the Lord to how lightning that flashes in the east is also visible in the west. In other words, it will be *very* noticeable. He further compared his coming during the Day of the Lord to the presence of vultures circling in the sky, which indicates the presence of a carcass. If you've ever seen vultures circling in the sky, you know they are hard to miss. These comparisons underscore the truth that Christ's coming during the Day of the Lord will be *very* apparent.

Let's continue reading Matthew 24:

Matthew 24:29-31

²⁹"Immediately after the tribulation of those days the sun will be darkened, and the moon will not give its light, and the stars will fall from heaven, and the powers of the heavens will be shaken.

³⁰Then will appear in heaven the sign of the Son of Man, and then all the tribes of the earth will mourn,

> and they will see the Son of Man coming on the clouds
> of heaven with power and great glory.
> [31]And he will send out his angels with a loud trumpet
> call, and they will gather his elect from the four winds,
> from one end of heaven to the other.

After the Great Tribulation, the sun and moon would be darkened, the stars would fall from heaven, and the powers of the heavens would be shaken. These combined events are mentioned in several Old Testament records, in Acts, and in the book of Revelation. They all refer to events that take place *during the Day of the Lord*.[150] Thus we see that Matthew 24:29-31 refers to events that occur during the Day of the Lord, not things that occur when Christ returns to gather the Church.

Further, verse 30 speaks of the "sign of the Son of Man in heaven," which will cause all the people of the earth to mourn. This is very different from what we read in the Church epistles, where the Church meets the lord in the air. In the verses about the Gathering Together, there was no mention of going through any kind of Great Tribulation. There was no mention of ALL the tribes of the earth being aware of his coming. There was no indication of his appearance to all the earth or any reference to mourning.

Perhaps the confusion arises because in verses 30-31 we read of clouds, a trumpet, and angels. As you may recall, clouds, a trumpet, and the archangel are also part of the coming of Christ for the Church (1 Cor. 15:51-58; 1 Thess. 4:13-18). However, there are notable differences as this chart shows:[151]

---

[150] See for example, Isa.13:6-13; Jer. 4:23-28; Joel 2:1-3, 10-11, 30-32, 3:14-16; Amos 5:18-20, 8:9; Acts 2:16-21; Rev. 6:12-17.
[151] Please see the outline at the end of this appendix for more details about the differences between Christ's return for the Church and his coming during the Day of the Lord.

Points of Comparison	1 Thess. 4:13-18/ 1 Cor. 15:51-58 (Gathering Together)	Matt. 24:29-31/ Rev. 1:7 (Coming of the Son of Man)
Timing	No indication of timing	Immediately after the tribulation
Who is involved from heaven?	Jesus Christ, the archangel	Son of Man, his angels
Who is gathered?	Dead in Christ, and those that are alive in Christ	His elect
Who witnesses Christ's coming?	Only the Church	All the tribes of the earth
Who does the gathering?	The Lord Jesus Christ himself	Angels
What effect on people?	Source of comfort for all Christians	Source of mourning for all the tribes of the earth

Let's finish reading Matthew 24:

Matthew 24:32-43

[32]"From the fig tree learn its lesson: as soon as its branch becomes tender and puts out its leaves, you know that summer is near.

[33]So also, when you see all these things, you know that he is near, at the very gates.

[34]Truly, I say to you, this generation will not pass away until all these things take place.

[35]Heaven and earth will pass away, but my words will not pass away.

[36]"But concerning that day and hour no one knows, not even the angels of heaven, nor the Son, but the Father only.

[37]For as were the days of Noah, so will be the coming of the Son of Man.

³⁸For as in those days before the flood they were eating and drinking, marrying and giving in marriage, until the day when Noah entered the ark,
³⁹and they were unaware until the flood came and swept them all away, so will be the coming of the Son of Man.
⁴⁰Then two men will be in the field; one will be taken and one left.
⁴¹Two women will be grinding at the mill; one will be taken and one left.
⁴²Therefore, stay awake, for you do not know on what day your Lord is coming.
⁴³But know this, that if the master of the house had known in what part of the night the thief was coming, he would have stayed awake and would not have let his house be broken into.

While the Scriptures reveal that some signs will precede the Lord's coming during the Day of the Lord, this passage indicates that no one knows precisely when this will occur. It is foolhardy, therefore, to hazard a guess.

Matthew 25

Matthew 25 continues with the topic of Christ's coming during the Day of the Lord.

Matthew 25:31-46

³¹"When the Son of Man comes in his glory, and all the angels with him, then he will sit on his glorious throne.
³²Before him will be gathered all the nations, and he will separate people one from another as a shepherd separates the sheep from the goats.
³³And he will place the sheep on his right, but the goats on the left.

³⁴"Then the King will say to those on his right, 'Come, you who are blessed by my Father, inherit the kingdom prepared for you from the foundation of the world.

³⁵For I was hungry and you gave me food, I was thirsty and you gave me drink, I was a stranger and you welcomed me,

³⁶I was naked and you clothed me, I was sick and you visited me, I was in prison and you came to me.'

³⁷Then the righteous will answer him, saying, 'Lord, when did we see you hungry and feed you, or thirsty and give you drink?

³⁸And when did we see you a stranger and welcome you, or naked and clothe you?

³⁹And when did we see you sick or in prison and visit you?'

⁴⁰And the King will answer them, 'Truly, I say to you, as you did it to one of the least of these my brothers, you did it to me.'

⁴¹"Then he will say to those on his left, 'Depart from me, you cursed, into the eternal fire prepared for the devil and his angels.

⁴²For I was hungry and you gave me no food, I was thirsty and you gave me no drink,

⁴³I was a stranger and you did not welcome me, naked and you did not clothe me, sick and in prison and you did not visit me.'

⁴⁴Then they also will answer, saying, 'Lord, when did we see you hungry or thirsty or a stranger or naked or sick or in prison, and did not minister to you?'

⁴⁵Then he will answer them, saying, 'Truly, I say to you, as you did not do it to one of the least of these, you did not do it to me.'

⁴⁶And these will go away into eternal punishment, but the righteous into eternal life."

In verse 31 and following, we read about Christ sitting on the throne of his glory, all the nations being gathered to him, and the separation between sheep and goats. However, in the records that speak about the gathering together of the Church, we don't read about thrones, all nations being gathered, or any separation between sheep and goats. This passage in Matthew 25 describes events during the Day of the Lord, not the gathering together of the Church.

Today, many point to dire happenings in the world, like wars, famines, earthquakes, and the like to suggest that the Day of the Lord is imminent or present or that the Great Tribulation has begun. But the Scriptures teach otherwise. Further, 1 Thessalonians 5:3 tells us that before the Day of the Lord comes, people will be talking about the great peace and security they are enjoying rather than all the tribulations they are going through! Jesus Christ said that before the Day of the Lord comes, people will be carrying on as usual—eating, drinking, and marrying like in the days of Noah. But then sudden destruction will come, and the events of the Day of the Lord will start to unfold. No one will escape.

However, the saints are *not* in that category because Christ will gather his Church before the events of the Lord's Day occur. It is a great comfort to know the difference, to be part of Christ's Church, and to look forward to the Gathering Together.

Comparing the Gathering Together and the Coming of the Son of Man

By way of summary, we offer an outline of the differences between Christ's coming for the Church and Christ's coming during the Day of the Lord. We refer to Christ's coming for the Church as the "gathering together," which is how the Scriptures refer to it; and Christ's coming during the Day of the Lord as the "coming of the Son of Man," which is how Jesus Christ referred to this event in the Gospels. We list some references that address these matters, but the list is not exhaustive.

Gathering Together:

2 Thessalonians 2:1
Now concerning the **coming of our Lord Jesus Christ and our being gathered together** to him, we ask you, brothers,

Other references: 1 Cor. 15:51-58; 1 Thess. 4:13-18

Coming of the Son of Man:

Matthew 24:30
Then will appear in heaven the sign of the Son of Man, and then all the tribes of the earth will mourn, and they will see the **Son of Man coming** on the clouds of heaven with power and great glory.

Other references: Dan. 7:13; Mark 13:26, 14:62; Luke 21:27; Rev. 1:7.

As to timing:

- The Gathering Together takes place before the Day of the Lord. No one knows when it will occur. (1 Thess. 4:13- 5:11; 2 Thess. 2:1-6)
- The coming of the Son of Man occurs during the Day of the Lord. It occurs after the Great Tribulation and after the shaking of the powers in heaven. Despite these signs, no one knows when it will occur. The Day of the Lord itself comes as a thief in the night, but it is after the departure of the Church. (Matt. 24:29-31; Mark 13:24-27; Luke 21:25-28)

As to when it was first revealed:

- The Gathering Together was revealed to Paul (1 Cor. 15:51-58; 1 Thess. 4:13-18; 2 Thess. 2:1). This information came by the "word of the Lord," and part of it was also a "mystery," thus indicating that it was not known before.

- The coming of the Son of Man is spoken of in the Old Testament and in the Gospels. (Dan. 7:13-14; Matt. 24:29-31; Mark 13:24-27; Luke 21:25-28; Rev. 1:7)

As to who is involved from the earth:

- The Gathering Together is for born-again Christians who are either living or dead at the time Christ returns. (1 Cor. 15:51-54; 1 Thess. 4:13-18)
- The coming of the Son of Man is witnessed by all nations. The Church will no longer be on the earth. After Jesus Christ sits on the throne of his glory, all the nations are gathered for judgment. (Matt. 19:28, 24:30, 25:31-41; Rev. 1:7, 20:11-15)

As to who is involved from heaven:

- The Gathering Together involves the Lord Jesus Christ and the archangel. (1 Thess. 4:16)
- The coming of the Son of Man involves the Lord Jesus Christ and all the holy angels. (Matt. 24:30-31; Mark 13:26-27; Luke 21:27)

As to who gathers the saints:

- At the Gathering Together, Christ himself comes with a summoning shout and gathers the saints. (1 Thess. 4:16-17)
- At the coming of the Son of Man, the angels are sent to gather the elect.[152] After Jesus Christ sits on the throne of his glory, all the nations are gathered for judgment. (Matt. 24:30-31, 25:31; Mark 13:27)

---

[152] The "elect" means chosen. Mark 13:19-20 refers to the time of tribulation. Verse 20 reads, "And if the Lord had not cut short the days, no human being would be saved. But for the sake of the elect, whom he chose, he shortened the days." Contextually, the elect refers to those who believe on Christ during the tribulation, which is part of the Day of the Lord. Later, in verses 26-27 we read, "And then they will see the Son of Man coming in the clouds with great power and glory. And then he will send out the angels and gather his elect from the four winds, from the ends of the earth to the ends of heaven." The elect are those who believe during the Day of the Lord; they are the ones gathered from the four winds. Today, we in the Church are also called "the elect of God" or "God's chosen ones" (Rom 8:33; Col 3:12; 2 Tim 2:10), but our gathering together occurs prior to the Day of the Lord.

As to the character of the event:

- The Gathering Together is to be anticipated with joy, rejoicing, and great expectation. There are no negative connotations associated with it for the Christian believer. Knowledge of Christ's Return is a source of comfort and edification. (1 Thess. 4:13, 18, 5:11)
- Except for the elect, the coming of the Son of Man causes mourning and wailing for people of the earth. It has associations with dread and fear. (Matt. 24:30; Rev. 1:7)

As to salvation:

- Those who are part of the gathering are already saved and in Christ. (Rom. 10:9-10)
- Those who believe during the Great Tribulation and the Day of the Lord are saved if they endure until the end. Those who are judged at the throne of his glory are saved depending on how they treat Christ's brethren, knowingly or unknowingly. (Matt. 24:13; 25:31-46)

As to the consequences of not being ready when Christ comes:

- Christians will be gathered together whether they watch and are awake or whether they are indifferent about Christ's return. (1 Thess. 5:9-10; 2 Timothy 2:19)
- Those who do not watch and do not endure are cast out when the Son of Man comes. Some form of punishment ensues. (Matt. 24:13; 25:31-46)

As to judgment of those in Christ:

- There is no judgment at the Gathering Together regarding the Christian's salvation, but there is judgment for reward (see Chapter 4: "The Reward").

- When the Son of Man comes with his angels, he sits on the throne of his glory, and all nations are gathered to him. He divides the sheep (righteous) and the goats (cursed). The cursed ones go into everlasting punishment and the righteous to life eternal. (Matt. 24:13, 25:31-46; Rev. 20:11-15)

Appendix B

Four Apparent Contradictions about the Inheritance

We have learned that one of the characteristics of the inheritance is that it is obtained through the merits of Jesus Christ. Once a person is born again of God's spirit, he receives the promise of eternal inheritance, also called the "inheritance of the saints in light" (Col. 1:12). There is nothing he can do that would alter the inheritance because it is eternal, imperishable, reserved in heaven. God Himself has qualified the saints to share in this inheritance. And yet there are four passages in the Bible that seem to indicate that one can lose or must earn the inheritance. We address these four apparent contradictions in this appendix.

#1 Apparent Contradiction

Let's start with Ephesians 5:

> **Ephesians 5:1-5**
> [1]Therefore be imitators of God, as beloved children.
> [2]And walk in love, as Christ loved us and gave himself up for us, a fragrant offering and sacrifice to God.
> [3]But sexual immorality and all impurity or covetousness must not even be named among you, as is proper among saints.
> [4]Let there be no filthiness nor foolish talk nor crude joking, which are out of place, but instead let there be thanksgiving.
> [5]For you may be sure of this, that everyone who is sexually immoral or impure, or who is covetous (that is, an idolater), **has no inheritance** in the kingdom of Christ and God.

Verse 5 specifies that everyone who is sexually immoral, impure, covetous, or idolatrous will have no inheritance in the kingdom of Christ and God. Does this include the child of God? If we keep reading, we will see to whom this verse refers:

Ephesians 5:6-8

[6]Let no one deceive you with empty words, for because of these things the wrath of God comes upon the sons of disobedience.
[7]Therefore do not become partners with them;
[8]for at one time you were darkness, but now you are light in the Lord. Walk as children of light

Verse 6 refers to the "sons of disobedience" and verse 8 to those in "darkness." In this context, these are figurative ways of signifying those who are not children of God. Those who have rejected Jesus Christ, the Messiah, will have no inheritance in the kingdom. If children of God behave in any of the above-mentioned sinful ways, will they lose their inheritance? No, because the inheritance is obtained through the finished work of Jesus Christ, not through one's works or behavior.

Furthermore, God has qualified the saints to share in the inheritance, so it is not dependent on their own merit. If the child of God could lose the inheritance, then that would mean it is not imperishable or incorruptible. This passage does not say that a son of God can lose his inheritance. Rather, it encourages the sons of God to demonstrate conduct befitting children of God and to walk in love, as is proper among the saints. They are encouraged to "walk as children of light," knowing they have a glorious inheritance coming and not to partake with those who walk in darkness.

#2 Apparent Contradiction

A second passage that seems to indicate that a Christian can lose his inheritance is found in Paul's first epistle to the Corinthian church.

1 Corinthians 6:9-11

9Or do you not know that the unrighteous will **not inherit** the kingdom of God? Do not be deceived: neither the sexually immoral, nor idolaters, nor adulterers, nor men who practice homosexuality,
10nor thieves, nor the greedy, nor drunkards, nor revilers, nor swindlers will inherit the kingdom of God.
11And such were some of you. But you were washed, you were sanctified, you were justified in the name of the Lord Jesus Christ and by the Spirit of our God.

At first blush, these verses seem to say that if someone does the things listed in verses 9 and 10, he will not inherit the kingdom of God. However, we have already seen that the inheritance is received on the merits of Jesus Christ. Any work a saint does, whether good or bad, cannot alter the surety of the inheritance. (This will affect the Christian's reward, however, as we have seen.)

Again, we must ask, to whom do verses 9 and 10 refer? They refer to "the unrighteous." As verse 11 states, all saints have been washed, sanctified, and justified in the name of the Lord Jesus Christ and by the spirit of God. It is the unrighteous who will not inherit the kingdom of God. Some of the Corinthians had come from a background that included the practices spoken of in verses 9 and 10, but they had been washed, sanctified, and justified in Christ. Subsequently, their inheritance was sure. This passage does not say they would lose their inheritance if they fell back into the abovementioned practices. Instead, this is an encouragement to walk in a manner befitting those who have an inheritance.

#3 Apparent Contradiction

We see a third apparent contradiction in Galatians.

Galatians 5:16-24

16But I say, walk by the Spirit, and you will not gratify the desires of the flesh.

¹⁷For the desires of the flesh are against the Spirit, and the desires of the Spirit are against the flesh, for these are opposed to each other, to keep you from doing the things you want to do.

¹⁸But if you are led by the Spirit, you are not under the law.

¹⁹Now the works of the flesh are evident: sexual immorality, impurity, sensuality,

²⁰idolatry, sorcery, enmity, strife, jealousy, fits of anger, rivalries, dissensions, divisions,

²¹envy, drunkenness, orgies, and things like these. I warn you, as I warned you before, that those who do such things **will not inherit** the kingdom of God.

²²But the fruit of the Spirit is love, joy, peace, patience, kindness, goodness, faithfulness,

²³gentleness, self-control; against such things there is no law.

²⁴And those who belong to Christ Jesus have crucified the flesh with its passions and desires.

Verses 19-21 list the works of the flesh, and then in verse 21, a warning is given: "those who practice such things will not inherit the kingdom of God." This seems to indicate that if a Christian practices the works of the flesh, he will not inherit the kingdom of God. How is this possible?

Once again, to whom do these verses refer? Verses 16-18 contrast those who walk by the spirit with those who carry out the desires of the flesh. Romans 8:9 tells us that those in the spirit cannot be "in the flesh" because they have the spirit of God dwelling in them. Putting these verses together, we are given to understand that verses 19-21 refer to those who are not born again of God's spirit. This passage does not say a Christian will lose his inheritance. Rather, it encourages born-again ones to walk by the spirit and to produce fruit of the spirit, not to fulfill the lusts of the flesh like those who do not have an eternal inheritance coming.

#4 Apparent Contradiction

Let's consider the fourth passage with an apparent contradiction.

Colossians 3:22-25

[22]Bondservants, obey in everything those who are your earthly masters, not by way of eye-service, as people-pleasers, but with sincerity of heart, fearing the Lord.

[23]Whatever you do, work heartily, as for the Lord and not for men,

[24]knowing that from the Lord you will receive the inheritance as your reward. You are serving the Lord Christ.

[25]For the wrongdoer will be paid back for the wrong he has done, and there is no partiality.

Verse 24 speaks of the inheritance as the reward.[153] Other translations render this verse:

Colossians 3:24 (KJV)

Knowing that of the Lord ye shall receive the reward of the inheritance: for ye serve the Lord Christ.

Colossians 3:24 (NASB95)

knowing that from the Lord you will receive the reward of the inheritance. It is the Lord Christ whom you serve.

Colossians 3:24 (YLT)

having known that from the Lord ye shall receive the recompense of the inheritance — for the Lord Christ ye serve;

---

[153] The word "reward" in Col. 3:24 is the Greek word *antapodosis*, which, according to Thayer, means "reward, recompense." The Greek word most often translated "reward" is *misthos*. The two words are synonyms. We discuss the meaning of *misthos* in detail in Chapter 4.

These translations more accurately reflect the genitive construction that is in the Greek. To understand what the phrase "reward of the inheritance" means, we need to learn about the genitive construction.

According to E. W. Bullinger, the genitive construction can fall into numerous classes.[154] In the chart below, we offer eight categories with their equivalent meaning, using the phrase "the reward of the inheritance."

Genitive Construction Categories	Equivalent Meaning
Genitive of Character	the inherited reward
Genitive of Origin	the reward originating from the inheritance
Genitive of Possession	the inheritance's reward
Genitive of Apposition	the reward consisting of the inheritance
Genitive of Relation	the reward pertaining to the inheritance
Genitive of Material	the reward made of the inheritance
Genitive of Contents	the reward filled with or containing the inheritance
Genitive of Partition	the reward sharing in or part of the inheritance

Given the other Scriptures that speak of this same topic, the phrase "reward of the inheritance" in Colossians 3:24 is a genitive of relation. It would therefore be translated as "the reward *pertaining* to the inheritance." This translation is also in keeping with the context.

In the context, servants are told to obey their masters with singleness of heart, working heartily out of reverence for the lord, and not to please men. If they do so, they will receive the reward pertaining to the inheritance. The context, then, is speaking about service. Furthermore,

---

154   Bulllinger, *The Companion Bible*, Appendix 17.

a warning is given: if a wrong is done, that also will be repaid in kind. Does this mean they would lose the inheritance? This contradicts Colossians 1:12, which states that God has qualified the saints to share in the inheritance. Does Colossians 3:24 now suggest that one must work for the inheritance? No, for this verse speaks of the possibility of them losing the *reward* pertaining to the inheritance, which is not the same thing.

Indeed, when Colossians 3:25 reads, "For the wrongdoer will be paid back for the wrong he has done, and there is no partiality," the wrong refers to those works that will not be rewarded but will be burned up. Taking into account the genitive construction and the context, we see that the phrase "the reward of the inheritance" refers to the reward associated with or pertaining to the inheritance; it signifies future reward. All Christians will receive the inheritance on the merits of Christ, but the reward that is associated with the inheritance will be received on the merits of the Christian's walk.

The four passages covered in this appendix contain apparent Bible contradictions that seem to say that a Christian can lose or must earn their inheritance. However, after considering the context, understanding to whom these passages refer, and taking into account the genitive construction, we see that there are no contradictions concerning the inheritance. Christians cannot lose their inheritance because it is eternal, unfading, and reserved in heaven for them.

Appendix C

The Judgment Seat of Christ

In chapter 4, we looked at key passages that speak about the reward and what will be rewarded. In this Appendix, we consider what the Scriptures say about *where* the reward will be received.

2 Corinthians 5:10-11

[10]For we must all appear before the **judgment seat** (*bēma*) of Christ, so that each one may receive what is due for what he has done in the body, whether good or evil.

[11]Therefore, knowing the fear of the Lord, we persuade others. But what we are is known to God, and I hope it is known also to your conscience.

According to verse 10, all Christians must appear before the judgment seat (*bēma*) of Christ. In the Greek New Testament, the word translated as "judgment seat" is *bēma*, meaning a "step or raised place... a tribune to speak from in a public assembly... the elevated seat of a judge."[155] Thayer notes that Herod built a *bēma*, "a structure resembling a throne at Caesarea, from which he viewed the games and made speeches to the people."[156] In ancient eastern culture, orators might sit on a *bēma* to make pronouncements, the idea being that having an elevated position would help to carry the voice. Or judges might sit on a *bēma* for judicial purposes, the idea being that having an elevated position connoted authority. One source even claims that the *bēma* was portable so that a Roman magistrate could carry it to various places under his jurisdiction.[157] In ancient Roman law courts, one *bēma* was provided

---

155   Bullinger, *A Critical Lexicon and Concordance*, s.v. "judgment seat."
156   Thayer, *A Greek-English Lexicon*. s.v. "*bēma*."
157   Panton, *The Judgment Seat of Christ*, 15 (fn).

for the accuser, and another for the accused.[158] To understand the word *bēma* as it is used in the Greek New Testament, we will look at all twelve of its occurrences.

Matthew 27:19

Besides, while he was sitting on the **judgment seat** (*bēma*), his wife sent word to him, "Have nothing to do with that righteous man, for I have suffered much because of him today in a dream."

John 19:13

So when Pilate heard these words, he brought Jesus out and sat down on the **judgment seat** (*bēma*) at a place called The Stone Pavement, and in Aramaic Gabbatha.

In these verses, Pilate sat down on the *bēma* to make a judgment.

Acts 7:4-5

4Then he went out from the land of the Chaldeans and lived in Haran. And after his father died, God removed him from there into this land in which you are now living. 5Yet he gave him no inheritance in it, not even a **foot's length** (*bēma*), but promised to give it to him as a possession and to his offspring after him, though he had no child.

Other translations render this phrase as "not even a square foot" (GNT), "not enough ground to set his foot on" (NIV), and "not even a foot of ground" (BSB). Here, *bēma* means a place to stand.

Acts 12:21

On an appointed day Herod put on his royal robes, took his seat upon the **throne** (*bēma*), and delivered an oration to them.

---

158   Bullinger, *A Critical Lexicon and Concordance*, s.v. "judgment seat."

In this verse, the *bēma* is an official seat where Herod made an oration.

Acts 18:12-17
¹²But when Gallio was proconsul of Achaia, the Jews made a united attack on Paul and brought him before the **tribunal** (*bēma*),
¹³saying, "This man is persuading people to worship God contrary to the law."
¹⁴But when Paul was about to open his mouth, Gallio said to the Jews, "If it were a matter of wrongdoing or vicious crime, O Jews, I would have reason to accept your complaint.
¹⁵But since it is a matter of questions about words and names and your own law, see to it yourselves. I refuse to be a judge of these things."
¹⁶And he drove them from the **tribunal** (*bēma*).
¹⁷And they all seized Sosthenes, the ruler of the synagogue, and beat him in front of the **tribunal** (*bēma*). But Gallio paid no attention to any of this.

In verses 12, 16, and 17, the *bēma* is a tribunal where Gallio sat to judge. The Jews brought Paul before Gallio for judgment, but he refused to judge these matters. Instead, he drove them from the tribunal where he was sitting. The Jews also brought Sosthenes, the ruler of the synagogue, and beat him in front of Gallio, who was still sitting on the tribunal.

Acts 25:6
After he stayed among them not more than eight or ten days, he went down to Caesarea. And the next day he took his seat on the **tribunal** (*bēma*) and ordered Paul to be brought.

Acts 25:10
But Paul said, "I am standing before Caesar's **tribunal** (*bēma*), where I ought to be tried. To the Jews I have done no wrong, as you yourself know very well.

Acts 25:17

So when they came together here, I made no delay, but on the next day took my seat on the **tribunal** (*bēma*) and ordered the man to be brought.

In Acts 25, Festus took his seat on the *bēma* to hear the accusations against Paul brought by the Jews who came down from Jerusalem. Paul was being tried there but opted to be tried before Caesar instead.[159] So in this occurrence, the *bēma* is where some ruler would make judgments.

So far, we have seen that in the Bible, Pilate sat on a *bēma* to judge, Herod sat on a *bēma* to make an oration, Gallio sat on a *bēma* to judge, Festus sat on a *bēma* to judge, and Caesar is referred to as judging from a *bēma*. In all these occurrences, *bēma* is where someone in authority sat to make a judgment or a pronouncement. Of the twelve occurrences of *bēma*, ten signify a place where someone in authority sat to judge.

Now let's read the other two occurrences of *bēma*.

Romans 14:10

Why do you pass judgment on your brother? Or you, why do you despise your brother? For we will all stand before the **judgment seat** (*bēma*) of God;

Some Bibles like the ESV have "the judgment seat of God" while others have "the judgment seat of Christ." The only other mention of the judgment seat of Christ is in 2 Corinthians 5:10.

2 Corinthians 5:10

For we must all appear before the **judgment seat** (*bēma*) of Christ, so that each one may receive what is due for what he has done in the body, whether good or evil.

---

[159] Though accused by the Jews, the apostle Paul was essentially found innocent by Gallio and Festus. He was forced to appeal for further judgment before Caesar, but it was not because he was guilty of anything. Even King Agrippa who heard Paul's case later said that Paul could have been set free had he not appealed to Caesar. No charge against Paul was proven. So, in all occurrences of this word *bēma* in the Gospels and in the book of Acts where judgment is carried out, no one is ever found guilty of any crimes.

In these verses, we read about the *bēma* of Christ, where each born again one must appear and where each one will receive "what is due for what he has done in the body." The phrase "done in the body" is a figurative way of saying what one has done in one's lifetime. These are the only two verses that speak of the *bēma* of Christ, where the believer will appear for judgment. Like all the other uses of *bēma*, this usage signifies a place of authority where one metes out judgment. The difference, of course, is that this is the *bēma* of CHRIST, and Christ is the one to carry out judgment.

How can a Christian, who is judged righteous, blameless, holy, and acceptable in Christ, be judged by Christ at the *bēma*? We've already looked at the record in 1 Corinthians 3, where we read that every man's *work* will be tested. Here again, in 2 Corinthians 5:10, we read that all Christians *must* appear before the judgment seat of Christ so that "each one may receive what is due for what he has *done* in the body, whether good or evil." What does it mean, "whether good or evil"? Taking this unclear phrase together with the clear verses of 1 Corinthians 3, we learn that those works which withstand the test of fire receive reward—the "good" of 2 Corinthians 5:10. Those works which do not withstand the test of fire will not receive reward—the "evil" of 2 Corinthians 5:10. Note how the NASB renders this verse:

2 Corinthians 5:10 (NASB95)
For we must all appear before the **judgment seat** (*bēma*) of Christ, so that each one may be **recompensed** for his deeds in the body, according to what he has done, whether good or bad.

The *bēma* of Christ is not a place where condemnation is pronounced, or punishment is given. Rather, the *bēma* of Christ is where every Christian's *work will be judged.* If the work abides, it will be rewarded. If it does not abide, it will be burned up.

The individual Christian has been judged righteous and blameless in Christ—that is an unchangeable truth. And so, when he stands before the judgment seat of Christ, it is to receive reward only, not punishment or condemnation. The believer is justified and sanctified by God because of the completed work of Jesus Christ, and no accusation can be held against him.[160] However, his work, service, and labor will be judged at the *bēma*. Works that are "good" will be rewarded; works that are "evil" will be burned up. It is paramount to keep this distinction in mind: at the *bēma*, the Christian is *not* on trial for his eternal salvation. It is his work alone that will be judged. About these truths, the Scriptures are clear.

Let's reread Romans 14:10-13.

Romans 14:10-13

[10]Why do you pass judgment on your brother? Or you, why do you despise your brother? For we will all stand before the **judgment seat** (*bēma*) of God;

[11]for it is written, "As I live, says the Lord, every knee shall bow to me, and every tongue shall confess to God."

[12]So then each of us will give an account of himself to God.

[13]Therefore let us not pass judgment on one another any longer, but rather decide never to put a stumbling block or hindrance in the way of a brother.

In verse 12, the words "to God" do not occur in the Greek, so it should read, "so then every one of us shall give account concerning himself." Every born-again one will stand before the judgment seat of Christ and will give an account of himself. Are Christians going to give an account for their sins? Of course not! In Christ, sins have been forgiven; in Christ, the born-again one has been made the righteousness of God. As we have seen in 1 Corinthians 3, every man's *work* shall be judged, not every man's *sin*. This is what the Christian will give an account of at the *bēma* of Christ.

As for who will be doing the judging at the *bēma*, the Scriptures say that all future judgment will be carried out by Jesus Christ, including the judgment that will take place at the *bēma*.

---

[160]   See Rom. 8:33-34

John 5:22

For the Father judges no one, but has given all judgment to the Son,

Acts 10:42

And he commanded us to preach to the people and to testify that he is the one appointed by God to be judge of the living and the dead.

2 Timothy 4:1

I charge you in the presence of God and of Christ Jesus, who is to judge the living and the dead, and by his appearing and his kingdom:

Indeed, the Scriptures attest that God has committed all judgment to His Son, the Lord Jesus Christ.[161]

In summary, the *bēma* is the judgment seat of Christ where every Christian's work will be judged. Works that abide will receive reward. Works that do not abide will not be rewarded, resulting in a loss. There are no punishments meted out at the *bēma* of Christ, only reward. At the *bēma,* it is Jesus Christ who will judge each saint's works.

---

[161] See also Acts 17:31 and Rom. 2:16. Jesus Christ will carry out judgment on more than one occasion. For example, he will judge ALL from his throne spoken about in the book of Revelation and in the Gospels. This judgment is not the same judgment he will make at the *bēma*. Further, Christ will delegate some judgment in the future, such as to the twelve apostles who will judge the twelve tribes of Israel and to the Church of God, who will also be called on to judge the world and angels (1 Cor. 6:1-4). However, a fuller discussion of these truths remains outside the scope of this appendix.

Appendix D
The New Body

We know from the records in 1 Thessalonians 4 and 1 Corinthians 15 that at Christ's return, all born-again ones will be changed: the dead in Christ will be raised and put on immortality, and those who are alive will be given incorruptible bodies. What will these changed, new bodies be like? How do they differ from our old bodies? In this appendix, we will look at verses that disclose details about the new body that awaits each Christian believer.

> **Philippians 3:20-21**
> [20]But our citizenship is in heaven, and from it we await a Savior, the Lord Jesus Christ,
> [21]who will transform our lowly body to be **like his glorious body**, by the power that enables him even to subject all things to himself.

The Christian's new body will be like Christ's glorious body, meaning his resurrected body. Therefore, it is instructive to consider some records that speak of Christ in his resurrected body. While we won't cover every description of Christ's appearances to his followers in his resurrected body, we will consider critical passages that shed light on the characteristics of that glorious body.

Characteristics of Christ's Resurrected Body

The Gospels tell us that Jesus Christ, in his resurrected body, appeared to Mary Magdalene first.

> **John 20:11-18**
> [11]But Mary stood weeping outside the tomb, and as she wept she stooped to look into the tomb.

¹²And she saw two angels in white, sitting where the body of Jesus had lain, one at the head and one at the feet.

¹³They said to her, "Woman, why are you weeping?" She said to them, "They have taken away my Lord, and I do not know where they have laid him."

¹⁴Having said this, she turned around and saw Jesus standing, but she did not know that it was Jesus.

¹⁵Jesus said to her, "Woman, why are you weeping? Whom are you seeking?" Supposing him to be the gardener, she said to him, "Sir, if you have carried him away, tell me where you have laid him, and I will take him away."

¹⁶Jesus said to her, "Mary." She turned and said to him in Aramaic, "Rabboni!" (which means Teacher).

¹⁷Jesus said to her, "Do not cling to me, for I have not yet ascended to the Father; but go to my brothers and say to them, 'I am ascending to my Father and your Father, to my God and your God.'"

¹⁸Mary Magdalene went and announced to the disciples, "I have seen the Lord"—and that he had said these things to her.

In this record, we see that Mary mistook the resurrected Christ for a gardener, which suggests that Christ appeared, at this point, like an ordinary human being.

After this encounter, Mary Magdalene told the disciples that Christ had risen, but they did not believe her. Shortly after that, Christ appeared to two men as they were walking into the country.

Mark 16:9-12
⁹Now when he rose early on the first day of the week, he appeared first to Mary Magdalene, from whom he had cast out seven demons.

¹⁰She went and told those who had been with him, as they mourned and wept.

¹¹But when they heard that he was alive and had been seen by her, they would not believe it.

¹²After these things he appeared in **another form** to two of them, as they were walking into the country.

Note that it says he appeared "in another form." In Greek, the word "form" means form, shape, or outward appearance. He appeared to Mary Magdalene in one form, shape, or outward appearance, and these two men in a different outward appearance. From this, we can gather that Jesus Christ could change his form, shape, or outward appearance in his resurrected body. How this took place is not explained in the Scriptures, but he could change to such a degree that he appeared one way to one person and another way to another person.

Let's read about his third resurrected appearance.

John 21:1-4

¹After this Jesus revealed himself again to the disciples by the Sea of Tiberias, and he revealed himself in this way.

²Simon Peter, Thomas (called the Twin), Nathanael of Cana in Galilee, the sons of Zebedee, and two others of his disciples were together.

³Simon Peter said to them, "I am going fishing." They said to him, "We will go with you." They went out and got into the boat, but that night they caught nothing.

⁴Just as day was breaking, Jesus stood on the shore; yet the disciples did not know that it was Jesus.

In his glorious, resurrected body, Jesus Christ was not immediately recognized by those who had known him intimately. Let's continue with the record.

John 21:5-14

[5]Jesus said to them, "Children, do you have any fish?" They answered him, "No."

[6]He said to them, "Cast the net on the right side of the boat, and you will find some." So they cast it, and now they were not able to haul it in, because of the quantity of fish.

[7]That disciple whom Jesus loved therefore said to Peter, "It is the Lord!" When Simon Peter heard that it was the Lord, he put on his outer garment, for he was stripped for work, and threw himself into the sea.

[8]The other disciples came in the boat, dragging the net full of fish, for they were not far from the land, but about a hundred yards off.

[9]When they got out on land, they saw a charcoal fire in place, with fish laid out on it, and bread.

[10]Jesus said to them, "Bring some of the fish that you have just caught."

[11]So Simon Peter went aboard and hauled the net ashore, full of large fish, 153 of them. And although there were so many, the net was not torn.

[12]Jesus said to them, "Come and have breakfast." Now none of the disciples dared ask him, "Who are you?" They knew it was the Lord.

[13]Jesus came and took the bread and gave it to them, and so with the fish.

[14]This was now the third time that Jesus was revealed to the disciples after he was raised from the dead.

Initially, the disciples did not recognize that the man on the shore was Jesus Christ. But after he instructed them to cast their net off the right side of the boat, where they pulled in a large catch, one of them recognized that it was the lord. After the miracle of this large catch, they finally recognized him.

If you think about someone you know exceptionally well, perhaps someone you see every day, would you be able to recognize them at a distance? Would you recognize your friend once they spoke to you? It's likely. But in these records, we see that men who had been with Jesus Christ and knew him intimately did not immediately recognize him. This suggests quite a changed appearance!

Let's next read the record in Luke that describes two men walking on the road to Emmaus. (Previously, we noted that he appeared to these two men in "another form" Mark 16:12.) As they walked, Jesus Christ appeared to them in his resurrected body.

Luke 24:15-17
¹⁵While they were talking and discussing together, Jesus himself drew near and went with them.
¹⁶But their eyes were kept from recognizing him.
¹⁷And he said to them, "What is this conversation that you are holding with each other as you walk?" And they stood still, looking sad.

In verse 16, we learn that these men did not recognize Jesus Christ, for their eyes "were kept" from recognizing him. The NASB translates verse 16 as "but they were prevented from recognizing him." Perhaps the two men did not recognize Jesus Christ because he looked nothing like he did before his resurrection, or maybe something took place to prohibit them from recognizing Jesus Christ. Whatever the cause, the men did not recognize Jesus Christ, even as he walked and talked with them for a considerable time.

Luke 24:30-31
³⁰When he was at table with them, he took the bread and blessed and broke it and gave it to them.
³¹And their eyes were opened, and they recognized him. And he vanished from their sight.

Only when Jesus Christ took bread, blessed it, broke it, and gave it to them to eat did the two men finally recognize him. After they finally realized it was him, Jesus Christ vanished out of their sight. This is an astonishing characteristic of Christ's resurrected glorious body—he could just disappear. The laws of physics, as we currently understand, do not apply to the lord's resurrected body, for he could vanish. While movies today, enhanced with special effects and CGI, can appear to make people or things disappear on the television and movie screen, to date, no one has been able to vanish out of sight. But Christ in his glorious body could!

After Jesus Christ vanished, the two men rushed back to Jerusalem to tell the eleven, and the others gathered with them that he had appeared to them in his resurrected body. While the two men were relating their experiences, Jesus Christ suddenly appeared and stood in their midst.

Luke 24:36-43

[36]As they were talking about these things, Jesus himself stood among them, and said to them, "Peace to you!"

[37]But they were startled and frightened and thought they saw a spirit.

[38]And he said to them, "Why are you troubled, and why do doubts arise in your hearts?

[39]See my hands and my feet, that it is I myself. Touch me, and see. For a spirit does not have flesh and bones as you see that I have."

[40]And when he had said this, he showed them his hands and his feet.

[41]And while they still disbelieved for joy and were marveling, he said to them, "Have you anything here to eat?"

[42]They gave him a piece of broiled fish,

[43]and he took it and ate before them.

Jesus Christ appeared amid the disciples, who were gathered together indoors. John 20:19 further tells us that this door was locked. Usually, if you want to join a group of people assembled in a locked room, you knock on the door and then enter when it's opened. But Jesus Christ did not enter through the locked door; he simply appeared in the room and stood among them! No wonder they were startled and frightened, thinking they had seen a spirit. Normal humans don't just suddenly appear in a room. Think about it. If you were gathered in a room with some friends, and someone suddenly appeared in the middle of your group, wouldn't you jump out of your skin? From this record, we again see that the laws of physics as we currently understand them do not seem to apply to the lord's resurrected body, for he could simply appear in a locked room without entering through a door or other opening.

Moreover, Jesus Christ could do everyday things like eat, walk, and talk in his resurrected body. He also invited the men to touch him because his body was composed of flesh and bones. In other words, it was not made from some nebulous matter with no corporeal substance.

Next, let's read the parallel record from John.

John 20:20-23
20When he had said this, he showed them his hands and his side. Then the disciples were glad when they saw the Lord.
21Jesus said to them again, "Peace be with you. As the Father has sent me, even so I am sending you."
22And when he had said this, he breathed on them and said to them, "Receive the Holy Spirit.
23If you forgive the sins of any, they are forgiven them; if you withhold forgiveness from any, it is withheld."

Jesus Christ showed the disciples his hands and side (Luke adds "feet") and encouraged them to touch him. After he showed them his hands, feet, and side, the disciples were glad. Why? Perhaps after seeing the wound marks from his crucifixion, they knew beyond a shadow of a doubt that he was, indeed, the resurrected Christ. Let's continue with the record.

John 20:24-25

[24]Now Thomas, one of the twelve, called the Twin, was not with them when Jesus came.

[25]So the other disciples told him, "We have seen the Lord." But he said to them, "Unless I see in his hands the mark of the nails, and place my finger into the mark of the nails, and place my hand into his side, I will never believe."

Thomas was not present when Jesus Christ initially appeared to the disciples. However, when the others reported to Thomas what they had seen, Thomas refused to believe them without seeing some tangible proof. He said, "Unless I see in his hands the mark of the nails and place my finger into the mark of the nails, and place my hand into his side, I will never believe" (John 20:25).

Jesus Christ did appear to Thomas eight days later.

John 20:26-29

[26]Eight days later, his disciples were inside again, and Thomas was with them. Although the doors were locked, Jesus came and stood among them and said, "Peace be with you."

[27]Then he said to Thomas, "Put your finger here, and see my hands; and put out your hand, and place it in my side. Do not disbelieve, but believe."

[28]Thomas answered him, "My Lord and my God!"

[29]Jesus said to him, "Have you believed because you have seen me? Blessed are those who have not seen and yet have believed."

When Jesus Christ did appear, and Thomas was present, he told Thomas to touch his hands and side so that he could believe. Thomas must have done so because his reverential declaration indicates that he was now witnessing Christ in his resurrected body. So again, we see that Christ's resurrected body was not made of vapor, but flesh and bones and that people could touch it. (These marks from the crucifixion were not apparent when he was walking with the two men on the road to Emmaus, suggesting that he could make these marks appear at will.)

In Acts 1:9 Jesus Christ was taken up into heaven in his resurrected body. The apostle Peter reveals that in his resurrected body, Christ could interact directly with those in the spiritual realm, including the spirits in prison (1 Pet. 3:19). Wherever these spirits are imprisoned, Jesus Christ was able to go into their presence and speak to them. The ability to travel to these places—heaven, spirits in prison—also indicates that Christ's glorious body was not limited by the laws of time and space as we currently understand them.

In sum, we have seen that in his resurrected body, Jesus Christ:

- could change form.
- could vanish.
- could appear suddenly.
- could appear in a room without going through the door or other opening.
- could appear in a form that was unrecognizable to those who knew him.
- was not limited by the laws of physics as we currently understand them.
- was not limited by the laws of time and space as we currently understand them.
- could do things people ordinarily do, like eat, drink, walk, talk, and cook.
- had flesh and bones and could be touched.
- could ascend to heaven.

The Scriptures declare that those in Christ will be changed and receive new bodies like Christ's glorious body. While the Scriptures do not say that our new bodies will be *exactly like* Christ's resurrected body, our new bodies will be *fashioned like* his glorious body.

1 Corinthians 15

1 Corinthians 15 addresses the matter of the resurrection from the dead. Some at Corinth were saying there was no resurrection of the dead, so the apostle Paul confronted this error by establishing that Christ had been raised from the dead and that those who are Christ's at his coming will also be raised from the dead. Then, in verse 35, Paul addressed two questions some had asked: 1) How are the dead raised? 2) What kind of bodies will they have?

1 Corinthians 15:36-41

[36]You foolish person! What you sow does not come to life unless it dies.

[37]And what you sow is not the body that is to be, but a bare kernel, perhaps of wheat or of some other grain.

[38]But God gives it a body as he has chosen, and to each kind of seed its own body.

[39]For not all flesh is the same, but there is one kind for humans, another for animals, another for birds, and another for fish.

[40]There are heavenly bodies and earthly bodies, but the glory of the heavenly is of one kind, and the glory of the earthly is of another.

[41]There is one glory of the sun, and another glory of the moon, and another glory of the stars; for star differs from star in glory.

Paul answered the first question—how are the dead raised? —by using the example of a seed. Before a seed can grow into a plant, it must "die" in the soil. Then it grows into a plant, which you can harvest. If you've ever seen a tomato seed sprout and eventually blossom into a three-foot-tall tomato plant, you know that there is a colossal difference between the body of the seed and the body of the plant. That's what Paul refers to in verses 36-38.

Though a seed doesn't literally die when it is planted, Paul spoke of it as "dying" (buried in the ground) and then coming back to life (growing into a plant). Jesus Christ also spoke of this process in John 12:24: "Truly, truly, I say to you, unless a grain of wheat falls into the earth and dies, it remains alone; but if it dies, it bears much fruit."[162] No one questions God's ability to turn a seed into a plant, which, in a sense, is bringing the dead back to life. So why should the Corinthians question God's ability to bring a dead body back to life?[163] Thus, the answer to the first question is that God knows *how* to give life to something that dies: He has demonstrated His power to do so with the simple seed.

To answer the second question—what kind of body will they have? —Paul provided a series of vivid comparisons in verses 37-41. Paul gave examples of how one type of body differs from another.

- A wheat seed's "body" differs from another type of grain seed's "body."
- Living bodies differ from one another. For instance, a human body is different from...
  o The body of animals.
  o The body of birds.
  o The body of fish.
- Heavenly bodies differ from earthly bodies.
- Heavenly bodies differ in brightness from one another.
  o The sun's brightness is different from the moon's brightness.
  o Each star differs from another star in brightness.

---

[162] In the context of John 12, Jesus Christ was speaking of his imminent death. He would first die and then, after being raised from the dead, he would also bear fruit. This means that others would live because of his resurrection. So, the implication is that prior to Christ's resurrection, his death must first take place. 1 Corinthians 15 also argues that it is because of the resurrection of Christ, others will be raised from the dead.

[163] The doubt someone displayed about God's ability to raise the dead is why Paul by revelation used such strong language calling the questioner: "You foolish person!" These questions were not posed out of a genuine desire to know, but to question the reality of the resurrection.

Any gardener knows that seeds vary widely in size, shape, color, texture, and so forth. They have different "bodies." Tiny poppy seeds are different from giant pumpkin seeds. Likewise, the body of a man is vastly different from the body of a cat, a hummingbird, or a cod fish. Similarly, heavenly bodies are different from earthly bodies. A star is different from a tree, for instance.

Further, celestial bodies differ from one another in brightness. No one would confuse sunlight with moonlight. And stars themselves also differ from one another in brightness. For instance, the North Star, or Polaris, is the brightest in the Ursa Minor constellation. It is easily distinguishable from all the other stars in that constellation.

With all these comparisons highlighting differences, is there any doubt that the emphasis here is on the differences between the old body and the new resurrected body to come?

Then comes a key phrase in verse 42, "So it is with the resurrection of the dead." If the reader misses the comparison, the Scriptures make it clear. Just as all the examples mentioned above have different bodies, man's current body also differs from his future resurrected body. These comparisons highlight and magnify the *difference* between man's current body and the new body he will receive at Christ's return.

Let's continue reading the chapter where the contrast between old and new continues.

1 Corinthians 15:42-49
[42]So is it with the resurrection of the dead. What is sown is perishable; what is raised is imperishable.
[43]It is sown in dishonor; it is raised in glory. It is sown in weakness; it is raised in power.
[44]It is sown a natural body; it is raised a spiritual body. If there is a natural body, there is also a spiritual body.
[45]Thus it is written, "The first man Adam became a living being"; the last Adam became a life-giving spirit.
[46]But it is not the spiritual that is first but the natural, and then the spiritual.

⁴⁷The first man was from the earth, a man of dust; the second man is from heaven.
⁴⁸As was the man of dust, so also are those who are of the dust, and as is the man of heaven, so also are those who are of heaven.
⁴⁹Just as we have borne the image of the man of dust, we shall also bear the image of the man of heaven.

Verses 45-49 compare the first man (Adam) and the second man (Jesus Christ). This set of contrasts further amplifies the difference between the old and new bodies. When verse 49 speaks of "the image of the man of heaven," it refers to Jesus Christ. Then in verse 50, we read: "I tell you this, brothers: flesh and blood cannot inherit the kingdom of God, nor does the perishable inherit the imperishable." In this verse, "flesh and blood" is a metonymy for the earthly or mortal body.[164] One of the reasons Christians will need new bodies is because flesh and blood—the old body—cannot inherit the kingdom of God!

Verses 45-49 also reveal that there are natural and spiritual bodies and a marked distinction between these two types of bodies. All earthly people are made like Adam in that they have natural bodies. All people born again of God's spirit have the promise of new bodies, which will be in the image of the man of heaven, Jesus Christ.

The numerous contrasts in 1 Corinthians 15:35-49 all serve to emphasize one central truth: the new body is VASTLY DIFFERENT. The following chart summarizes the contrasts between the old and new body mentioned in 1 Corinthians 15:42–49:

Old Body	New Body
Perishable	Imperishable
In dishonor	In glory (or honor)
In weakness	In power
A natural body	A spiritual body
Like Adam	Like the last Adam (Jesus Christ)

---

[164] *Metonymy* is a noun or name put for another noun or name. Hans, *Go Figure!* 49.

Old Body	New Body
Living being	Living spirit
Natural (earth, dust)	Spiritual (heaven)
Image of the man of dust	Image of the man of heaven

Whether dead or alive at the time of Christ's Return, all Christians will be changed—all will receive their new bodies, which will be like Christ's glorious, resurrected body. Isn't that something to look forward to?

Appendix E

Jesus Christ's Teachings on Reward

In studying the topic of reward, we have relied on the teachings of Jesus Christ from the Gospel records, for no one taught more about heavenly reward than he did. Regarding his teachings on reward, let's first note that Jesus Christ spoke to his disciples, not the crowds.[165] These teachings on reward address the topic of commitment, not salvation. Christ's disciples were not limited to the Gospel time, for disciples were to be made of all nations (Matt. 28:19-20), and "disciples" are referred to in the book of Acts. Indeed, after Pentecost, Christian believers are called "disciples."

Acts 9:26
And when he [Paul] had come to Jerusalem, he attempted to join the disciples. And they were all afraid of him, for they did not believe that he was a **disciple**.

Acts 9:36
Now there was in Joppa a **disciple** named Tabitha, which, translated, means Dorcas. She was full of good works and acts of charity.

Acts 16:1
Paul came also to Derbe and to Lystra. A **disciple** was there, named Timothy, the son of a Jewish woman who was a believer, but his father was a Greek.

---

[165] The only two times he was not specifically speaking to his disciples was when he addressed the rich young ruler (Matt. 19:16; Mark 10:17; Luke 18:18) and the chief Pharisee (Luke 14:1).

Acts 21:16

And some of the **disciples** from Caesarea went with us, bringing us to the house of Mnason of Cyprus, an early **disciple**, with whom we should lodge.

Paul, Tabitha, Timothy, and Mnason were called "disciples." They were not simply born-again ones; they were born-again ones who had demonstrated commitment to the Lord Jesus Christ. The term "Christian" implies that a person is born again, having Christ in them. One can be born again in a moment of time. However, "disciple" implies devotion and commitment to Jesus Christ and the Gospel. Disciples abide in his word. Thus, we understand that Christ's teachings on reward, addressed to his disciples, offer valuable instruction to his disciples today.

The following table lists most records where Jesus Christ taught about reward. He used various terms and expressions to speak about the reward, such as "treasure in heaven," "reap eternal life," "Father will honor him," etc. In the chart, note to whom he was speaking.

Record	Verses where reward is mentioned	Whom he was addressing	Notes
Matt. 5-7	Matt. 5:12, 46, 6:1, 2, 4, 5, 6, 16, 18, 19, 21	Disciples (Matt.5:1)	Commonly called the "Sermon on the Mount." The crowds may have been listening also, but he addressed the disciples.
Matt. 10	Matt. 10:41-42	Twelve disciples (Matt.10:1, 11:1)	The sending out of the twelve.

Record	Verses where reward is mentioned	Whom he was addressing	Notes
Matt. 16:13-28	Matt. 16:27	Disciples (Matt. 16:13, 20, 21, 24)	
Matt. 19:16-20:16; Mark 10:17-31; Luke 18:18-30	Matt. 19:21, 28, 29; Mark 10:21, 29-31; Luke 18:18, 29-30	Rich young ruler, disciples (Matt.19:16ff; Mark 10:17ff; Luke 18:18ff)	Though he was directly addressing a rich ruler, the disciples were in earshot and were listening.
Mark 9:33-50	Mark 9:41	The twelve (Mark 9:35)	
Luke 6:17-7:1	Luke 6:23, 35	Disciples (6:17, 20)	There were multitudes present, but verse 20 says, "he lifted up his eyes on his disciples, and said…"
Luke 12:1-59	Luke 12:8, 9 (acknowledge/ deny implies reward), 21, 33-34, 42, 43	Disciples (12:1, 22)	Many people were present, but Luke 12:1 shows that he spoke these things to his disciples.
Luke 14:1-24	Luke 14:14	Ruler of the Pharisees (Luke 14:1)	An exception— he is not called a disciple.

Record	Verses where reward is mentioned	Whom he was addressing	Notes
Luke 22:14-38	Luke 22:28-30	Twelve apostles (Luke 22:14)	
John 4:5-42	John 4:36, 37	Disciples (John 4:31, 33)	
John 12:20-36	John 12:24-26	Andrew and Philip (John 12:22-23)	

Jesus Christ himself set the standard for and the definition of discipleship:

John 8:31-32
[31]So Jesus said to the Jews who had believed him, "If you abide in my word, you are truly my **disciples**,
[32]and you will know the truth, and the truth will set you free."

Jesus Christ gave two criteria for being a disciple: believe on him and abide in his word.

Note what Jesus Christ also said about discipleship in the following passage:

Luke 14:25-33
[25]Now great crowds accompanied him, and he turned and said to them,
[26]"If anyone comes to me and does not hate his own father and mother and wife and children and brothers and sisters, yes, and even his own life, he **cannot be my disciple**.

²⁷Whoever does not bear his own cross and come after me **cannot be my disciple.**

²⁸For which of you, desiring to build a tower, does not first sit down and count the cost, whether he has enough to complete it?

²⁹Otherwise, when he has laid a foundation and is not able to finish, all who see it begin to mock him,

³⁰saying, 'This man began to build and was not able to finish.'

³¹Or what king, going out to encounter another king in war, will not sit down first and deliberate whether he is able with ten thousand to meet him who comes against him with twenty thousand?

³²And if not, while the other is yet a great way off, he sends a delegation and asks for terms of peace.

³³So therefore, any one of you who does not renounce all that he has **cannot be my disciple.**

Jesus Christ made a distinction between the crowds and his disciples: "If anyone comes to me and does not hate his own father and mother and wife and children and brothers and sisters, yes, and even his own life, he cannot be my disciple" (v. 26). Was Jesus Christ literally teaching people to hate their family members and their own lives in order to become disciples? Of course not. He was speaking about commitment and priorities. In other words, would they take up their responsibility (this is the meaning of "bearing the cross"), or would they be distracted by earthly responsibilities? To highlight this truth, Jesus Christ gave the illustration of a man who builds a tower and a king preparing for war: both must count the cost before undertaking their objectives. Similarly, those who wanted to be the lord's disciples had to consider the cost of discipleship. They had to reorder their priorities. Thus, we can see that Jesus Christ required commitment from those who wanted to be his disciples.

Salvation vs. Reward

One reason many may not fully appreciate Christ's teachings on reward is by mistaking them as teachings on salvation. His disciples had already believed in him, so he did not need to speak about salvation. Let's note the following record:

> **Matthew 16:24-27**
> [24]Then Jesus told his **disciples**, "If anyone would come after me, let him deny himself and take up his cross and follow me.
> [25]For whoever would save his life will lose it, but whoever loses his life for my sake will find it.
> [26]For what will it profit a man if he gains the whole world and forfeits his soul [life]? Or what shall a man give in return for his soul [life]?
> [27]For the Son of Man is going to come with his angels in the glory of his Father, and then he will **repay** each person according to what he has done.

When we studied this record in chapter 4, we noted that Jesus Christ was speaking about commitment. He was asking his disciples to give up their own self-interests and follow him.

Some think that because he spoke about forfeiting the "soul," he was referring to salvation. They suggest that "losing the soul" means losing salvation. The word translated "soul" twice in verse 26 is the same word translated "life" twice in verse 25.[166] Jesus Christ was speaking about what someone *did* with their life and about the *profit* of that life. His rhetorical questions implied that a man who dedicated his whole life to gaining the world in fact lost his life, meaning that he wasted it. Jesus Christ was teaching his disciples about commitment, about denying themselves and taking up the cross to follow him. He spoke about the

---

[166] The word "life" and "soul" are from the same Greek word: *psuchē* which means breath life. *Psuchē* is never used in association with eternal life. The Greek word associated with eternal life is *zōē*.

future when he would come with his angels and "repay each person according to what he has done." So, it is clear that he was not speaking about salvation, but about reward. The context indicates that those who committed themselves to following and serving him would be rewarded, but those who committed themselves to worldly pursuits would lose out. In essence they would "lose" or waste their lives.

Confusing reward with salvation has caused many to miss out on the valuable teachings of Jesus Christ on this subject. But understanding to whom he was speaking – disciples in this case – helps us to gain a greater appreciation of the reward.

Repaid at the Resurrection of the Just

While Christ's teachings on reward in the Gospels offer unparalleled understanding, we must carefully note that some things he said were superseded by new revelation given to the Church. For example, consider what Jesus Christ said as to *when* the disciples would receive reward:

Luke 14:13-14
[13]But when you give a feast, invite the poor, the crippled, the lame, the blind,

[14]and you will be blessed, because they cannot repay you. For you will be repaid at the resurrection of the just."

He spoke of the reward at the resurrection of the just.

Matthew 16:27
For the Son of Man is going to come with his angels in the glory of his Father, and then he will repay each person according to what he has done.

Jesus Christ also spoke of giving out the reward when he came with his angels in the glory of his Father. However, Paul received revelation concerning the Gathering Together, which was still a secret at the time of Jesus Christ's teaching in the Gospels (see 1 Cor. 15:51ff). For the Church, new revelation indicated that the reward would be given at the judgment seat of Christ, not at the resurrection of the just:

2 Corinthians 5:9-10

[9]So whether we are at home or away, we make it our aim to please him.

[10]For we must all appear before the judgment seat of Christ, so that each one may receive what is due for what he has done in the body, whether good or evil.

Born-again ones will receive their reward at the *bēma*, the judgment seat of Christ. Information regarding where the saints will receive their reward *did* change from the Gospel period to the Church age.

No matter the subject, the applicability of a teaching in the Gospels cannot contradict Scripture directly addressed to the Church. Jesus Christ's teachings to his disciples on the reward offer essential knowledge for the Church today.

Appendix F

"Lest I Be Disqualified"-A Study of 1 Corinthians 10:1-14

If you recall, 1 Corinthians 10:1 immediately follows 1 Corinthians 9:27 where Paul wrote, "But I discipline my body and keep it under control, lest after preaching to others I myself should be disqualified." What would disqualify Paul from receiving the prize? The answer may be found in 1 Corinthians 10:1-14. But to fully understand this passage, it's essential to read and consider the Old Testament references and quotes that occur in the first ten verses. The following chart lists 1 Corinthians 10:1-10 with the corresponding Old Testament records. Before proceeding, the reader is encouraged to read these verses in 1 Corinthians and the associated Old Testament records.

Verse from 1 Corinthians 10	Old Testament Records
v. 1	Exod. 13:21-14:31
v. 3	Exod. 16:1-36
v. 4	Exod. 17:1-17;Num. 20:8-12, 24
v. 7	Exod. 32:6
v. 8	Num. 25:1-18 or Exod. 32
v. 9	Num. 21:4-9
v. 10	Num. 16:41-50

Let's start with the first two verses.

1 Corinthians 10:1-2

¹For I do not want you to be unaware, brothers, that our fathers were **all** under the cloud, and **all** passed through the sea,

²and **all** were baptized into Moses in the cloud and in
the sea,

The fathers spoken of in verse 1 refer to the children of Israel whom
Moses led out of Egypt. The cloud refers to the pillar of cloud that God
provided for them, as we can see from the following verses:

Exodus 13:21-22
²¹And the LORD went before them by day in a pillar
of cloud to lead them along the way, and by night in a
pillar of fire to give them light, that they might travel
by day and by night.
²²The pillar of cloud by day and the pillar of fire by
night did not depart from before the people.

God miraculously provided a pillar of fire to give them light so they could
travel at night and a pillar of cloud by day. In 1 Corinthians 10:1, passing
through the sea refers to that miraculous event when God caused a strong
east wind to divide the waters of the Red Sea so that the children of Israel
could pass on dry ground (Exod. 14). Note how "all" were under the
cloud and "all" passed through the sea. This refers to all of the Israelites
who were led by Moses out of Egypt. All passed through the Red Sea
unscathed, and all were blessed by the protection the pillars provided.

1 Corinthians 10:3
and **all** ate the same spiritual food,

Verse 3 also states that "all" Israelites ate the same spiritual food. Verse
3 refers to a record in Exodus 16 where God provided manna for the
people of Israel when they were in the wilderness. The Israelites had
journeyed until they came to the wilderness of Sin, between Elim and
Sinai. At that time, the congregation grumbled against Moses and
Aaron, saying that they would rather have died in Egypt than die of
hunger in the wilderness. In response, God gave Moses the following
instructions:

Exodus 16:4-5

⁴Then the LORD said to Moses, "Behold, I am about to rain bread from heaven for you, and the people shall go out and gather a day's portion every day, that I may test them, whether they will walk in my law or not.
⁵On the sixth day, when they prepare what they bring in, it will be twice as much as they gather daily."

Moses related this to all the people, yet some disobeyed. When they stored more than they needed, the manna rotted and stank. God gave further instructions to Moses regarding the manna.

Exodus 16:23-26

²³he said to them, "This is what the LORD has commanded: 'Tomorrow is a day of solemn rest, a holy Sabbath to the LORD; bake what you will bake and boil what you will boil, and all that is left over lay aside to be kept till the morning.' "
²⁴So they laid it aside till the morning, as Moses commanded them, and it did not stink, and there were no worms in it.
²⁵Moses said, "Eat it today, for today is a Sabbath to the LORD; today you will not find it in the field.
²⁶Six days you shall gather it, but on the seventh day, which is a Sabbath, there will be none."

Moses related this to all the people, yet some disobeyed again. Despite the unambiguous instructions, some of them went out on the Sabbath to collect manna, only to find none just as God had said.

Let's return to 1 Corinthians 10.

1 Corinthians 10:4-5

⁴and **all** drank the same spiritual drink. For they drank from the spiritual Rock that followed them, and the Rock was Christ.

> [5]Nevertheless, with **most** of them God was not pleased,
> for they were overthrown in the wilderness.

Note how all drank the same spiritual drink. The repetition of "all" in 1 Corinthians 10:1-4 draws attention to the fact that *all* of them had the pillar of cloud and fire, *all* of them passed unharmed through the Red Sea, *all* of them ate the miraculously provided manna, *all* of them drank of the miraculously provided water. We will address verse 4 in a moment, but let's consider what it means in verse 5 when it says that God was "not pleased." This employs a figure of speech, *litotes*, understatement that uses a negative to express the positive to a high degree.[167] Keeping the figure in mind, the first part of verse 5 might read, "Nevertheless with most of them God was extremely displeased."

To what does this "spiritual rock" in verse 4 refer? To answer this, we need to consider a passage from Exodus:

Exodus 17:1-7
[1]All the congregation of the people of Israel moved on from the wilderness of Sin by stages, according to the commandment of the LORD, and camped at Rephidim, but there was no water for the people to drink.
[2]Therefore the people quarreled with Moses and said, "Give us water to drink." And Moses said to them, "Why do you quarrel with me? Why do you test the LORD?"
[3]But the people thirsted there for water, and the people grumbled against Moses and said, "Why did you bring us up out of Egypt, to kill us and our children and our livestock with thirst?"
[4]So Moses cried to the LORD, "What shall I do with this people? They are almost ready to stone me."
[5]And the LORD said to Moses, "Pass on before the people, taking with you some of the elders of Israel,

---

[167] Hans, *Go Figure!* 89.

314

and take in your hand the staff with which you struck the Nile, and go.

⁶Behold, I will stand before you there on the rock at Horeb, and you shall strike the rock, and water shall come out of it, and the people will drink." And Moses did so, in the sight of the elders of Israel.

⁷And he called the name of the place Massah and Meribah, because of the quarreling of the people of Israel, and because they tested the LORD by saying, "Is the LORD among us or not?"

In this record, the children of Israel had moved from the wilderness of Sin and were now camped at Rephidim, where there was no water to drink. Again, the Israelites argued with Moses, accusing him of bringing them out of Egypt so that he could kill them with thirst. And yet once again, God miraculously provided for Israel. God instructed Moses to take some elders with him and to strike the rock at Horeb. When he did, water came out for the Israelites to drink. The rock at Horeb was a literal rock, but it also served as a type of the coming Christ.[168]

Let's return to 1 Corinthians 10.

1 Corinthians 10:6-7

⁶Now these things took place as examples for us, that we might not desire evil as they did.

⁷Do not be idolaters as some of them were; as it is written, "The people sat down to eat and drink and rose up to play."

In verse 6, these things serve as an example for Christians *to avoid*. Verse 7 is a partial quote from Exodus 32:6, which reads, "And they rose up early the next day and offered burnt offerings and brought peace offerings. And the people sat down to eat and drink and rose up to play." This refers to the time when Aaron and the children of Israel made a

---

[168] "Type" is a figure of resemblance that can be an example, pattern, mark, or form. For more, see also Zuck, *Basic Bible Interpretation*, 169-184.

molten calf and worshipped it (Exod. 32:1-10). According to one biblical scholar, "to play" suggests "drunken and immoral activities so common to idolatrous fertility cults in their revelry."[169] This play included loud shouting, singing, and dancing (Exod. 32:17-19). This riotous behavior was part of Israel's idolatrous worship of the golden calf.

Let's return to 1 Corinthians 10.

1 Corinthians 10:8
We must not indulge in sexual immorality as some of them did, and twenty-three thousand fell in a single day.

In this verse, we read that 23,000 Israelites died ("fell") in a single day because they indulged in sexual immorality. In this context, sexual immorality may refer to the base sexual practices that accompanied pagan worship, or it may refer to the worship of other gods itself. Either way, "sexual immorality" in this verse is linked to idolatry.

There are several records from the Old Testament that verse 8 may refer to. The first is Exodus 32:28 where we read that about 3,000 men died on the day that Moses came down from Mount Sinai and confronted Aaron and the children of Israel about their idolatrous worship of the golden calf. The Levites killed the 3,000 at God's command. Further, in Exodus 32, we read about a plague God sent on the people because they made and worshipped the calf Aaron made. While there is no specific number mentioned, it is possible that 20,000 died in this plague. That would equal 23,000 people who died in one day because of their idolatry.

A second possible reference is Numbers 25:1-18, where we read that 24,000 Israelites died of a plague brought about because of their idolatrous worship of Baal and other false gods. The chiefs of all the people were hanged separately, and it's possible that there were 1000 of them. If we subtract the leaders who were hanged separately, that leaves 23,000 who died that day. In both cases, 23,000 Israelites died in a single day because of idolatrous worship.

---

[169]   MacArthur, *The MacArthur Study Bible*, 192.

Let's return to 1 Corinthians 10.

1 Corinthians 10:9-10

9We must not put Christ to the test, as some of them did and were destroyed by serpents,

10nor grumble, as some of them did and were destroyed by the Destroyer.

Verse 9 refers to the following passage in Numbers 21.

Numbers 21:4-9

4From Mount Hor they set out by the way to the Red Sea, to go around the land of Edom. And the people became impatient on the way.

5And the people spoke against God and against Moses, "Why have you brought us up out of Egypt to die in the wilderness? For there is no food and no water, and we loathe this worthless food."

6Then the LORD sent fiery serpents among the people, and they bit the people, so that many people of Israel died.

7And the people came to Moses and said, "We have sinned, for we have spoken against the LORD and against you. Pray to the LORD, that he take away the serpents from us." So Moses prayed for the people.

8And the LORD said to Moses, "Make a fiery serpent and set it on a pole, and everyone who is bitten, when he sees it, shall live."

9So Moses made a bronze serpent and set it on a pole. And if a serpent bit anyone, he would look at the bronze serpent and live.

Many of the people of Israel died when bitten by fiery serpents because they spoke against God and Moses (vv. 5-6). Yet when Moses interceded for the people, God mercifully provided a way for them to live after these deadly vipers had bitten them.[170]

Let's return to 1 Corinthians 10. Verse 10 speaks of the Israelites grumbling and being destroyed by the Destroyer. In the Bible, there are numerous references to Israel's grumbling and to the Destroyer. While it's unclear which record or records this refers to, one example of Israel's grumbling followed by their destruction may be found in Numbers 16:41-50. Another example may be found in Numbers 21:5-6, which we just read.

Let's return to 1 Corinthians 10.

> **1 Corinthians 10:11-14**
> [11]Now these things happened to them as an example, but they were written down for our instruction, on whom the end of the ages has come.
> [12]Therefore let anyone who thinks that he stands take heed lest he fall.
> [13]No temptation has overtaken you that is not common to man. God is faithful, and he will not let you be tempted beyond your ability, but with the temptation he will also provide the way of escape, that you may be able to endure it.
> [14]Therefore, my beloved, flee from idolatry.

Once again, we read that what happened to the Israelites serves as an example. The passage then gives two warnings that frame a promise. First, Paul warns the saints to take heed lest they fall. Second, he issues a blunt statement: "flee from idolatry." Twice we read that the Israelites served as examples not to follow. Twice we read about warnings, including "flee idolatry."

---

[170] 1 Corinthians 10:9 reads, "we must not put Christ to the test." But how could the Israelites put Christ to the test if he had not yet been born? According to some critical Greek texts, the word "Christ" should be "Lord." The Israelites put the Lord God to the test by questioning His goodness and His willingness to provide for them.

Sandwiched between these two warnings is a marvelous promise, given in verse 13:

- No temptation is unique to the individual.
- God is faithful.
- God will not allow one to be tempted beyond one's ability.
- God will provide a way of escape from temptation so that one may be able to endure it.

The temptation in this passage refers to the sins Israel committed in the wilderness, which included rebelling against God, murmuring against God, Moses, and Aaron, and committing fornication and idolatry. Remember that 1 Corinthians 10:1-14 follows 1 Corinthians 9:27, where Paul writes about the possibility of his being disqualified from receiving the prize.

What could disqualify him? Imitating Israel's sin of disobedience and idolatry. The Corinthians were warned not to imitate Israel and forfeit the prize through their disobedience and idolatry. We should also recall Colossians 2:18 where the saints are warned about the worship of angels and other idolatrous practices that would disqualify and rob them of the prize (see Chapter 6: "The Crown").

Conclusion

In this appendix, we have seen that in 1 Corinthians 10:1-14, there are numerous quotations from and references to Old Testament records about Israel's sin and idolatry during their time in the wilderness. Despite God's miraculous provision for them—the cloud by day, the pillar of fire at night, the parting of the Red Sea, the provision of quails and manna and water—Israel rebelled against God and worshipped false gods in the wilderness. They disobeyed God's commands regarding the manna. They continually grumbled against Moses and Aaron. They grumbled against God, doubting His willingness and ability to provide for them in the wilderness. They accused Moses of wanting to kill them in the wilderness. They incited Aaron to build a golden calf, which they worshipped. As such, they serve as examples for the Church to avoid. These examples are for the Church's instruction. Just as most of the Israelites forfeited going into the Promised Land because of their rebellion, so too can a son of God forfeit the prize by imitating Israel.

In Numbers 14, we read Moses's prayer for God to forgive Israel immediately after their worship of the Golden Calf:

> **Numbers 14:19-24**
> [19]Please pardon the iniquity of this people, according to the greatness of your steadfast love, just as you have forgiven this people, from Egypt until now."
> [20]Then the LORD said, "I have pardoned, according to your word.
> [21]But truly, as I live, and as all the earth shall be filled with the glory of the LORD,
> [22]none of the men who have seen my glory and my signs that I did in Egypt and in the wilderness, and yet have put me to the test these ten times and have not obeyed my voice,
> [23]shall see the land that I swore to give to their fathers. And none of those who despised me shall see it.
> [24]But my servant Caleb, because he has a different spirit and has followed me fully, I will bring into the land into which he went, and his descendants shall possess it.

God pardoned the Israelites according to Moses's request, yet they still were not permitted to enter the Promised Land.

First Corinthians 10 tells us that all the children of Israel were under the cloud, all passed through the sea, all were baptized into Moses, all ate the same spiritual food, and all drank the same spiritual drink, but God was not pleased with most of them. In a similar vein, all born-again ones are righteous, sanctified, redeemed, justified, and have an inheritance. All run in the race, yet not all will receive the crown. Christians must heed the warnings of 1 Corinthians 10:1-14 lest they disqualify themselves from receiving the prize.

Appendix G

A Study of *Kathizō* (Seated)

Ephesians 2:4-6
[4]But God, being rich in mercy, because of the great love with which he loved us,
[5]even when we were dead in our trespasses, made us alive together with Christ—by grace you have been saved—
[6]and raised us up with him and **seated** us **with** (*sunkathizō*) him in the heavenly places in Christ Jesus,

In chapter 8 we noted that in the Greek New Testament, the word translated as "seated with" (v. 6) is *sunkathizō*, a compound word from *sun*, meaning together, and *kathizō*, meaning to sit. With a view to clarifying what it means to be "seated with" Christ in the heavenly places, we offer this appendix listing all 48 occurrences of the verb *kathizō* in the Greek New Testament.

Few occurrences of *kathizō* mean literally to sit or to rest. Instead, most of the time, *kathizō* refers to sitting on a seat to perform functions such as teaching, judging, exercising authority, and calculating. As we read each use, the reader needs to consider the word in its immediate and remote context. The following table lists all occurrences of *kathizō*. We've arranged them topically but understand that other groupings might work. Our objective here is to show that sitting indicates more than just taking a seat and resting.

Usage	Verses
Sit down with the purpose of teaching	Matt. 5:1 …the mountain: and when he sat down, his disciples came… Mark 9:35 And he sat down and called the twelve… Luke 4:20 …the attendant and sat down… Luke 5:3 …the land. And he sat down and taught… John 8:2 …unto him, and he sat down and taught them. Acts 8:31 …to come up and sit with him. Acts 16:13 …a place of prayer, and we sat down and spoke… Acts 18:11 And he stayed a year and six months teaching…
Sit to rest, meaning to stay	Acts 2:3 …of fire appeared to them and rested on each one of them.
Sit down	Matt. 13:48 …sat down and sorted the good… 1 Cor. 10:7 …written, "The people sat down to eat and drink…."
Sit down to judge	Mark 11:2 …no one has ever sat. Untie it and… Mark 11:7 …and he sat on it [colt]. Mark 12:41 And he sat down opposite the treasury and watched… Luke 19:30 …colt tied, on which no one has ever yet sat. Luke 22:30 …my kingdom and sit on thrones judging… John 12:14 …a young donkey and sat on…[170] John 19:13 …Jesus out and sat down on the judgment seat… Acts 25:6 …the next day he took his seat on the tribunal… Acts 25:17 …on the next day took my seat on the tribunal… 1 Cor. 6:4 …such cases, why do you lay them before those who…

---

[171] According to some ancient Eastern cultures, a ruler riding on a donkey's colt indicated the carrying out of judgment. In the Bible, judges or rulers would sometimes ride on donkeys as an indication of their position. (See Judg. 5:10, 10:3-4, 12:13-14).

Usage	Verses
Exercising authority	Matt. 20:21 ...two sons of mine are to sit, one at your right... Matt. 20:23 ...but to sit at my right hand... Matt. 23:2 ...and the Pharisees sit on Moses' seat... Mark 10:37 ...Grant us to sit, one at your right... Mark 10:40 ...but to sit at my right... 2 Thess. 2:4 ...so that he takes his seat in the temple of God...
To sit, with the location of sitting being a "throne," indicates authority	Matt. 19:28 ...Son of Man will sit on his glorious throne... Matt. 19:28 ...will also sit on twelve thrones... Matt. 25:31 ...will sit on his glorious throne. Acts 2:30 ...set one of his descendants on his throne... Acts 12:21 ...his royal robes, took his seat upon the throne... Rev. 3:21 ...I will grant him to sit with me on my throne... Rev. 3:21 ...also conquered and sat down with my Father on his throne. Rev. 20:4 ...saw thrones, and seated on them were to those whom the authority to judge was committed.
To sit, location being God's right hand- indicates authority	Mark 16:19 ...into heaven and sat down at the right hand of God. Eph. 1:20 ...from the dead and seated him at his right hand... Heb. 1:3 ...making purification for sins, he sat down at the right hand of the Majesty on high... Heb. 8:1 ...high priest, one who is seated at the right hand of the throne of the Majesty in heaven... Heb. 10:12 ...for sins, he sat down at the right hand of God... Heb. 12:2 ...the shame, and is seated at the right hand of the throne of God...

Usage	Verses
Sit down to wait	Matt. 26:36 ...to his disciples, "Sit here, while I go..." Mark 14:32 ...to his disciples, "Sit here while I pray." Luke 24:49 ...upon you. But stay in the city... Acts 13:14 ...they went into the synagogue and sat down.
Sit down to calculate, write	Luke 14:28 ...sit down and count the cost... Luke 14:31 ...king in war, will not sit down first and deliberate... Luke 16:6 '...and sit down quickly and write fifty.'

From this, we gather that the reasons for sitting are to:

- Sit down to teach.
- Sit down to rest.
- Sit down to judge.
- Sit down to exercise or indicate authority.
- Sit down to wait.
- Sit down to calculate, write.

Even in modern usage, the word "seat" can connote a position of authority. For example, when we say that someone is "running for a seat in the Senate," we mean much more than seeking a place to sit.

While we won't discuss every occurrence of *kathizō*, we will take the time to consider some. Most references have to do with sitting down to exercise some kind of authority. For instance, some speak of Jesus Christ being seated at God's right hand and exercising authority.

Ephesians 1:19-23

[19]and what is the immeasurable greatness of his power toward us who believe, according to the working of his great might

[20]that he worked in Christ when he raised him from the dead and **seated** (*kathizō*) him at his right hand in the heavenly places,

²¹far above all rule and authority and power and dominion, and above every name that is named, not only in this age but also in the one to come.
²²And he put all things under his feet and gave him as head over all things to the church,
²³which is his body, the fullness of him who fills all in all.

Mark 16:19

So then the Lord Jesus, after he had spoken to them, was taken up into heaven and **sat** (*kathizō*) down at the right hand of God.

Hebrews 1:3

He is the radiance of the glory of God and the exact imprint of his nature, and he upholds the universe by the word of his power. After making purification for sins, he **sat** (*kathizō*) down at the right hand of the Majesty on high,

Hebrews 8:1

Now the point in what we are saying is this: we have such a high priest, one who is **seated** (*kathizō*) at the right hand of the throne of the Majesty in heaven,

Hebrews 10:12

But when Christ had offered for all time a single sacrifice for sins, he **sat** (*kathizō*) down at the right hand of God,

Hebrews 12:2

looking to Jesus, the founder and perfecter of our faith, who for the joy that was set before him endured the cross, despising the shame, and is **seated** (*kathizō*) at the right hand of the throne of God.

The right hand represents power and authority. Therefore, Jesus Christ's being seated at God's right hand implies having a position of power and authority.

In the book of Revelation, some are described as sitting on thrones with Jesus Christ:

> **Revelation 3:21**
> The one who conquers, I will grant him to **sit** (*kathizō*) with me on my throne, as I also conquered and **sat** (*kathizō*) down with my Father on his throne.

> **Revelation 20:4**
> Then I saw thrones, and **seated** (*kathizō*) on them were those to whom the authority to judge was committed. Also I saw the souls of those who had been beheaded for the testimony of Jesus and for the word of God, and those who had not worshiped the beast or its image and had not received its mark on their foreheads or their hands. They came to life and reigned with Christ for a thousand years.

It's clear that those sitting on thrones exercise authority.

In the following verse, note the correlation between sitting and judging.

> **Matthew 19:28**
> Jesus said to them, "Truly, I say to you, in the new world, when the Son of Man will **sit** (*kathizō*) on his glorious throne, you who have followed me will also **sit** (*kathizō*) on twelve thrones, judging the twelve tribes of Israel.

Jesus Christ made this promise to the twelve apostles. In this instance, judging carries with it the connotation of ruling and exercising authority.

In Matthew 20:20-21 and Mark 10:35-37, 40-43, James and John, together with their mother, asked Jesus Christ to sit at his right and left hand. These were singular positions of rulership and authority.

We see this same usage in the following verses:

Matthew 23:2-3
²"The scribes and the Pharisees **sit** (*kathizō*) on Moses' seat, ³so do and observe whatever they tell you, but not the works they do. For they preach, but do not practice.

In sitting in Moses' seat, the Pharisees exercised rule over the people.

Matthew 25:31-32
³¹"When the Son of Man comes in his glory, and all the angels with him, then he will **sit** (*kathizō*) on his glorious throne.
³²Before him will be gathered all the nations, and he will separate people one from another as a shepherd separates the sheep from the goats.

Sitting on "his glorious throne" implies more than a place to sit but has the connotation of rulership and judgment.

In some ancient Eastern cultures, a ruler riding on a donkey's colt indicated the carrying out of judgment.[172] In the Bible, judges or rulers sometimes rode on donkeys to indicate their position and function. (See Judg. 5:10, 10:3-4, 12:13-14). Therefore, when we read that they brought a colt for Jesus to sit (*kathizō*) on, we know that this signified more than a mode of transportation (Mark 11:7).

Note the following references to carrying out judgment or exercising authority after being seated:

Luke 22:30
that you may eat and drink at my table in my kingdom and **sit** (*kathizō*) on thrones judging the twelve tribes of Israel.

---

[172] Wierwille, *Jesus Christ Our Passover*, 43-45.

John 19:13
So when Pilate heard these words, he brought Jesus out and **sat** (*kathizō*) down on the judgment seat at a place called The Stone Pavement, and in Aramaic Gabbatha.

Acts 2:30
Being therefore a prophet, and knowing that God had sworn with an oath to him that he would **set** (*kathizō*) one of his descendants on his throne,

Acts 12:21
On an appointed day Herod put on his royal robes, took his **seat** (*kathizō*) upon the throne, and delivered an oration to them.

In his first epistle to the Corinthians, Paul asked, why would you set those who have no authority in the Church in a position to judge?

1 Corinthians 6:4
So if you have such cases, why do you **lay** them **before** (*kathizō*) those who have no standing in the church?

And in 2 Thessalonians, Paul wrote:

2 Thessalonians 2:3-4
³Let no one deceive you in any way. For that day will not come, unless the rebellion comes first, and the man of lawlessness is revealed, the son of destruction,
⁴who opposes and exalts himself against every so-called god or object of worship, so that he takes his **seat** (*kathizō*) in the temple of God, proclaiming himself to be God.

In sitting in the temple of God, the man of lawlessness elevates himself to a position of high authority, proclaiming himself to be God.

From considering the uses of the verb *kathizō*, we see that in addition to physically sitting someplace, *kathizō* often carries the connotations of authority, judgment, and rulership. While *kathizō* can indicate resting or sitting after completing a task, it may have a different connotation depending on the PLACE of sitting, such as a throne, judgment seat, or in the heavenlies. Thus, when we read in Ephesians 2:6 that the Church is "seated together with him [Christ] in the heavenly places," we understand that this seating carries the connotation of having authority.

Appendix H

Some Words and Expressions that Signify Reward

In the Bible, the word "reward" means wage or compensation.[173] For example, we read about the reward in the following passages:

Reward

Matthew 5:11-12

[11]"Blessed are you when others revile you and persecute you and utter all kinds of evil against you falsely on my account. [12]Rejoice and be glad, for your **reward** is great in heaven, for so they persecuted the prophets who were before you.

Luke 6:22-23

[22]"Blessed are you when people hate you and when they exclude you and revile you and spurn your name as evil, on account of the Son of Man! [23]Rejoice in that day, and leap for joy, for behold, your **reward** is great in heaven; for so their fathers did to the prophets.

Luke 6:35

But love your enemies, and do good, and lend, expecting nothing in return, and your **reward** will be great, and you will be sons of the Most High, for he is kind to the ungrateful and the evil.

---

[173] Every use of the word "reward" in the verses in this appendix is translated from the Greek word *misthos.*

Matthew 10:41-42

[41]The one who receives a prophet because he is a prophet will receive a prophet's **reward**, and the one who receives a righteous person because he is a righteous person will receive a righteous person's **reward**.
[42]And whoever gives one of these little ones even a cup of cold water because he is a disciple, truly, I say to you, he will by no means lose his **reward**."

The word translated as "reward" in these examples is *misthos* in the Greek New Testament. It means compensation and refers to the future reward for the believer. In these examples (and many others), it's plain to see that "reward" refers to a literal reward that will be given out.

However, other words and expressions used in the Bible also indicate future reward, future compensation. In these cases, the wording is figurative, so the meaning might not be readily apparent. The following chart offers *some* ways future reward is figuratively referred to in the Bible. (That's not to say, however, that these expressions always signify future reward. The context would determine their meaning.) Except where noted, these verses are covered in detail in the body of the book, so a full explanation here is not warranted.

No.	Word/Expression	Scriptures
1	treasure in heaven	Matt. 6:20, 19:21; Mark 10:21; Luke 12:33, 18:22
2	treasure	1 Tim. 6:19
3	fruit for eternal life	John 4:36
4	fruit that increases to your credit	Phil. 4:15-17
5	not be unfruitful	Titus 3:14
6	prize	1 Cor. 9:24; Phil. 3:14
7	crown ("wreath" ESV)	1 Cor. 9:25; 2 Tim. 4:8; James 1:12; 1 Pet. 5:4
8	eternal life	Matt. 19:29; Mark 10:30; Luke 18:30

No.	Word/Expression	Scriptures
9	reap eternal life	Gal. 6:8
10	take hold of eternal life	1 Tim. 6:12
11	promise for the life to come	1 Tim. 4:8
12	recompense at the resurrection of the just	Luke 14:12-14
13	honor	John 12:26
14	commendation from God	1 Cor. 4:5
15	receive what is due	2 Cor. 5:10
16	receive back from the lord	Eph. 6:8
17	acknowledge before my Father in heaven	Matt. 10:32
18	loses his life...will find it; repay each person according to what he has done	Matt. 16:25-27; Mark 8:35; Luke 9:24
19	set over all his possessions	Luke 12:44
20	repaid at the resurrection of the just	Luke 14:14
21	more will be given	Luke 19:26
22	labor is not in vain	1 Cor. 15:58
23	things that belong to salvation	Heb. 6:9
24	richly provided entrance into the kingdom	2 Pet. 1:11

Treasure

Matthew 6:19-21

[19]"Do not lay up for yourselves treasures on earth, where moth and rust destroy and where thieves break in and steal, [20]but lay up for yourselves **treasures in heaven**, where neither moth nor rust destroys and where thieves do not break in and steal.

[21]For where your treasure is, there your heart will be also.

In verse 20, does the phrase "treasures in heaven" mean that there will be pots of gold or chests filled with precious jewels in heaven? No, this refers to future reward. We see this figurative expression in other verses as well.

Matthew 19:21
Jesus said to him, "If you would be perfect, go, sell what you possess and give to the poor, and you will have **treasure in heaven**; and come, follow me."

Mark 10:21
And Jesus, looking at him, loved him, and said to him, "You lack one thing: go, sell all that you have and give to the poor, and you will have **treasure in heaven**; and come, follow me."

Luke 18:22
When Jesus heard this, he said to him, "One thing you still lack. Sell all that you have and distribute to the poor, and you will have **treasure in heaven**; and come, follow me."

Luke 12:33
Sell your possessions, and give to the needy. Provide yourselves with moneybags that do not grow old, with a **treasure in the heavens** that does not fail, where no thief approaches and no moth destroys.

In these verses, the phrase "treasure in heaven" signifies reward. (In Luke 12:33, the phrase "moneybags that do not grow old" also refers to reward.)

1 Timothy 6:17-19
[17]As for the rich in this present age, charge them not to be haughty, nor to set their hopes on the uncertainty

of riches, but on God, who richly provides us with everything to enjoy.

[18]They are to do good, to be rich in good works, to be generous and ready to share,

[19]thus storing up **treasure** for themselves as a good foundation for the future, so that they may take hold of that which is truly life.

In 1 Timothy 6:17-19, Paul encouraged those "rich in the world" to "take hold of that which is truly life." According to the context, they do this by doing good, being rich in good works, by being ready to share generously. They are "storing up treasure for themselves as a good foundation for the future." In this passage, the word "treasure" signifies future reward.

Fruit

John 4:31-37
[31]Meanwhile the disciples were urging him, saying, "Rabbi, eat."

[32]But he said to them, "I have food to eat that you do not know about."

[33]So the disciples said to one another, "Has anyone brought him something to eat?"

[34]Jesus said to them, "My food is to do the will of him who sent me and to accomplish his work.

[35]Do you not say, 'There are yet four months, then comes the harvest'? Look, I tell you, lift up your eyes, and see that the fields are white for harvest.

[36]Already the one who reaps is receiving wages and gathering **fruit** for eternal life, so that sower and reaper may rejoice together.

[37]For here the saying holds true, 'One sows and another reaps.'

In verse 36, when Jesus Christ refers to gathering "fruit for eternal life," is he speaking about apples, oranges, and bananas? No. "Fruit for eternal life" is figurative for reward.

In this context, we see that Jesus Christ had just spoken to a Samaritan woman at Jacob's well and that the woman believed he was the Christ. She went back to tell others. In the meantime, his disciples went into the city to buy food. When they returned, they saw Jesus Christ talking to this Samaritan woman. In verse 31, they spoke about physical food, but Jesus Christ is speaking about spiritual food—that is, doing the will of God and accomplishing His work. The harvest he referred to in verse 35 is people, like the Samaritan woman, who believed he was the Christ. In verse 36, the "one who reaps" refers to the woman who went and spoke about the Messiah to the other Samaritans. She is the one "gathering fruit for eternal life," meaning reward. If you read the following verses, you will see many Samaritans believed after hearing from the Samaritan woman. Jesus stayed with the Samaritans for two more days, and even more believed!

Philippians 4:15-17

[15]And you Philippians yourselves know that in the beginning of the gospel, when I left Macedonia, no church entered into partnership with me in giving and receiving, except you only.
[16]Even in Thessalonica you sent me help for my needs once and again.
[17]Not that I seek the gift, but I seek the **fruit** that increases to your credit.

Some versions render the latter part of verse 17 as "fruit that may be credited to your account" (Berean Literal Bible); "fruit that may abound to your account" (KJV); and "more [fruit] be credited to your account" (NIV). So, what account is Paul referring to?

The words "fruit" and "seek" give us a clue. Fruit comes from planting a seed and then reaping. Fruit is not a one-for-one exchange, either. One seed yields much more than one piece of fruit. In this context, then, Paul refers to the Philippians' financial giving as something that would produce fruit that would be credited to their account. While "fruit" in verse 17 may refer to the blessings for giving in the present, it also refers to the blessings of future reward for giving.

Prize/Crown

1 Corinthians 9:24-25

[24]Do you not know that in a race all the runners run, but only one receives the **prize**? So run that you may obtain it.

[25]Every athlete exercises self-control in all things. They do it to receive a perishable wreath, but we an imperishable.

In verse 24, the "prize" refers to a specific type of reward.

Philippians 3:13-14

[13]Brothers, I do not consider that I have made it my own. But one thing I do: forgetting what lies behind and straining forward to what lies ahead,

[14]I press on toward the goal for the **prize** of the upward call of God in Christ Jesus.

As discussed in chapter 6, the prize refers to the crown given to those who fulfill the criteria outlined in the Scriptures.

2 Timothy 4:7-8

[7]I have fought the good fight, I have finished the race, I have kept the faith.

[8]Henceforth there is laid up for me the **crown** of righteousness, which the Lord, the righteous judge, will award to me on that day, and not only to me but also to all who have loved his appearing.

1 Corinthians 9:25
Every athlete exercises self-control in all things. They do it to receive a perishable **wreath**, but we an imperishable.

James 1:12
Blessed is the man who remains steadfast under trial, for when he has stood the test he will receive the **crown** of life, which God has promised to those who love him.

1 Peter 5:4
And when the chief Shepherd appears, you will receive the unfading **crown** of glory.

The crown or wreath refers to a specific type of future reward in these verses.

Eternal Life

The phrase "eternal life" is a metonymy for reward in several verses.

Matthew 19:29
And everyone who has left houses or brothers or sisters or father or mother or children or lands, for my name's sake, will receive a hundredfold and will inherit **eternal life**.

Mark 10:29-30
[29]Jesus said, "Truly, I say to you, there is no one who has left house or brothers or sisters or mother or father or children or lands, for my sake and for the gospel, [30]who will not receive a hundredfold now in this time, houses and brothers and sisters and mothers and children and lands, with persecutions, and in the age to come **eternal life**.

Luke 18:29-30

29And he said to them, "Truly, I say to you, there is no one who has left house or wife or brothers or parents or children, for the sake of the kingdom of God,
30who will not receive many times more in this time, and in the age to come **eternal life**."

In these verses, the phrase "eternal life" is a metonymy to refer to things associated with eternal life, like the reward. Jesus Christ is not asking his disciples to give up houses, parents, family, and so forth, for his sake so that they might gain eternal life. Instead, he is saying that in doing so, they would be rewarded for their commitment.

Galatians 6:7-10

7Do not be deceived: God is not mocked, for whatever one sows, that will he also reap.
8For the one who sows to his own flesh will from the flesh reap corruption, but the one who sows to the Spirit will from the Spirit reap **eternal life**.
9And let us not grow weary of doing good, for in due season we will reap, if we do not give up.
10So then, as we have opportunity, let us do good to everyone, and especially to those who are of the household of faith.

Romans 6:23 says, "the free gift of God is eternal life in Christ Jesus our Lord." One cannot work ("reap") to receive eternal life. Here "eternal life" is put by metonymy for things pertaining to eternal life, such as reward. The saints are encouraged not to "grow weary in doing good" and to take every opportunity to "do good to everyone... especially to those who are of the household of faith." Doing good is not a requirement for salvation, but "doing good" can yield reward.

1 Timothy 6:11-12

[11]But as for you, O man of God, flee these things. Pursue righteousness, godliness, faith, love, steadfastness, gentleness.

[12]Fight the good fight of the faith. Take hold of the **eternal life** to which you were called and about which you made the good confession in the presence of many witnesses.

In verse 12, the man of God is encouraged to "take hold of the eternal life." Since eternal life is a gift and not something one can earn, the expression "take hold of the eternal life" in this passage is a figurative way to signify the reward.

Promise

1 Timothy 4:7-8

[7]Have nothing to do with irreverent, silly myths. Rather train yourself for godliness;

[8]for while bodily training is of some value, godliness is of value in every way, as it holds **promise** for the present life and also for the life to come.

Training oneself in godliness brings blessings in this life and also for the "life to come." Since we can do no work to obtain salvation and the associated blessings, the promise for life to come is in the category of reward. In contrast, bodily training only has some value for this life. However, training in godliness yields profit in this life and reward in the future.

Praise and Glory and Honor

1 Peter 1:7

so that the tested genuineness of your faith—more precious than gold that perishes though it is tested by fire—may be found to result in **praise and glory and honor** at the revelation of Jesus Christ.

In this verse, the phrase "praise and glory and honor" signifies recognition, a figurative expression meaning future reward.

Commendation from God

1 Corinthians 4:5
Therefore do not pronounce judgment before the time, before the Lord comes, who will bring to light the things now hidden in darkness and will disclose the purposes of the heart. Then each one will receive his **commendation** from God.

The phrase "commendation from God" signifies future reward.

Receive

2 Corinthians 5:10
For we must all appear before the judgment seat of Christ, so that each one may **receive what is due** for what he has done in the body, whether good or evil.

The phrase "receive what is due" signifies future reward.

Ephesians 6:5-9
[5]Bondservants, obey your earthly masters with fear and trembling, with a sincere heart, as you would Christ,
[6]not by the way of eye-service, as people-pleasers, but as bondservants of Christ, doing the will of God from the heart,
[7]rendering service with a good will as to the Lord and not to man,

⁸knowing that whatever good anyone does, this he will **receive back from the Lord**, whether he is a bondservant or is free.

⁹Masters, do the same to them, and stop your threatening, knowing that he who is both their Master and yours is in heaven, and that there is no partiality with him.

Though this section explicitly addresses bondservants and their relationship to earthly masters, the application extends to "whatever good anyone does (bond or free)." Those who serve as if they were serving Christ, "doing the will of God from the heart," will be repaid by the lord. In this context, to "receive back from the lord" signifies reward.

Other Expressions

Acknowledged before my Father in heaven

Matthew 10:32-33
³²So everyone who acknowledges me before men, I also will **acknowledge before my Father who is in heaven**, ³³but whoever denies me before men, I also will deny before my Father who is in heaven.

If we were to continue reading the context of this chapter and arrive at verses 41 and 42, we would understand that "acknowledgment" signifies reward.

Lose his life for my sake shall find it

Matthew 16:24-27
²⁴Then Jesus told his disciples, "If anyone would come after me, let him deny himself and take up his cross and follow me.

342

²⁵For whoever would save his life will lose it, but whoever **loses his life for my sake will find it.**
²⁶For what will it profit a man if he gains the whole world and forfeits his soul? Or what shall a man give in return for his soul?
²⁷For the Son of Man is going to come with his angels in the glory of his Father, and then he will repay each person according to what he has done.

Note that the context is speaking of taking up the cross, meaning denying one's self-interests for the interests of Christ. Further, Jesus Christ is addressing his disciples. According to Jesus Christ, a disciple was someone who believed on him and continued in his word (John 8:31). In John 5:24, 6:40, 47, 11:25 and other records, Jesus Christ said that those who believe on him have eternal life. Thus to "lose the soul" in Matthew 8:25 cannot mean to lose eternal life.

In addition, the words "life" and "soul" are translated from the same Greek word *psuchē*, which means breath life. It is *never* used in association with eternal life. (The Greek word associated with eternal life is *zōē*.) If we were to translate *psuchē* consistently, verse 26 would read, "For what will it profit a man if he gains the whole world and forfeits his *life*? Or what shall a man give in return for his *life*?" Therefore, gaining the whole world, spending one's life in self-interest, would mean forfeiting one's life. There would be no reward for that individual, for he had wasted his life not following Christ, but his own interests. Mark 8:34-38 and Luke 9:23-26 use a similar expression and also mean eternal reward.

Set over all his possessions

Luke 12:42-44
⁴²And the Lord said, "Who then is the faithful and wise manager, whom his master will set over his household, to give them their portion of food at the proper time?

343

⁴³Blessed is that servant whom his master will find so doing when he comes.

⁴⁴Truly, I say to you, he will **set him over all his possessions**.

In Luke 12:35-40, Jesus Christ taught a parable. In it, he spoke of the need for servants to be faithful managers to be ready when the master returned. In verse 42, we read about the faithful and wise manager who would be blessed upon his master's return. As a reward, that master would set the trustworthy manager "over all his possessions." As a result, he would receive a position of authority and responsibility for his faithful service to the master. This signifies future reward.

Repaid at the resurrection of the just

Luke 14:12-14

¹²He said also to the man who had invited him, "When you give a dinner or a banquet, do not invite your friends or your brothers or your relatives or rich neighbors, lest they also invite you in return and you be repaid.

¹³But when you give a feast, invite the poor, the crippled, the lame, the blind,

¹⁴and you will be blessed, because they cannot repay you. For you will be **repaid at the resurrection of the just**."

To be repaid at the resurrection of the just signifies reward.

Things that belong to salvation

Hebrews 6:9-10

⁹Though we speak in this way, yet in your case, beloved, we feel sure of better things—**things that belong to salvation**.

¹⁰For God is not unjust so as to overlook your work and the love that you have shown for his name in serving the saints, as you still do.

The context of Hebrews 6 refers to those who "fall away," meaning they stop living fruitful Christian lives. These saints are encouraged instead to continue in the works they had been doing so they would "inherit the promises" (Heb. 6:12). The things that belong to salvation include reward. Salvation is by grace, inheritance is by grace, and many other things that God has given with salvation are by grace. Therefore, anything that the saints are encouraged *to do* to receive something back would fall into the reward category.

Richly provided entrance

2 Peter 1:5-11

⁵For this very reason, make every effort to supplement your faith with virtue, and virtue with knowledge,
⁶and knowledge with self-control, and self-control with steadfastness, and steadfastness with godliness,
⁷and godliness with brotherly affection, and brotherly affection with love.
⁸For if these qualities are yours and are increasing, they keep you from being ineffective or unfruitful in the knowledge of our Lord Jesus Christ.
⁹For whoever lacks these qualities is so nearsighted that he is blind, having forgotten that he was cleansed from his former sins.
¹⁰Therefore, brothers, be all the more diligent to confirm your calling and election, for if you practice these qualities you will never fall.
¹¹For in this way there will be **richly provided for you an entrance into the eternal kingdom** of our Lord and Savior Jesus Christ.

We know that the Scriptures teach that entrance into the kingdom is via the new birth and not by any work a person does. And so, in speaking of a "richly provided entrance" into the kingdom, Peter is speaking figuratively of future reward.

Appendix I

Frequently Asked Questions

Most of these questions come from students who participated in our live seminars, while others have come from correspondences. While this is not a complete list of all the queries we've received over the years, it does represent the most-asked questions. We hope you find them helpful and encouraging. (In most cases, we retained the original wording of the questions.)

Questions about the Reward

1   Why study the topic of reward?

The reward is spoken about throughout the Scriptures, so it merits our attention. It is a topic that Jesus Christ frequently addressed in his earthly ministry, especially as a motivation to serve when enduring affliction. We study the reward because it is a blessing to know, at least in part, what is in store for the Church in the future ages.

For more information, see Chapter 4: "The Reward."

2   Is the topic of reward important?

The reward is one incentive to live a life of service and commitment to the Lord Jesus Christ and the Gospel. The carnal Christian may follow worldly pursuits and not grow in the knowledge of the truth, not put on the mind of Christ, and not seek to excel in spiritual matters. However, studying the topic of the reward helps one understand what is at stake, that serving will benefit us now and be rewarded in eternity.

For more information, see Chapter 4: "The Reward."

3 Where does the idea of rewards come from?

Eternal reward is God's idea. The reward is mentioned throughout the Scriptures, even at the close of the book of Revelation, where Jesus Christ says, "Behold, I am coming soon, bringing my recompense (*misthos*) with me, to repay each one for what he has done" (Rev. 22:12).

> For more information, see Chapter 4: "The Reward."

4 Can you lose previously gained rewards?

No, the Scriptures do not indicate that it is possible to lose rewards. A person may lose out on gaining *future* reward, or he may lose out on receiving the crown if he does not fulfill the criteria outlined in the Scriptures. But the believer cannot lose any reward he has already attained for his service because it would be unrighteous for God to forget his labor (Heb. 6:10). Anything that merits a reward will be rewarded. However, anything that does not stand the test of fire, as specified in 1 Corinthians 3, will be burned. We have also seen in the Scriptures that saints can live unfruitful lives. Indeed, a believer might spend his entire life serving himself or other gods, and then his reward at the *bēma* of Christ would be pretty minimal, wouldn't it? God would have all to bear fruit until Christ returns or they fall asleep. In fact, believers are encouraged to get the "full reward" mentioned in 2 John 1:8, including the crown.

> For more information, see Chapter 4: "The Reward."

5 How serious is the loss suffered if my work is burned?

No man, except the Lord Jesus Christ, walks perfectly with God. So, it isn't too hard to imagine that Christians will not be rewarded for some of the works they have done, those things that are not built on the foundation of Jesus Christ. Things like causing division in the fellowship of the saints or promulgating the wrong doctrine are works that will be burned up at the *bēma* of Christ. Those works will not be rewarded. But once they have been burned, "every man will have praise of God" for what remains.

In chapter 4, when we examined 1 Corinthians 3:17 ("If anyone destroys God's temple, God will destroy him."), we discussed the meaning of "destroy." It spoke to the seriousness of the loss. Other Scriptures also indicate that the loss for returning to the "defilements of the world" is serious.

2 Peter 2:20-22

[20]For if, after they have escaped the defilements of the world through the knowledge of our Lord and Savior Jesus Christ, they are again entangled in them and overcome, the last state has become worse for them than the first.

[21]For it would have been better for them never to have known the way of righteousness than after knowing it to turn back from the holy commandment delivered to them.

[22]What the true proverb says has happened to them: "The dog returns to its own vomit, and the sow, after washing herself, returns to wallow in the mire."

Verse 20 says that the "last state is worse than the first," meaning that not knowing the way of righteousness is better than knowing it and then turning back from it. This cannot literally be true and is, in fact, a figure of speech hyperbole. Certainly, being born again and having eternal life is better than not being born again. And so, in using hyperbole in verse 21, Peter draws attention to the seriousness of returning to the world's defilements. As we have noted, it is God's will that Christians receive a "full reward." It's one thing to occasionally do works that will not receive a reward versus quitting on the Christian life altogether and not finishing the race. We know that no crown will be rewarded to those who abandon their Christian service. Not receiving a reward, like the crown, is a severe loss, indeed.

> For more information, see Chapter 4: "The Reward."

6   How do rewards fit with grace? Do rewards repudiate grace?

For an answer to this question, see Chapter 5: "Reward and Grace."

7   What is rewarded? What are rewards given for?

For an answer to this question, see Chapter 4: "The Reward."

8   What will the reward be?

Jesus Christ spoke about a righteous man's reward and a prophet's reward, indicating different categories or degrees of reward. Paul, by revelation, said that each person would receive his own reward according to his own labor. Someone may labor a little and another much. So, we know that there will be various degrees of reward. We also understand from the Scriptures that the reward involves receiving positions of authority in future ages. For example, Jesus Christ told the twelve Apostles that they would sit on twelve thrones judging the Twelve Tribes of Israel because of their all-out commitment to him and the Gospel. We also learned that the crown signifies some type of specific reward and that the crown likely signifies having a position of authority in the kingdom of God. Even though we have learned that there are degrees of reward, that the reward includes having positions of authority in Christ's kingdom, and that the reward is of great value, we don't know all there is to know about this topic. This is merely our current understanding of the reward.

> For more information, see Chapter 7: "The Nature of the Reward."

9   Do the teachings of Christ in the Gospels about the reward apply to the Church?

For an answer to this question, please see Appendix E: "Jesus Christ's Teachings on Reward."

10 *Are rewards given to motivate the believer?*

According to Romans 12:1, the encouragement to serve is in consideration of the "mercies of God." Jesus Christ has laid down his life for us so that we can serve him and not be the servants of men. So, the beseeching to serve in Romans 12 is in light of God's mercy and what He has already done for us in Christ.

However, God's Word also encourages us to abound in the work of the lord because our labor is not in vain in the lord, meaning that such work will be profitable now and will be rewarded in the future. While the reward may motivate one to serve, it is not the *only* motivation. Love for and thanksgiving to God are also motivators. Interestingly, in the Scriptures, the reward is often held up as a motivation when the service is challenging to carry out or when one is persecuted, reviled, and afflicted for Christ's sake. During difficult times, it's easy to see how some may want to forsake their Christian service. At times like this, the promise of future reward can be an incentive indeed.

The allure of the world can also stop people from continuing in their service to God, and the reward is a motivation to overcome such distractions. For instance, Jesus Christ taught that the cares, riches, and pleasures of this life could choke the Word of God in one's life so that they become unfruitful (Luke 8:14). We also read about Demas, who forsook Paul, having loved this present age (2 Tim. 4:10) and about those enemies of the cross of Christ who minded earthly things (Phil. 3:18-19). Those who are tempted to forsake the things above for those on this earth may be motivated to change their orientation—from present and earthly to eternal and heavenly—when they consider the promise of future reward.

> For more information, see Chapter 4: "The Reward," and Chapter 6: "The Crown."

11 When are the rewards given out?

When Christ returns, the reward will be given out at the Judgment seat (*bēma*) of Christ. The reward for others who are not part of the One Body of Christ will be given at the resurrection of the just.

For more information, see Appendix C: The Judgment Seat of Christ

12 Does the word "reward" only refer to future compensation?

The word "reward" in the English Bible can refer to a future reward, a reward in this life, or both. It depends on the context. For example, when Jesus Christ sent out the twelve and the seventy, he told them not to take anything with them for their journey because the laborer was worthy of his reward. He meant they would have their physical needs met by those they ministered to. In addition, Jesus Christ also spoke about praying in secret and the Father seeing in secret, rewarding openly. In this instance, the reward could mean compensation in this life, payment in the next, or both. So, checking the context when the reward is spoken of is important.

For more information, see Chapter 4: "The Reward."

13 Should we worry about "earning rewards" in everything we do?

Biblically speaking, we are not to be anxious or worried about anything (Phil. 4:6). Further, there is no appeal to "earn" reward, nor are there instructions to worry about losing reward. However, there are exhortations to labor, serve, endure, pray, be thankful, stand, and so forth. The reward will be given out, but changing our focus from serving to earning the reward may cause us to scrutinize every action to the point of distraction. Worse, we could adopt a pharisaical attitude of ourselves and others. We may remonstrate to someone, "Don't do that—you won't get a reward!" but such thinking is far from what the Scriptures teach regarding the loving relationship between a servant and his master.

In the Scriptures, we read the exhortation to do all things "heartily as unto the lord" (Col. 3:23). We read the appeal "to seek the things which are above, where Christ sits at the right hand of God" (Col. 3:1) and set our thoughts on "the things above and not on the earth" (Col. 3:2). While appeals such as these direct our attention from earthly to heavenly, there is no exhortation to assess each of our actions so that we can calibrate how much reward we are racking up. Better to be focused on serving than to be concerned about amassing reward. In studying the parable of the Workers in the Vineyard (Matt. 20:1-16) in chapter 4, we came to understand that the Master's generous giving exceeded the ability of anyone to "earn" by their own labors. Therefore, our focus should be on pleasing the Master with our service rather than on what we are getting back in return.

For more information, see Chapter 4: "The Reward."

14 Will rewards really be given out?

Yes, if God's Word is correct.

Perhaps because there aren't detailed descriptions of the reward in the Scriptures and probably because it is hard for people to grasp the concept of a heavenly reward, people sometimes wonder, "Will rewards *really* be given out?" The Scripture clearly states that every man will receive his own reward according to his own labor. There is no doubt that Jesus Christ will give out rewards at the *bēma*. When a person labors at a job, they expect to get compensated. When it comes to worldly things, there is no question that a laborer is to be paid. Why is it so hard to imagine that God would give out a reward or compensation for labor done in His name? God is the One who established the truth that a laborer deserves his wage. When Jesus Christ sent out the twelve and the seventy to preach the gospel, he expected them to be recompensed for their service. Christ also taught about works that would be repaid at the resurrection of the just. Clearly, this is a future repayment for something done in this life. Compensation for labor done is God's design. So, will rewards really be given out? YES!

15 Will I lose out on the reward if I don't work hard enough?

While hard work is certainly not discouraged by the Scriptures (see, for instance, 1 Cor. 15:58), it is not, in itself, a guarantee of reward. But, as we've seen, a reward is given for work, service, and labor built upon the foundation of Jesus Christ.

A believer may work hard but not be engaged in doing God's will. Paul said that he labored more abundantly than all the other apostles, but it was not his effort alone; God's grace was with him. Jesus Christ only did the works His Father directed him to do. Further, Paul labored under the grace of God, and he labored by walking with God. Both Paul and Jesus Christ worked hard, but not without divine direction.

> For more information, see Chapter 4: "The Reward."

16 If the reward is such a big deal, then why isn't there more information about it in the Bible?

If you simply do a word study on "reward" in the Bible, you will find relatively little information compared to, say, the topic of faith or believing. Perhaps one of the reasons for this question is that the word "reward" is a general term, meaning "compensation." But many other terms are used in the Scriptures that signify reward such as "treasure in heaven," "rich toward God," "set to your account," "lay hold on eternal life," "reap in due season," "exceeding heavy weight of glory," "glory and praise and honor," "an abundant entrance into the kingdom of God," and by metonymy, "eternal life." Once these and other expressions are familiar, it is easy to see that the information concerning future compensation is not as limited as some may think.

In addition, if you have a broad scope of the Bible, you know that the topic of the Hope permeates its pages. Believers from the Old Testament, like Abraham, looked forward to the coming of Christ, and this affected the way they lived. Hebrews 11 speaks of Abraham and others who considered themselves "strangers and pilgrims in the earth," meaning that they did not focus on earthly things as if that were the only reality. Abraham was told he would be the "heir of the world," but this promise would not be fulfilled in his lifetime. People like Abraham and others were clearly looking to God as their reward.

Moreover, Jesus Christ taught much about the future reward to his disciples. The topic of future reward is broad in the Bible, but one must look past doing a simple word study to appreciate just how broad it is.

> For more information, see Appendix H: "Words and Expressions that Signify Reward."

17 Why doesn't God tell us exactly what we get?

What God chooses to reveal in His Word is His business. There is plenty of information in the Scriptures to indicate that the reward will be fantastic and that it will be worth *far more* than any sacrifice on our part. It will also be far more than the most significant earthly gain. Understanding the benevolence of God and the exceeding riches of His grace, we should not doubt the blessings that God has in store for His children. In fact, the pattern that we see in the Scriptures is that God blesses His people beyond what they could ask or think! It's not a stretch to say that if we were left to determine our own reward, we would probably short-change ourselves. However, God, by His nature, is generous beyond measure. In the coming ages, He will show us the "immeasurable riches of His favor in kindness toward us in Christ Jesus" (Eph. 2:7).

> For more information, see Chapter 4: "The Reward."

18 Isn't it enough that we have salvation? Why be concerned with reward?

The salvation we have received is called "a great salvation," and indeed, salvation unto eternal life is a priceless gift of God's grace through Jesus Christ. But the Scriptures also speak of things that "accompany" salvation: reward, the prize, reigning with Christ, and so on. Being assured of salvation isn't an excuse to live a life unworthy of the heavenly calling. It is not an excuse to be entangled again with the things of this world. Salvation gives us an excellent framework in which to conduct our lives. That is, we have the opportunity to serve God joyfully and freely, knowing we have been saved from the wrath to come. Salvation is genuinely remarkable. But the saved one is called *to serve*, and the degree to which one serves God is the degree to which one is rewarded. Salvation makes that service available. Being saved is not the whole story for the Christian believer. We are saved to serve.

For more information, see Chapter 4: "The Reward."

19 Is it selfish or mercenary to think about future rewards?

That is a good question! Perhaps it helps to remember that the idea of future reward is God's idea. Thinking about the promise of future reward and being motivated by that promise, especially when times are tough, is not mercenary or selfish. Certainly, many of us would serve God simply out of love and thanksgiving. But God has extended His grace and kindness towards us by promising us a future reward for work, service, and labor. So, while thinking about future reward may be frowned upon by some religious persons, God wants us to know about future reward, and He has set them forth as one motivation to remain faithful, especially when facing trials and afflictions for the Gospel's sake.

For more information, see Chapter 4: "The Reward."

20 What good is a reward in heaven when I am on the earth where the persecution is taking place?

The reward in heaven will endure forever, whereas the persecution is temporary. The Scriptures teach that the sufferings of this present time are not even worth comparing to the future glory that awaits the Church. So, while no persecution or tribulation is enjoyable, it is *temporary.* Further, if the persecution or tribulation is on account of

Christ, and if the person endures during this suffering, they will be rewarded. The suffering is temporary; the reward is eternal.

For more information, see Chapter 4: "The Reward."

21 How can I be sure that my labor will stand the test of fire?

Please see Chapter 4: "The Reward" for an answer to this question.

22 What about people who have never heard about the reward?

Some men and women who have been motivated throughout the ages to serve the One True God may not have understood very much about the reward. But because God recognizes labor and rewards every man according to his own labor, they will not lose out simply because they did not know about the reward.

In the parable of the workers in the vineyard, some labored for the master without an agreed-upon wage but were still rewarded. The parable teaches us that the master would not allow anyone to be short-changed regarding rewarding, whether they knew about it or not. Many have truly served the One True God, hoping for nothing in return.

For those who are taught about the reward, however, this knowledge may serve as motivation to persevere in serving the living God.

23 Are you sure there aren't degrees of importance regarding work, service, and labor in the Body of Christ?

This question may arise because people with higher skills are usually paid more than less skilled laborers in our culture. A surgeon receives more compensation than someone who mows lawns. So, it may not be a question of whether one type of work is more important than another, but if a kind of work is more valuable than another. Not in the Body of Christ. 1 Corinthians 3 teaches that the reward is received according to the labor, not the *type* of labor. The apostle Paul reproved the Corinthians for valuing one minister above another. He reminded them that each one would receive his own reward for his own labor. In 1 Corinthians 12:12-27, we read that God has determined that *each* member in the body of Christ is indispensable. Indeed, God has arranged, composed, and appointed the different parts of the Body of Christ as it pleased Him. In the world, there are different wages based on the types of labor, but not in the Body of Christ. In the Body of Christ, one type of labor is not more important than another and will not be rewarded more than another.

Questions about the New Body

24 What age will we be in our new bodies?

Since we will live eternally in the ages to come, the short answer is "ageless." This question may be asked because people die at different ages, and the questioner wants to know what age they will be once they receive their new bodies. It is a natural tendency to think of the new bodies and the life to come in terms of the current life we know. But we know that there is a vast difference between our current bodies and our new bodies, and that would include age. What's more, if you think about it, the concept of age is grounded in a finite measure of time. We think of youth and middle age and elderly because our time is finite, meaning it has an end. But because we will be in heaven in our new bodies for eternity, the idea of age will, perhaps, be irrelevant.

For more, see Appendix D: "The New Body."

25 What will we do in heaven? Where will we live?

While some people think heaven consists of floating around in the clouds doing nothing, that is not what the Scriptures indicate. For one thing, the Church will judge the world and angels (1 Cor. 6:2-3). For another, the world to come is subject to Christ, which also implies that there will be work and responsibility. In the new authority structure in Christ, of which the Church is part, there will be responsibilities to carry out. Finally, the Church is already seated in the heavenly places in Christ (Eph. 2:6), which also implies responsibilities for the saints. It would be guesswork to determine what we will be responsible for, but there will be things to do.

Perhaps the idea of work or responsibility does not mesh with some people's concept of heaven. This may be due to the frustration brought about by Adam's sin and the accompanying curse. The "thorns and thistles" that come along with work in this life (Gen. 3:17-19) can rob someone's joy as they work. But with the new heavens and earth, work will not be accompanied by frustration because there will be no more curse. Before Adam sinned, his keeping of the garden would have been a joyful task. But after the curse on the ground was pronounced, he would "in pain...eat of it all the days of his life" (Gen. 3:17). Without any curse to frustrate us, work will once again be a blessing, and we will have the privilege to serve our God in whatever capacity He deems best.

As to where we will live, we should note that there will be people in both the new heaven and new earth, but the Church's citizenship is *in heaven*. The promise of inheriting the earth belongs to believers from the Old Testament. The inheritance of the Christian is *in heaven*.

For more information, see Chapter 7: "The Nature of the Reward."

26 Will we eat in heaven?

It seems likely that we will eat in heaven, or at least have the capacity to eat, for we know that Jesus Christ ate in his resurrected body. As for what we eat, God will provide the food or the means to get the food necessary for our new bodies. Or maybe we won't need to eat at all!

Other Questions

27 What does 1 Corinthians 3:17 mean by "God will destroy him"?

1 Corinthians 3:17 says, "If anyone destroys God's temple, God will destroy him. For God's temple is holy, and you are that temple." The

thought of being destroyed by God is rather frightening, to say the least. In chapter 4 we noted that the word "temple" is "sanctuary." This verse contains a figure of speech where the word "temple" is a metaphor for the Church. Contextually, to destroy the temple means to harm the Church.

In the Greek New Testament, the words translated as "destroys" and "destroy" (v. 17) are *phtheirō*, meaning "to spoil, corrupt, to bring into a worse state."[174] Note how this word is used in 2 Corinthians 11:

2 Corinthians 11:3-4

[3]But I am afraid that as the serpent deceived Eve by his cunning, your thoughts will be **led astray** (*phtheirō*) from a sincere and pure devotion to Christ.

[4]For if someone comes and proclaims another Jesus than the one we proclaimed, or if you receive a different spirit from the one you received, or if you accept a different gospel from the one you accepted, you put up with it readily enough.

By preaching another Jesus or another gospel, some would pervert the Gospel of Christ and thus cause the minds of the believers to be led astray. Teaching the wrong doctrine is one of the ways someone could destroy the Church.

Moreover, the words "If anyone destroys God's temple, God will destroy him" also contain the figure of speech *hyperbole* or exaggeration. This figure underscores the seriousness of the matter. It is not literally true that God would destroy a born-again one. It is figurative to say that that person will suffer a loss of reward. Identifying the figures of speech and reading the context helps us to understand this potentially unclear verse.

So when someone destroys the Church, they are spoiling it, corrupting it, and generally bringing it to a worse state. When one studies the broader context of Corinthians, it is easy to see that some were doing such things by teaching wrong doctrine, causing division

---

174   Bullinger, *A Critical Lexicon and Concordance*. s.v. "destroy."

and putting stumbling blocks in front of the believers. Thus, to destroy the temple of God means to harm the Church and "God will destroy him" means that his work will be burned, indicating loss.

For more information, see Chapter 4: "The Reward."

28 Will animals be with us in heaven?

On one hand, no Scripture says Fluffy has eternal life. In fact, in the Psalms, man is compared to the "beasts that perish" (Ps. 49:12, 20), so we know that beasts do perish. That is, they do not have eternal life. This question might be posed by those who are particularly fond of a pet, and the thought of not seeing it again is painful. However, we know that with the fulfillment of our hope, there will be no more sorrow. So even if animals are not in heaven, this fact will not cause us sorrow. On the other hand, no Scripture says animals will not be with us in eternity, and we know that there were animals in the original creation, in the Garden of Eden. We also know that all creation will be delivered from the bondage of corruption, including animals. So perhaps animals will accompany us in heaven. We will have to wait and see.

29 Why does God withhold the date of Christ's return?

It is God's prerogative to do so, and He must have a good reason for not giving us the exact date of Christ's return. God always has good reasons to keep things secret. We know that the mystery was kept secret because had God revealed it, the rulers of this age "would not have crucified the lord of glory" (1 Cor. 2:8), and thus God's plan of salvation would have been thwarted. Jesus Christ told his disciples that it was not for them to know "the times or the seasons that the Father has fixed by his own authority (Acts 1:7)." Jesus Christ also said that there were things in the future that even he and the angels in heaven did not know (Mark 13:32). Whatever the reason, it is perfectly wise and just for God to not reveal the exact date of Christ's return. However, He has revealed plenty for us to be excited about as we await that day!

30 Will everyone be judged, even those who are not born again?

Yes, all the world will be judged, as Romans 2 (and other Scriptures) make clear. Thankfully, the born-again ones have been justified in Christ and have nothing to fear. The Christian's works—not their standing before God—will be judged and either rewarded or burned up. Because there will be a resurrection of both the just and unjust (in addition to the Gathering Together), the rest of humankind will be judged at some point in the future.

31 What language will we speak?

Whatever language God deems appropriate, and we know that angels also have languages (1 Cor. 13:1). Perhaps we will even speak multiple languages. Stay tuned.

32 What will happen to born-again people who were evil-doers and persecutors?

It is regrettable, but throughout the history of the Church, born-again ones have instigated evil toward their fellow brethren. In Acts 20:29-30, Paul warned the Ephesian elders of men, meaning fellow believers, who would do evil things among them. The book of 2 Timothy records the evil deeds of many who had turned away from the truth. So, it is sad, to say the least, when Christians become evil doers. What will happen to them when they are brought before the judgment seat of Christ? We have already considered 1 Corinthians 3 in detail, and we know their salvation is never in question. However, their evil works will be burned up on that day. They will not receive reward for those evil deeds. Having studied the great value of the reward, we understand that this is no slight loss.

For more information, see Chapter 4: "The Reward." See also question #27.

33 If the bēma is for rewards, why does the Word of God talk about receiving for evil and good?

The phrase "receiving evil and receiving good" in 2 Corinthians 5:10 is a figure of speech meaning not receiving reward and receiving reward.

For more information, see Chapter 4: "The Reward."

34 What does it mean when it says we will give an account for the words we speak?

The questioner may have two verses mixed up.

Matthew 12:36
I tell you, on the day of judgment people will give account for every careless word they speak,

Romans 14:12
So then each of us will give an account of himself to God.

In Matthew 12:36, we read that it is on the Day of Judgment when people will give an account for every careless word they have spoken. The Day of Judgment is not for born-again ones. Matthew 12:37 goes on to say, "for by your words you will be justified, and by your words, you will be condemned." Christians are justified by believing in Christ and not by their words. And so, this verse does not apply to born-again ones.

In Romans 14:12, we read that each born-again one will give an account of himself to God. This takes place at the *bēma* of Christ. Contextually, this verse occurs in a section that admonishes sons of God not to judge one another. How believers conduct their lives in the sight of the lord will be judged by the lord; therefore, it is not up to us to judge. Romans 14:12 says that each one will give an account for him or herself. From our study of the Judgment Seat of Christ, we know that this pertains to reward.

For more information, see Chapter 4: "The Reward."

35 Are halos, harps, and wings required?

Yes, each person will receive one or more of these celestial accessories once they reach heaven. Just kidding. Seriously, all these items come from religious and traditional works, not from the Scriptures.

36 Why has so much time passed already? Why hasn't God sent Christ back?

God will send Christ back in the "fullness of times." His wisdom is unquestionable in this regard. However, his sense of time and ours is not the same (2 Peter 3:8). In 2 Peter 3:9, we read, "The Lord is not slow to fulfill his promise as some count slowness, but is patient toward you, not wishing that any should perish, but that all should reach repentance." In other words, God is patient, not wanting any to perish. He would prefer ALL to receive eternal life. Note also what Hebrews 10 says about Christ's return:

> **Hebrews 10:36-37**
> [36]For you have need of endurance, so that when you have done the will of God you may receive what is promised. [37]For, "Yet a little while, and the coming one will come and will not delay;

He will come and not delay!

37 What will happen to babies who have died?

The apostle Paul wrote:

> **1 Corinthians 7:13-14**
> [13]If any woman has a husband who is an unbeliever, and he consents to live with her, she should not divorce him.

¹⁴For the unbelieving husband is made holy because of his wife, and the unbelieving wife is made holy because of her husband. Otherwise your children would be unclean, but as it is, they are holy.

A child born into a family with only one believing parent is considered "holy." So, it stands to reason that this type of grace, perhaps greater, will be extended to babies of the saints at the time of Christ's return. If God is concerned with a sparrow, how much more would He care about a helpless human baby?

38 What happens to the dead who are cremated?

Whether a person is interred in the ground, cremated, or buried at sea, it does not matter since all men are taken from dust, and all will return to dust, one way or another (Gen. 3:19). The new body they receive is not affected by the method of burial.

For more information, see Appendix D: "The New Body."

39 In Matthew 24, what do those who are "taken" and "left" refer to?

Let's consider this question by looking at the context.

Matthew 24:36-42
³⁶"But concerning that day and hour no one knows, not even the angels of heaven, nor the Son, but the Father only.
³⁷For as were the days of Noah, so will be the coming of the Son of Man.
³⁸For as in those days before the flood they were eating and drinking, marrying and giving in marriage, until the day when Noah entered the ark,
³⁹and they were unaware until the flood came and swept them all away, so will be the coming of the Son of Man.

⁴⁰Then two men will be in the field; **one will be taken and one left**.

⁴¹Two women will be grinding at the mill; **one will be taken and one left**.

⁴²Therefore, stay awake, for you do not know on what day your Lord is coming.

Jesus Christ was referring to his coming during the Day of the Lord, not during the gathering together of the Church. In speaking about the Day of the Lord, he compared it to the time of Noah when the flood came upon them unawares and "swept them all away." The coming of the Son of Man at that time will also take people by surprise, and some will be "swept away," meaning they will not escape the judgment. Jesus Christ is not referring to taking one to heaven and leaving another. He is saying that some will be left alive, and some will die during the Day of the Lord.

> For more information, see Appendix A: "The Day of the Lord."

40 What is the "hope" referenced in Romans 5:3-5? Do these all refer to the hope of Christ's return or to a general hope and expectation in God's ability to deliver time and time again from the suffering as we endure?

Let's read the passage in question.

Romans 5:1-5

¹Therefore, since we have been justified by faith, we have peace with God through our Lord Jesus Christ.

²Through him we have also obtained access by faith into this grace in which we stand, and we rejoice in **hope** of the glory of God.

³Not only that, but we rejoice in our sufferings, knowing that suffering produces endurance,

⁴and endurance produces character, and character produces **hope**,

[5]and **hope** does not put us to shame, because God's love has been poured into our hearts through the Holy Spirit who has been given to us.

The word "hope" occurs in verses 2, 4, and 5. In verse 2, born-again ones rejoice in the hope of God's glory. The word "hope" in this verse refers to the future glorification of all believers with Christ, which is part of the hope of Christ's return.

Verses 3-4 speak of rejoicing in suffering. This does not mean we are happy to be suffering but that we can rejoice *during* suffering. Why? Because patiently enduring suffering produces endurance, and endurance produces character, which produces hope. In verse 4, "hope" refers to the expectation of God's deliverance. In other words, because we endure in believing when we are suffering affliction, this produces character. We know God has delivered us from past difficulties, and we trust He will deliver us from the present afflictions. This character, in turn, produces the expectation that God will again deliver us.

Finally, in verse 5, the word "hope" is preceded by an article and should read, "and *the* hope does not put us to shame." This refers to the hope of Christ's return.

Bibliography

Allen, Stuart. *Letters from Prison*. Short Run Press: Exeter, Great Britain, 2001.

Allen, Stuart. "The Second Epistle to Timothy." *The Berean Expositor.* Vol. 48:4 (1975-1976), 81-87.

Broneer, Oscar. "The Apostle Paul and the Isthmian Games." *The Biblical Archaeologist.* Vol. 25, No. 1, Feb. 1962, pp. 1-31.

Bullinger, E. W. *The Companion Bible: The Authorized Version of 1611 with the Structures and Critical, Explanatory, and Suggestive Notes and with 198 Appendixes*. Grand Rapids: Kregel Publishing, 1999.

Bullinger, E. W. *A Critical Lexicon and Concordance to the English and Greek New Testament*. Grand Rapids, Zondervan, 1982.

Bullinger, E.W. *How to Enjoy the Bible*. London: Samuel Bagster & Sons Ltd., 1970.

Bullinger, "The Practical Power of our Hope," *Things to Come*. Vol. 1-2 (1894-1896): 31.

Carden, Robert. *One God: The Unfinished Reformation*. 3rd. Edition., Naperville, IL: Grace Christian Press, 2005.

Coneybeare W.J. and J.S. Howson. *The Life and Epistles of St. Paul*. Grand Rapids: Eerdmans, 1856.

Cummins, Walter J. ed. and trans., *A Journey Through the Acts and Epistles: The Authorized King James Version with Notes and a Working Translation of the Book of Acts and the Church Epistles, and the Personal Epistles of Paul*. Vol. 1. Franklin, Ohio. Scripture Consulting, 2006.

Ellicott, C. J. 1897. *A New Testament Commentary for English Readers*. London: Cassell and Co. 1897. Digital.

Freeman, James M. *Manners and Customs of the Bible*. Plainfield, NJ: Logos International, 1972.

"George Mueller Quotes." *George Mueller*. Org. 17 Feb. 2021. https://www.georgemuller.org/quotes/category/eternity

Gower, Ralph. *The New Manners and Customs of Bible Times*. Chicago: Moody Press, 1987.

Hans, Julia B. *Go Figure! An Introduction to Figures of Speech in the Bible*. Bloomington, IN: Westbow Press, 2018.

MacArthur, John, Author and Gen. Ed. *The MacArthur Study Bible*. Nashville, TN: Thomas Nelson, 2006.

Mueller, George. *A Narrative of Some of the Lord's Dealings with George Mueller Written by Himself*. London: J. Nisbet Publishers, 1845.

Panton, D.M. *The Judgement Seat of Christ*. Hayesville, NC: Schoettle Publishing Co., 1984.

Strong, James. *The New Strong's Expanded Exhaustive Concordance of the Bible*. Nashville: Thomas Nelson, 2010.

Swaddling, Judith. *The Ancient Olympic Games*. London: The British Museum Press, 2015.

Thayer, Joseph Henry. *A Greek-English Lexicon of the New Testament*. Grand Rapids: Baker Book House, 1977.

Welch, Charles H. *An Alphabetical Analysis Part 1*, London: The Berean Publishing Trust, 1955.

Welch, Charles H. *The Berean Expositor*, Vol. 45 (1969-79). London: Berean Publishing Trust, reprinted 2000.

Wierwille, Victor Paul. *Are the Dead Alive Now?* New Knoxville, OH: American Christian Press, 1971.

Wierwille, Victor Paul. *Jesus Christ Our Passover*. New Knoxville, OH: American Christian Press, 1980.

Wierwille, Victor Paul. *Jesus Christ Our Promised Seed*. New Knoxville, OH: American Christian Press, 1982.

Zuck, Roy B. *Basic Bible Interpretation: A Practical Guide to Discovering Biblical Truth*. Colorado Springs, CO: David C. Cook, 1991.

Scripture Index

Also by Julia Hans

Books

Go Figure! An Introduction to Figures of Speech in the Bible. Westbow Press: Bloomington, IN, 2018.

Lamps, Scrolls, and Goatskin Bottles: A Handbook of Bible Customs for Kids. Standard Publishing, Cincinnati, OH, 2000.

Booklets

All Sufficiency in All Things at All Times: A Study of 2 Corinthians 8 and 9

'I Am So Troubled I Cannot Speak": What the Psalms of Lament Teach Us

For You Have the Poor Always with You

To purchase, please visit our website:

onthingsabove.org

About the Authors

Ravi and Julia Hans have been married for more than 35 years and have taught the Bible in home fellowships, churches, seminars, and online for nearly four decades. An electrical engineer by trade, Ravi has taught God's Word in Canada, India, and the United States. Julia is a national award-winning essayist and college professor who has published two books on the Bible. They can be reached at their website: https://www.onthingsabove.org

Printed in the United States
by Baker & Taylor Publisher Services